UNIVERSITY OF
WINCHEST

Martial R
Tel

SAMUEL SMILES

AND THE CONSTRUCTION *of*

VICTORIAN VALUES

SAMUEL SMILES

AND THE CONSTRUCTION *of*
VICTORIAN VALUES

ADRIAN JARVIS

SUTTON PUBLISHING

First published in 1997 by
Sutton Publishing Limited · Phoenix Mill
Thrupp · Stroud · Gloucestershire · GL5 2BU

British Library Cataloguing in Publication Data
A catalogue record for this book is available from the British Library

ISBN 0-7509-1128-X

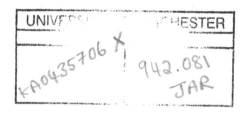

TM ALAN SUTTON™ and SUTTON™ are the
trade marks of Sutton Publishing Limited

Typeset in 10/15.5 pt New Baskerville.
Typesetting and origination by
Sutton Publishing Limited.
Printed in Great Britain by
Hartnolls, Bodmin, Cornwall.

Contents

List of Plates

Acknowledgements

For a man whose works sold very widely and often in large numbers during his lifetime, some of Smiles' books are hard to find. The Inter-Library Loans section at the Sydney Jones Library, University of Liverpool, succeeded in obtaining several of his more obscure works, notably *Brief Biographies* and an American edition of *The Life of George Stephenson*. Liverpool City Libraries, Manchester Central Library, Leeds City Library and the Bodleian Library searched some of their more distant stacks for me and produced further rarities, while the British Library found me the sole copy of the truly appalling dramatisation of *The Life of George Stephenson*, a work whose existence was revealed to me by Peter James, Principal of the London Academy of Music and Dramatic Art.

On the archival front, Virginia Murray at John Murray and the staff at the West Yorkshire Record Office (Leeds) and at Haddington Library all made me feel genuinely welcome and gave me a great deal of help in finding what I wanted. Mary Murphy and Carol Arrowsmith at the Institution of Civil Engineers were immensely helpful.

Most of the research for this book was carried out as a spare-time project, and I owe a great deal to people who have patiently discussed Smiles and allied topics with me, either face to face or in correspondence, provided references and made helpful suggestions. It is impossible to mention everyone, but also impossible to omit the following. E.F. Clark, Past-President, the Newcomen Society, took an interest from the start, but specifically it was he who suggested holding the mini-conference 'Perceptions of Great Engineers', whose proceedings, edited by Denis Smith, appear in the bibliography. This introduced me to a number of kindred spirits, especially the other contributors, who provided much food for thought. Victoria Haworth, Secretary of the Robert Stephenson Trust, has not only encouraged me constantly but has showered me with information and copies of documents from her large research collection. I don't know what Rank Xerox would do without her – and I'm not too sure what I would either.

Special thanks are due to Dr Simon Dentith, formerly of Liverpool University, now at Cheltenham and Gloucester College of Higher Education. His interest in Smiles began from the opposite direction to mine – from literature rather than from engineering – but of course we were bound to meet in the middle. This we did, and he kindly agreed to read the draft of this work, and made many helpful suggestions and comments. In one or two places I have noted his dissent from opinions I have expressed: I should here specifically exonerate him from any responsibility for my view of Weber's work ethic, which I portray as a once-brilliant idea, now past its sell-by date, a view he definitely does not share. I also claim sole intellectual property in any errors which may remain.

Married authors usually praise the forbearance of their partners in what sometimes seems a rather hollow convention. In this case my wife (or should I say help-meet?) Anthea has put up with about eight years of appalling untidiness, having to ask three times for domestic chores to get done and being offered convenience food or Dial-a-Pizza when it was my turn to do the cooking. Apart from once borrowing my car and having the gall to complain because it had not been cleaned for fifteen months, she has never failed to support and encourage me. But her help went far beyond mere tolerance, for she has read numerous drafts, discussed them and commented on them. If I reveal that she is a costume historian, the provenance of information about *Vestiarum Scoticum* will become evident.

Finally, I would like to thank Roger Thorp and his colleagues at Sutton Publishing. I trust that their faith in the project will be justified in the same way that John Murray's was when he took on a text that Routledge had rejected in 1855, namely *Self-Help*.

Introduction

Samuel Smiles was born in 1812 and died in 1904. His first published works appeared in Edinburgh newspapers before the accession of Queen Victoria, and his first hard-back book the year after her coronation. At an unknown date towards the end of his life he became senile, but he was still capable of a lucid letter at least as late as 1899. Earlier in the 1890s he had produced two substantial works: a house history of John Murray (his publisher for thirty-five years) and a biography of Josiah Wedgwood. During that amazingly long writing career he produced some thirty books, another thirty or so substantial pamphlets and articles in journals, several hundred slighter articles and an even larger number of newspaper articles and editorials.

Yet from that prodigious output, he is remembered (if at all) almost entirely for two works, namely *Self-Help* and *Lives of the Engineers*. The latter is often seen as an extended book of exemplars of the former, so that Smiles is inextricably associated with the image of *Self-Help*. What visions of Victorian earnestness and outward moral probity are conjured up by its title and by the sober advice given therein. How frequently we may find index entries for Smiles in works on nineteenth-century history or literature which prove on investigation merely to be mentions of 'Samuel Smiles, of *Self-Help* fame . . .' leading into some crushing denunciation of the hypocrisy of Victorian respectability.

The sheer volume and variety of his output become an obstruction to the formation of a detached and scholarly view of the man and his work. That is probably why this is only the third book published about one of the nineteenth century's more prolific and successful authors. (Unless one counts T. Bowden Green's somewhat quirky offering as a fourth!) There have been relatively numerous papers on aspects of his work, but an overview of his output poses considerable challenges in more ways than one. Among these, it has to be admitted, is the fact that to the modern reader his writing can be slow-moving and over-burdened with detail. *Life and Labour* especially is virtually impossible to read in a comfortable armchair! Even Aileen Smiles, whose book is really an abridgement of Smiles' *Autobiography* with the addition of some more general family history and some affectionate reminiscences of 'Granpa', admits that his books could be boring.

That is no excuse for neglecting or belittling Smiles. I have a personal dislike of writers of the 'never use a word where a paragraph will do' school, notable among whom for present purposes is Smiles' near-contemporary Thomas Carlyle. The average reader would not be impressed by my diligence if I wrote that it might seem surprising that no comparisons had been drawn between Smiles' ideas and those of Carlyle, but this was because I found Carlyle boring and could not be bothered to read him. Yet, as emerges in the main text, people have repeatedly done this in Smiles' case.

There is another difficulty with Smiles' work. While I repudiate the suggestion that he gradually sold out on the radical views he held in his thirties, it is true that his views evolved over the years: with a writing life of sixty years he would have needed to be not merely an ideologue but a monomaniac for it to be otherwise. That evolution, taken together with the variety of his writing, gives his work something of the quality of the Bible (or *Mein Kampf*), namely that with a little patience it is possible to find a quotation to support any statement whatever. Over the years I have amassed quite a substantial card index of quotations: I hope I have not used it unfairly. However, I cannot deny that any other recent writer on Smiles might be able to use just the references in my card index, never mind the whole of Smiles' work, to come to very different conclusions.

Much of this book, as the title implies, sets out to weigh Smiles against modern perceptions of typical Victorian respectability. I venture to suggest that I have proved that he initially fits the stereotype rather badly. However, his views were extremely widely disseminated, and had such influence that the stereotype may be thought to shift towards, and in some measure comply with, his views. That is why I leave until the last chapter any lengthy consideration of what we mean by Victorian attitudes and values.

Whenever one works on an individual for a long time, one unconsciously develops a personal, and probably quite irrational, impression of what they were really like. My late father was a lifelong, albeit low-key, Sherlock Holmes enthusiast and had read all the stories several times during his lifetime. To him, the only actor who played Holmes convincingly was Basil Rathbone, because he was the one who corresponded to the unconscious picture my father had formed when first reading the books as a youth. This is an entirely separate question from the actual relative talents of, say, Basil Rathbone and Peter Cushing. I have my own personal picture of Smiles, which I hope will emerge from the main text. Obviously I also hope my readers will agree with me, but I must concede that it is a subjective impression, albeit one based on a more thorough reading of Smiles than that effected by some of the people about whom I am rude.

Smiles is, to me, the arch-synthesist. A man of constant moderation in almost everything, he could find enthusiasm, admiration and even affection for an astonishing variety of people and views. Of course he had his *bêtes noires*, especially in his days of anti-Corn Law campaigning, but they are few. Of course he could write angrily, and he did so on a number of topics, but he was scarcely ever bitter. In the *Self-Help* series, we may find that almost everyone and everything which is treated disparagingly may in fact be gathered under the single heading of 'sham'. The key epithets that underpin so much of the Smiles philosophy are 'true' and 'truly'. He had little time for denominational religion, yet could twice refer sympathetically to St Ignatius Loyola in *Self-Help*. Sincerity and truth were what mattered, and he clearly regarded the saint as possessing both. Never mind that large numbers of the older-fashioned Protestants of his day still associated Loyola with the foundation of an elite corps of zealots who were a key element in the long-term popish plot to take over the world.

What Smiles established was, I suggest, a simple secular religion in which he included what he considered to be the essential points of Christianity while discarding those parts which he saw as leading to intolerance and hatred. As we shall see, Smiles had possibly the longest legs in nineteenth-century Britain when it came to straddling fences, but he did so not because he was indecisive or unsure of his ground but because he was a natural cooperator and synthesist. Between the grim and dangerous days of his childhood and the altogether gentler climate of his old age, Britain had undergone a silent and bloodless revolution. The London Dock Strike of 1889 may have been fairly bitter, but it cannot be compared with atrocities like Peterloo. Threats of unemployment due to technological advances might be met with strikes or protest marches, perhaps some casual street violence: they were not met with organised arson such as that which confronted John Rennie or Matthew Boulton. I do not believe that I am making too lofty a claim for Smiles by suggesting that he played his part – quite an important one – in this process. If I were writing the 'Victorian' volume of a new series on the history of Britain I might be tempted to tweak Christopher Hill's tail by entitling it 'The Century of Peaceful Revolution'.

There is one area in which I feel I owe readers an explanation, namely that of the referencing of this book. In the interests of producing a reasonably continuous and readable account for the general reader, I have tried to keep references to the minimum. On the other hand, for the scholarly reader, I have attempted to provide sufficient references. Clearly these are incompatible objectives, and the solution I have adopted is that where I recognise that the text is either producing new information or attacking an established point of view I have inserted references fairly thick and fast. Where, on the other hand, I am being either discursive or relatively uncontroversial, or am writing about things which I imagine are pretty common knowledge among aficionados, I have inserted references much more sparsely. In some places I have also clustered references for exactly the same reasons. If I have fallen between two stools I can only apologise: to mix metaphors, my fence-straddling ambitions may be worthy of Smiles, but my legs are not as long.

The mention of 'two stools' prompts an association of ideas which may be thought to form an additional claim for attention to Samuel Smiles. We all know about the two cultures (cf. C.P. Snow), and I regret my ignorance of particle physics as much as I do the propensity of engineers for writing sentences in which a present participle is used as a main verb. My interests in the field of history of engineering and engineering management could scarcely be called encyclopaedic, yet I have lectured in no fewer than five different faculties of the University of Liverpool. How can something that seems to me to be a coherent subject fall within each of the obviously diverse disciplines of arts, sciences, engineering, social and environmental studies and education? If I fall between stools, is that my fault, or does it indicate that universities place their stools too far apart?

These interdisciplinary divisions were incipient at the time Smiles was writing all his best-known books. If there is one serious adverse criticism I could make of his work it is that this is one fence he did not straddle, nor did he even make any serious attempt. His engineers are men alone, unaided on the one hand by scientists and on the other by scholars in the humanities. 'Book-learning' is disparaged and the promoted artisans who became great engineers are allowed little credit for their theoretical or mathematical achievements. Engineers whose contribution was primarily in those fields, such as Rankine or Bidder, are conspicuous by their absence. It may be possible to attribute to Smiles the 'dirty-handed' image which has tended to demean engineering and ultimately to pull down the status of the profession from the very lofty heights to which he sought to elevate it. The position has been reached where an economic historian was able to attribute the decline in the status and remuneration of late Victorian clerks to the fact that they did not have specific restricted skills like those of joiners or engineers!

That has been the long-term result, but it is one for which we should not, perhaps cannot, really blame Smiles. His ideology of engineering was actually a characteristic fence-straddling exercise. At the time he formed his ideas about the engineers, there were indeed two cultures. On the one hand, there were the 'promoted artisans' and on the other the gentlemen 'natural philosophers'. The latter group had two critical disadvantages in terms of finding favour in Smiles' pages: quite a few of them were of landed origin and – there's worse to come – some of them were French. But they were the ones who published things, and Smiles knew as well as we do that the judgement of history favours the victors and the literate. That, I suggest, is why he donned his crusader's armour and put forth a case which we now recognise as leaning far too much in favour of the intelligent self-improving son of toil. Long before Wimbledon was televised, the British exhibited a paradoxical (and probably insincere) love of the underdog. Smiles, with his characteristically astute knowledge of his readers, used that instinct to bridge the two cultures of *his* age. If we try to assess him in terms of the two cultures of *our* age we do him an injustice and ourselves a disservice. We might as well attack him for his inadequacy at computer programing or his lack of appreciation of the work of Picasso.

John Murray was the publisher of many important books. Byron was one of his authors, Darwin another. Shelf-yards of recent books have been published on the works of these and other Murray authors. Smiles is not halfway to a shelf-foot yet. Mill's *Essay on Liberty*, just as the *Origin of Species*, was published in the same year as *Self-Help*. It is open to question whether any of these great works had more influence, direct or indirect, on the ordinary lives and attitudes of everyday people than did the far more mundane works of Smiles.

I suppose I must end by levelling with my readers. What I really admire and envy in Smiles is his endless benign optimism. Where the uncovering of Robert Maxwell's theft of millions made me despair of modern business practice, Smiles could write cheerfully of George Hudson in the past tense, confident that the lesson had been learned and things would be better in the future. He was wrong, of course, but as Aileen Smiles emphasises, 'this true Victorian was always happy'. When I read in the press that the Institute of Human Ageing at the University of Liverpool has found the basis of a means whereby we might live to be 140, I immediately envisage the total destruction of the pension industry, mass suicide of actuaries and the collapse of the property market. Samuel Smiles would, I am sure, have received such news as evidence of the continued improvement of mankind, and signed a contract with John Murray for a series of books on such subjects as 'Life and Work after Life's Centenary'. He could have added an extra volume to *Lives of the Engineers* featuring two Liverpool dock engineers, Thomas Steers and Jesse Hartley, both of whom worked until they were eighty.

I have tried to avoid the emotional excesses to which biographers fall victim, but I have to end by admitting that the more I came to know the man through his works, the more I admired him. No doubt some future researcher on the subject will discover that Smiles had some dubious relationship with Jane Carlyle, Eliza Cook or Mrs Schimmelpenninck. If he did, I genuinely hope he enjoyed it (though from what I know of them it seems unlikely) but it's his writing that matters. In my opinion, it matters a great deal.

CHAPTER ONE

The Early Years

About 18 miles out of Edinburgh, the A1 bypasses a smallish town called Haddington and sweeps on to Berwick-upon-Tweed. In 1812, however, the road went through the town and for those who had preferred the speed of the stage coach to the comparative comfort of the coastal packet it was time for a change of horses. Time also, no doubt, for some to fall victim to the multifarious rip-offs practised on travellers throughout the coaching world. Coaching stages were busy places, where people congregated not only to travel, but to collect and dispatch packages, to seek news, to gossip, to perpetrate assorted felonies. Haddington was a market town as well, with all the noise and bustle which that status implied.[1]

The population of the town at the beginning of the nineteenth century was only about four thousand, but the influxes to its market, its coaching and its local role as a 'central place' meant that it supported a fair number of shops and small businesses, one of which was that of Samuel Smiles, General Merchant, 61 High Street. It was here, on 23 December 1812, that Samuel Smiles' wife Janet, 'Mrs Smiles of the shop', gave birth to her third child, subsequently named after his father. These were the days of large families and high infant mortality, and Mrs Smiles continued to bear children until 1831, when Christian, youngest of eleven, was born. Of this large brood, three died in infancy.[2] However, young Samuel appears to have been a robust child – his *Autobiography* contains no mention of childhood illnesses. In his schooldays he enjoyed good health[3] – and he outlived both Queen Victoria and the nineteenth century, dying in 1904 at the age of ninety-two.

Haddington was famously described by another of its famous children, Jane Welsh Carlyle, as 'the dimmest, deadest spot in the Creator's universe . . . the very air one breathes is impregnated with stupidity'.[4] But Mrs Carlyle has not been generally noted for her capacity for contentment, and the young Samuel Smiles found better things in Haddington than met her possibly jaundiced eye. One of Smiles' most endearing characteristics was his consistent optimism and his quest to see the best in people and places. His view of his upbringing in Haddington begins 'A good education is equivalent to a good fortune'. Referring to John Knox's maxim 'Let the common people be taught', he praises the education available in 'A poor and sterile country [which] was made strong by its men'. The first encounter with school which he describes was at Patrick Hardie's private school, and when Hardie was appointed to the Burgh School, Smiles followed him there. Despite the fact that Hardie was 'a tyrant and a toady' Smiles was generous enough to describe him as also being a good teacher, even if 'I cannot tell how thankful I was to be taken away from Hardie's School and sent to the Classical School in the adjoining building'. There he was taught by Rector Graham, who was, he says, loved by every boy in the school and who imparted every branch of learning in a pleasant and cheerful way.

Smiles then digresses into the favourite biographical trope which requires that boys who do well at school do badly in later life, and vice versa, a device which was to recur many times in his biographical writings. As we find that the young James Brindley became a millwright of prodigious skills despite, not because of, his apprenticeship under an allegedly drunken and incompetent oaf named Bennett, so, in the *Autobiography*:

> What became of the favourites at the one school and the prize boys at the other? I do not think that any of them made a mark in the world. Some became insufferable prigs, stuck up with self-conceit. The prize boys began as prodigies and ended as failures.

While, on the other hand

> The most successful of my schoolfellows in after years was originally a dunce. Hardie could not flog arithmetic into him. Teacher after teacher tried him and the result was the same.

Smiles does not see the need to mention that he himself had made some considerable mark in the world, though he does perhaps reveal a slight glow of self-satisfaction, if not 'self-conceit':

I was only an average boy, distinguished for nothing but my love of play . . . I fear I was fonder of frolic than of learning. I could not have been very bright, for one day, when Hardie was in one of his tyrannical humours he uttered this terrible prophecy in a loud voice: 'Smiles! you will never be fit for anything but sweeping the streets of your native borough.'

Coming from one who has just praised the benefits of education, this device, which clearly implies that teachers are incompetent even at recognising, much less fostering, talent in children, seems out of place. Smiles, however, is rarely illogical or inconsistent, and the apparent discord is easily resolved: 'On the whole, provided there was perseverance, those young men succeeded the best from whom little was expected.'

Travers has placed a curious interpretation on this aspect of Smiles' schooling, suggesting that it resulted 'in a lasting sense of the injustice of the power of money and the exclusiveness of the power structure', when it seems to the present writer merely to be a use of a stock story line, employed in much the same way as some of the more improbable ones discussed in Chapter 6, below.[5]

Smiles' account of his youth now touches on the subject of religion. He explains how 'heredity also had much to do with my being and instincts' and implicitly gives the credit for any moral worth he might possess to the upbringing he received, one component of which was the Cameronian tradition in his father's side of the family. A little later, he mentions his last meeting with his ninety-year-old grandfather, still an elder of the Cameronians, and writes of the old man with evident respect and affection.[6]

Yet, when his mother asked him whether he would like to enter the ministry when he grew up, he 'said decidedly' that he would not. He then explains at some length how it came about that he did not want to be a minister. There is a description of the traditional Cameronian Sunday – 'the "day of rest" was to us [the children] the most exhausting and unpleasant of the week.'[7] His typical Sunday certainly sounds uninviting enough, but there was a worse disincentive to the ministry:

Our preacher was a combative man. He preached the narrowest Calvinism and there was far more fear than love in his sermons . . . Our minister was a good and hard-working man. He, no doubt, gave us all that he had to give; but he was wearisome and unsympathetic; and his doctrines, though intended to frighten us into goodness, had perhaps the very opposite effect.

The very opposite effect? What, in a man who has been pictured as the very type-specimen of Victorian middle-class respectability and described by a scholarly commentator as 'both a representative and an eminent Victorian',[8] was 'the very opposite effect' which showed its first signs when he was thirteen years of age?

SAMUEL SMILES AND RELIGION

Smiles has long been described as the author of 'The Gospel of Work', and it is well known that a cased set of *Self-Help, Character, Thrift* and *Duty* was published in Argentina under the collective title of *The Social Gospel.*[9] It has also been suggested that his *Lives of the Engineers* deals with a communion of 'self-made saints'.[10] These slightly irreverent remarks both hint at and also serve partially to conceal a clear perception of what Smiles' own religious views actually were.

Both *Lives of the Engineers* and *Self-Help* and its sequels were comparatively expensive books: few editions of any of them cost less than six shillings, which put them beyond the reach of all but the most enthusiastic and substantial of the working classes. *Self-Help* has been described as 'so deeply expressive of the spirit of its own times'[11] and passing references to Smiles' works as typical of their times have been so numerous that his name can be used as a form of shorthand for the values of conventional middle-class Victorian men. Harriet Ritvo, in a paper on Victorian dog breeding did so: 'The bulldog's rise was an analogue of the rags to riches, or better still, pluck and luck stories of Victorian mythologists like Samuel Smiles.'Smiles will be defended against the vile calumny of 'pluck and luck' at a later stage. The point made here is simply that Ritvo was able to assume that the mere use of his name in this context was sufficient to conjure up a picture. Had she endured the tedium of actually reading Smiles she would eventually have found his angry denunciation of dependence on luck.[12] Yet the picture remains, so, in that respect, she was right, albeit at the expense of mythologising the alleged mythologist. The beauty of myths is that they demand neither effort nor references: plain old prejudice does well enough.

To a large section of the British population between 1850 and 1880, when Smiles wrote most of his popular works, and all those for which he is best remembered, 'pluck and luck' would, if they thought about it, cause great offence. The 1851 census of churchgoers indicated that some 58 per cent of the population attended church regularly and it seems a fair guess that a significant majority of the presumably rather earnest members of the rising or aspiring middle classes would find it socially difficult, and possibly difficult in their working lives as well, not to participate in some form of organised Christianity. With what degree of regularity or sincerity they attended churches we need neither investigate nor care. That some may have gone to cultivate business contacts, to attempt to negotiate advantageous marriages for their offspring after the services or merely to appear respectable, is not material. We are not here to judge collective, anonymous and totally unquantifiable motives. What is material is that, in common with many authors, they at least paid lip service to Christianity and many, of course, took their religion very seriously and honestly tried to live by it.

When these Christians, whatever their denomination, went to church, one of the things they spent their time doing was saying prayers. Some prayers are concerned only with praise or worship of God, but most involve some sort of request. Among the supplicants might be a few grubby souls who sought divine intervention in the price of coffee futures, but everyone without exception made such requests as that they be led not into temptation. They believed, in short, not only that there was an omniscient, omni-present God, but also that He guided the affairs of mankind.

Travers regards the Calvinist influence of Smiles' childhood as highly important, formative even. The index to his book contains far more entries under the heading 'Smiles: influence of Calvinism on' than under any other. It is true that some parts of the suggested connection work well: 'This Calvinistic emphasis on the individual covenant [with God] and the self-reliance of the individual in religious matters, was to pass over into a secular self-reliance in all Smiles' books.'[13]

This reflects the fact that Travers' book is largely expressed in terms of the Weber thesis, about which this author has severe doubts, expressed at pp. 122–5 below. For present purposes, however, we need merely note that Travers recognises the somewhat traumatic nature of Smiles' early experiences with religion, but nevertheless asserts that Smiles 'remained a deeply religious person'. Perhaps he did, but there must be serious doubts as to the nature of his religious beliefs.

The works of Smiles, which the prayerful people mentioned above bought by the hundred thousand, contain scant recognition of their views. Mentions of God are few, mentions of Jesus exceptional. When God is mentioned at all He is usually depersonalised as 'The Creator', 'The Almighty', or even, most impersonally, 'Providence'. In the great parade of success stories in *Lives of the Engineers*, not one of the men who rose from humble origins to be rich, famous and hugely beneficial to their fellow men, is said to have owed anything to the help of God. They succeeded through inborn genius, through hard work, perseverance, integrity, intellectual curiosity, devotion to their fellow men – just about anything, in fact, except the grace of God, to which many an 1850s author would have felt bound to refer. Furthermore, we seek in vain for an account of how the great Thomas Telford demonstrated his practical skills by repairing the fabric of the church of which he was a warden. He didn't, because he wasn't. John Rennie could mend a stage-coach axle, and George Stephenson could show a navvy how to shovel spoil.[14] Did either of them even attend church, much less demonstrate their humility in greatness there? Smiles is silent. Did great engineers die at peace with God? Brindley died of overwork and on his deathbed was not commending his soul to God but telling people how to puddle a canal.[15] Rennie similarly worked until he died. Stephenson and Watt spent their declining years respectively gardening and in the famous 'garret workshop'. We can find exceptions, of course: Myddleton was a church warden and Smeaton, when he knew death was close, is reported to have 'expressed his thankfulness to the Almighty' and to have exhibited a belief in the hereafter. Even when Smiles does have to record the death of someone who was an orthodox Christian, he avoids words such as God and heaven if he can.[16]

Apart from the childhood references cited above, Smiles makes no mention in his *Autobiography* of ever having gone to a church except for the occasional wedding, funeral or other special occasion. One of the few of which some account is given is the thanksgiving service in Westminster Abbey for the Queen's Golden Jubilee. Few authors would have failed to remark upon God's numerous blessings on the Queen and her people, perhaps even adding some suggestion that it might be nice if they were to continue. Smiles, as usual, does not mention the name of God.[17]

Self-Help and its companions contain huge numbers of mentions of individuals, varying from quite substantial cameo biographies down to very brief passing references. One of the striking features of these mentions is the degree of religious toleration exhibited. Just as Smiles could write with equal sympathy of the persecution of Roman Catholics in Ireland and of the Huguenots in France, so he could make laudatory references with complete impartiality to, for example, St Ignatius Loyola and John Knox.[18] One suspects that neither of these worthies would have been delighted with his account of the other.

The suspicion begins to dawn that Smiles was not just devoid of the religiosity with which some contemporary writers felt it necessary to adorn their books. That, too, he could tolerate – he writes not unkindly of Mrs Schimmelpenninck, a prominent figure in the 1850s whose writings have all the incisiveness of a barrel of syrup.[19] If he could tolerate all these things, perhaps it was because he did not care about any of them. Certainly his granddaughter's affectionate biography of him gives some support for such a view:

> Someone (was it Robert Owen?) said that man's first duty is to be happy, that a happy man is the religious man. If that is the case, Samuel Smiles was most religious, for, although he did not often go to Church, unless to hear a really BROAD sermon, this true Victorian was always happy . . .[20]

This is one of the very few pieces of positive evidence we have of any kind of religious observance. Another, unearthed by R.J. Morris, is that in the early 1840s, Smiles rented a pew in the Mill Hill Unitarian Chapel, Leeds. Morris attributes this to a 'recent break with a harsh Presbyterianism reflected in an early letter from his father'.[21] At the risk of carping, it might be pointed out that the letter cited is dated 17 October 1829. Given that Smiles' father died of cholera in 1832, it is a comparatively late letter, but the damage had in any case been done some three years previously, when young Sam announced to his mother that he would 'no' be a minister'.

Several writers have noted in passing that the Cameronians' beliefs and practices were very strict, narrow and austere.[22] Since their history is little known outside Scotland and a few parts of North America, it may be worth giving a very brief account of them. Their name derives from Richard Cameron, who was killed by government troops in 1680. He was a field preacher who assumed leadership of a group which felt that the mainline

Covenanters – themselves capable of being a fairly truculent body – had become compliant and sold out their principles. Cameron, with a band of armed men, solemnly declared war on all who supported Charles Stuart in his tyranny and repudiated the succession of the 'papist' James. His successors, Donald Cargill and James Renwick, were executed respectively in 1681 and 1688. At the root of these troubles lay that old chestnut which had so exercised the mind of medieval Christendom: the relationship between Church and State. The Cameronians began their corporate existence as an aggressive and highly uncooperative group of people: while the passage of time may have delayed their resort to force, they remained aloof from the growth of moderation in the Church in Scotland and did not lose their separate identity. When the disruption of 1843 led to the emergence of the Church of Scotland in recognisably the form we know today, the Cameronians again adopted a pugnacious posture which was responsible for widespread disagreement and unpleasantness.[23]

But long before then, one specific aspect of their aspirations towards Church government of secular affairs had burned itself into the memory of young Samuel Smiles. Two things from his childhood he remembered with particular disgust: one was the practice of whipping burglars at the cart's tail. Smiles' views of crime and punishment were not especially liberal, but he had no time for violence or brutality, be it military, criminal, judicial or pedagogical. The second thing he remembered is more revealing: 'There was another exhibition at our meeting house, quite as offensive as whipping men at the cart's tail. That was, publicly rebuking men and women on the cutty stool.'[24] He goes on to explain that the cutty stool was a 'sort of pillory, erected for the punishment of those who have transgressed in the article of chastity'.

We have identified a number of things in which Smiles did not believe, and a couple of reasons why he did not believe in them. If we may believe his *Autobiography* he seems to have regarded organised religion largely as a source of intolerance and aggression. Was he, though, like James Kitson who is said to have first suggested that he write *The Life of George Stephenson* or Henry Booth who played such a large part in the execution of the Liverpool and Manchester Railway, a Unitarian? The evidence of Morris suggests that he must have had some inclination in that direction, but any long-term commitment is doubtful. Unitarians stood aloof from much of the sectarian wrangling which seemed so harmful and irrelevant to Smiles, and their cultured and rational outlook is eminently compatible with most of Smiles' writings. He wrote kindly of both James and Harriet Martineau and the fact that Unitarians were rich and influential out of all proportion to their rather small numbers meant that some of them could be seen as the kind of genuine success story which appealed to Smiles. But they still built elaborate churches and employed a liturgy loosely based on the Anglican: above all they believed in a God to whom it was worth addressing requests on the grounds that He might choose to act on them.

In 1871, Smiles suffered a stroke which completely disabled him for a time. Qualified in early life both as a surgeon and a physician, there is no doubt that he knew how likely it was that another, fatal, stroke would soon follow. Of course we now know that he made an almost complete recovery, so that eventually the only noticeable reminder was a fairly regular buzzing sound in his ears. But in 1872 he did not know that: he thought he was due shortly to meet his Maker. Or did he? Early the following year, a small pamphlet was privately printed which was intended to be the preface to the forthcoming Italian edition of *Character*, entitled *A Memoir of the Author*. The only copy found during research for this book is in the Smiles Collection at the West Yorkshire Record Office, and its cover bears the name of John Hartree, husband of Smiles' eldest daughter Janet. Of the surviving personal papers of Samuel Smiles, a significant proportion is made up of letters to or from Janet, or 'Gingers' as he called her, which, rightly or wrongly, creates the impression that she was his favourite child. This document cannot have been written by Smiles – he had not yet taught himself to write again[25] – but neither could it have been written by 'Gingers' or anyone else, because it contains reminiscences with which only he would have been familiar. Therefore we are forced to picture a poignant scene in which the ageing author dictates to his favourite daughter, or possibly to his wife, what he believes to be his own obituary. What Christian or Unitarian would resist the temptation to thank God for a life he had thoroughly enjoyed and to express trust in his Maker's allowing him a place in the great publishing house in the sky? From the skewed and ill-controlled lips of the invalid there escapes not a word. No thanks, no hope, and no lying back to commit his soul to his Maker, only a ferocious will to recover and to live, which may suggest a conviction that there would be no hereafter in which to carry on writing. All of which is well for us who wish to study him, for some of his best and most useful work was yet to come, including the *Autobiography*, without which we would know so little of the man.

Despite his eschewal of organised religion, Smiles was not without religious views or beliefs. As we work our sometimes weary way through some of his lesser works such as *Life and Labour* we might identify him with an updated version of Renaissance humanism. That he believed in a Creator is clear, but he mainly pictures the achievements of the Creator as vicarious, performed by the agency of men to whom He had granted the requisite qualities.[26] We do not, however, need to stray by several centuries and a thousand or two miles to find connections: some may be found in and around that 'dimmest and deadest' place, Haddington. Not everyone in and around Haddington was narrow or combative.

The strictures of Mrs Carlyle notwithstanding, Haddington offered a remarkable range of intellectual activities for a small town. Foremost among these were the educational opportunities offered by the School of Arts, established in 1821, which provided instruction in mathematics, science and many other subjects. Even before that, in 1818, a society had been founded to that end, but it scarcely measured up to its successor, which was helped into being by the Principal of Edinburgh University and the Professor of Hebrew and Oriental Languages. Meetings were held in a variety of places over the years, including the council chamber, the parish school and at least two different chapels, but eventually the school rented a room of its own. By 1823, there were eighty members, and the list of subjects covered is impressive.[27] We cannot tell what the standard of the teaching was, though when we find Smiles' *bête noire* Patrick Hardie offering a course in 1825 which included 'Dynamics, Mechanics, Hydrostatics, Pneumatics, Acoustics, Magnetism and Electricity' we may have our fears. On the other hand, Smiles spoke warmly of the lectures on chemistry by Dr Lorimer, and of the remarkable theories of the nature of matter advanced by Samuel Brown.[28]

In 1826, the school achieved a decided coup when it secured a lecture from Revd Thomas Chalmers DD, Professor of Moral Philosophy at the University of St Andrews. A committed and prominent Evangelical, Chalmers was a top-flight intellectual whose view of religion was much less concerned with the invocation of graphically described horrors of hell upon anyone who disagreed with him than were the preachings of lesser men who followed broadly similar doctrines.[29] In 1813, he had been criticised for his contribution 'Christianity' in the *Edinburgh Encyclopaedia*, on the grounds that he was testing the truth of the faith by inductive reasoning.[30] Wanting for himself the right to dissent, he supported the right of Roman Catholics to do likewise at a time when describing the Pope as nothing worse than the Antichrist would have been considered fifth-columnism among the Cameronians. More important for present purposes, he regarded relief of the able-bodied poor as an attempt, doomed to failure, to fly in the face of the laws of nature. As an Evangelical, his solution to the social and political problems of Scotland would work through the widespread adoption of the true faith. But two of its manifestations would be a more egalitarian society and one in which the upper classes would serve as a standing moral example to the lower.[31] Such views could easily be secularised, and they were by Smiles. Chalmers' young pupil, Edward Irving (who was later among the founders of the Catholic Apostolic Church), lived in Haddington for a while, and got himself into trouble for some unwise preaching, which was interpreted as casting doubt on the doctrine of the Trinity.[32] Whatever men such as these may have been, narrow they were not, and to a young man disillusioned by Cameronian rigidity, contact with them must have suggested other lines of religious enquiry. There existed in Haddington the opportunity to encounter unorthodox religion at a high intellectual level.

Behind specific contacts such as these were more general influences which may have worked on the young Smiles. Older histories of religion in the nineteenth century concentrate mainly on the doctrines, liturgies and organisation of the innumerable denominations and sects which vied to save men's souls. Recent works on the subject are fewer in number, and tend to be a rather specialist field, but it becomes clear that for some repulsive and quite numerous elements of the population, religion then fulfilled the role that football or some political groups do now. It provided a common identity for a bunch of thugs who wanted to go out and have a really good fight. Haddington provided the correct intellectual answer to that as well, for it was quite extraordinarily well provided with libraries. There was the town's library, though 'Most of the books were theological but some of the later additions were valuable',[33] a distinction which would not necessarily have met with universal approval in the drawing rooms to which Mrs Schimmelpenninck addressed her writings. Smiles goes on to explain that Hardie was the librarian there – the man seems to turn up everywhere – and when Smiles took out Gibbon's *Decline and Fall* 'he havered a bit to me, in his dictatorial way, as to how I was to read it'. What should Hardie have been telling Smiles if not that Gibbon's religious scepticism made him a dangerous man to read? There were other libraries

– Begbie's Library, the East Lothian Itinerating Library, the Subscription Library, Tait's Library and Niell's Library. He became a voracious reader, a habit which he maintained for most of his life and which is obvious from the enormous breadth of knowledge necessary to have written his books. Later, when he returned to Haddington in 1833, he 'devoured poetry, especially Shelley and Keats. I afterwards rose to Coleridge and Wordsworth.'[34] All of these were generally recognised as great poets, and few cultured people would have taken any exception to Coleridge or Wordsworth. But Shelley was, of course, notorious for his atheism, and it cannot be said that any of the other three was an entirely orthodox Christian.[35] Poetry was another point of contact with high-level heterodoxy.

We have seen that Smiles was repelled by the narrowness and aggression of the Cameronians, and that the unusually broad cultural facilities of Haddington made it eminently possible for him to encounter a variety of degrees of unorthodoxy, through to and including atheism. We have found *prima-facie* evidence that he may have embraced some form of theism, but all that we have proven is that he was not a practising orthodox Christian. The next step is to try to establish what he was.

We may begin by discounting atheism. In his successive careers as a doctor, a newspaper editor, a railway manager and a popular author, openly avowed atheism would have been socially unacceptable. If he had indeed been an atheist we should never find the evidence of it, for had it been readily discernible we should never have heard of Smiles, or not, at least for any of the things for which he is actually known. Either he was not an atheist, or he concealed it with complete effectiveness. When Sam Jnr flirted with atheism, this was the substance of his father's warning to him. Travers points out that a passage in *Duty* argues that religion is a stabilising influence, and that without it we might have had an equivalent of the French Revolution in Britain. But when Smiles sums up the message of the chapter in which Travers' quote occurs his coda is 'The race is for Life.' Not salvation, life.[36]

Even more briefly may we dispose of the possibility of agnosticism: that Smiles, whose endlessly confident assertions and anecdotes spelled out the answer (in his own eyes at least) to the central problems of nineteenth-century life could be unsure whether there was a God or not is simply inconceivable. Let us, therefore, test the theist explanation.

To begin with, Smiles, like several of the engineers whose biographies he wrote, was a freemason. Now there have been generations of Christians of many denominations who have not found freemasonry and Christianity incompatible. That question is not really relevant. If, however, one considers the religious element within freemasonry itself, then we have a supreme being – the great architect – who constructed the universe and gave man the necessary skills, and a book of instructions, to enable him to look after himself. That is in no way incompatible with the *Self-Help* view that man's future is in his own hands and can be improved – or ruined – by the adoption of standards of behaviour entirely within his own control. It did not imply an acceptance of a completely mechanistic universe, indeed Smiles poured scorn on Robert Owen's mechanistic view: it was better to be a 'pagan suckled in a creed outworn than believe in this spinning jenny of a universe . . . '.[37] But what damned Owen was his lack of any idea of 'moral sublimity', that is to say the exercise of such moral qualities as self-help and thrift. This is, in short, the difference between deism, which may be roughly aphorised as the doctrine of the 'Divine Clockmaker', and theism.

Theism was a comparatively acceptable creed, particularly in intellectual circles: it was the highest common factor which could form a basis for the reconciliation of a wide variety of Christian and other beliefs. In this context it is worth remembering that any denunciation of any religion whatsoever is hard to find in Smiles – but denunciations of the behaviour of the adherents of religions are plentiful. Theism also had support from such widely respected philosophers as Rousseau (recovering from his Jacobin image) and John Stuart Mill. It was eminently compatible with the views put forward in Adam Smith's influential *Wealth of Nations*. The writings of Jeremy Bentham, which seemed to some to offer the solution to the 'Condition of England Question', were a positive encouragement to theism. In 1859, Charles Darwin posed no problems to the theists, any more than did those who had partly anticipated his theory (including, of course, Grandfather Erasmus). To committed Christians of whatever denomination, all this proved was that theism was so vague a belief that it was compatible with absolutely anything. To Smiles, however, Christianity as then practised was itself compatible with almost any atrocity one cared to name, and Chapters 5 and 6 of *Duty, The Huguenots* and *The History of Ireland* name plenty.

Chapter 12 of *Duty*, on missionary activities, is illustrative of Smiles' dilemma. Missionaries were brave and persevering, missionaries had the courage of their convictions. They taught the heathen useful skills to the overall benefit of mankind:

The once naked, filthy savages became clothed and cleanly. Idleness gave place to industry, they built houses and cultivated gardens. Provision for the wants of the mind kept pace with those of the body; they reared schools for the young and chapels for the old.[38]

Those of us who write books while ignoring the lawn growing above the window frame may doubt that all of these were unmitigated blessings, whatever benefits they may have bestowed on British soap and textile manufacturers, to say nothing of printers. But there seems little reason to doubt Smiles' sincerity in seeing these as improvements. In all these respects, missionaries were not merely good men, but good enough to constitute a praiseworthy example to be held up for imitation. Yet one cannot help but feel that the benefits he describes were not those for which the missionaries risked a close encounter with a barbecue. Smiles could also write on the very next page: 'Professing Christians, like vendors of bad coinage, often expose genuine religion to suspicion.' He enlarged on this by quoting the well-known Scottish divine, Dr Thomas Guthrie:

> . . . and how are you to keep the world from saying 'Ah! your man of religion is no better than others; nay he is sometimes worse. With what frightful prominence does this stand out in the never-to-be-forgotten answer of an Indian Chief to the missionary who urged him to become a Christian. The plumed and painted savage drew himself up in the consciousness of superior rectitude, and with indignation quivering on his lip and flashing in his eye, he replied – 'Christian lie! Christian cheat! Christian steal, drink, murder! Christian has robbed me of my lands, and slain my tribe!' Adding, as he haughtily turned away – 'The Devil, Christian! I will be no Christian!'

This probably fictitious tale was told as a warning to Christians, but it contains an interesting underlying question. What was the source of the Indian chief's 'superior moral rectitude'? The crimes he enumerated were also sins, but how, as a mere 'plumed and painted savage', did he know that? Whether or not Christians lived up to their professions becomes secondary, because the key moral values are not the subject of divine revelation but are common to all men. They might, indeed, have been built in by the Great Architect. And what was the 'genuine religion' which might be exposed to suspicion?

It has already been mentioned that Smiles is often unforthcoming on the religious views of the subjects of his biographies. Robert Dick, however, forms a notable exception. In the main, Smiles wrote biographies only of people of whom he approved[39] and there were few of whom he approved more strongly than Robert Dick, baker, of Thurso. Certainly Dick was a remarkable man: at the British Association meeting at Leeds in 1858, no less a personage than Sir Roderick Murchison, Director-General of the Geological Survey, had this to say of him:

> I found, to my humiliation, that this baker knew infinitely more of botanical science – ay, ten times more – than I did; and that there were only some twenty or thirty British plants that he had not collected . . . and he is so excellent a botanist that he might well have been a professed ornament of Section D (Zoology and Botany).[40]

This baker had distinctive views on religious matters. When Hugh Miller (who is mentioned many times in Smiles' works) finally lost his reason, Dick, who knew him well and corresponded with him regularly, attributed it to his efforts to reconcile biblical creationism with recent discoveries in geology. It had become clear that at least the chronology, and possibly much else besides, in the Book of Genesis, did not tally with the evidence being wrung out of fossils – evidence of which Dick was one of the wringers.

> Dick was of opinion that Hugh Miller published the book [*Testimony of the Rocks*] quite as much to please the dominant religious party in Scotland, as to satisfy the convictions of his own mind. Indeed, he traced the beginnings of Hugh Miller's insanity to the over-stimulation of his brain, for the purpose of meeting the exigencies of his position as a scientific man and a religious journalist.[41]

We may perhaps note in passing that 'over-brainwork' was a theme close to Smiles' heart, and one of which he had unfortunate personal experience. A long chapter in *Life and Labour* treats of the problems, and amid a sad procession of anecdotes of intellectual self-destruction we find the following remark: 'Brain workers, of all others, require the most repose; and every attempt to stimulate the thinking organ into abnormal activity should above all things be avoided.'[42]

Dick is credited with a number of quite bitter remarks about organised Christianity:

I candidly say that it is very hard that you cannot enjoy yourself for one day among the rocks without being assailed for it by ignorant W.W.'s, be they clerical or not. Great stir about tyrannical Popery at present; but query – may there not be among ourselves Moderate Popes, Free Popes and such like? Plenty, I guess. . . .

[These papers] shall be duly pondered and considered – ay, on mountain tops, even at early dawn or sober eve, when the twinkling stars and the soothing winds tell their own tale of nature's happiness in their own dear way. . . .

No, no! I have thrown Calvin's theory to the winds. There are as many Gospel theories as there are geological; and all are at liberty to behold their own likeness in their own mirror.[43]

Smiles goes on to report that Dick found Miller's attempted synthesis in *Testimony of the Rocks* 'does not solve the great problem . . . nor will it convert geologists . . .'. Yet this is not necessarily the most logical place in the book for Smiles to point out that Dick had provided large amounts of valuable information for Miller and that Miller's biographer had ignored more than a hundred of Dick's letters which were in his possession: 'But not a word is said there as to Hugh's greatest helper.'[44] The implication is not enlarged upon, but it seems likely that Smiles intended to suggest that religious considerations had led to a distortion of the truth. Certainly Dick is portrayed by Smiles as having little time for Miller's attempts to sustain the Mosaic cosmogony, and that despite the respect Smiles accorded Miller.

In another place, George Shearer, corresponding in his youth with Dick, tried to draw him on his views of the Mosaic cosmogony and was brushed off as having insufficient maturity and experience to consider such issues. Later in life, Shearer wrote: 'I took his reply in excellent part. I felt that, when he wrote it, he thought that the unthinking may easily be orthodox, and that the loudest professors were sometimes the shabbiest actors in the drama of life.'[45] Smiles' comment on this quotation is that 'Dick was of opinion that dogmatism in interpretation was equally out of place in geology as in divinity.' Dick's open-minded approach made it easy for him to receive new ideas, and he took Darwin's theory of evolution on board with almost casual ease, while admitting that he had only read reviews of his work, not the work itself. In a paragraph of a letter using the words 'The Almighty', 'God' and the 'Maker' he simply explains that his God made the world, but that there is no reason why we need assume that it has remained unchanged ever since: '*first stocks* must have had a Creator. . . . There is an over-ruling Hand everywhere' [italics in original].[46]

In the same way that Smiles has exposed much more of Dick's religous views than is the case with most of the subjects of his biographies, so his account of his subject's death is much fuller. Smiles now seems somewhat ambivalent, for on Dick's deathbed, the minister of the parish

> prayed with him and read to him the fourteenth chapter of St. John. Christ's words were a great consolation to Dick on his bed of death. Mr Miller [the minister] says of him that 'he was the most humble believer that he ever met'.[47]

The mention of the name of Christ is unusual, and the reference to John 14 might be thought finally to establish that Dick was, after all, an orthodox Christian, for it contains such well-known verses as

> In my Father's house are many mansions: if it were not so, I would have told you. I go to prepare a place for you. . . .
> I am the way, the truth and the life: no man cometh unto the Father but by me. . . .
> I will not leave you comfortless: I will come to you.[48]

Smiles completes the narrative simply:

> In the morning of the 24th of December, Robert Dick's spirit returned to Him who gave it. Towards the end, his sufferings left him, and he died quietly and peacefully. He was left in the hands of the Wise and Loving.

Which, taken at face value, would establish that the entire account here given of Dick's religious views, and thus by implication, of Smiles', is false. But was 'the Wise and Loving' the God of orthodox Christianity? The minister was, after all, only doing his duty in providing Christian comfort to a dying man, and he very probably read John 14 to most or all of them. When the people of Thurso felt almost universal pity for Dick's long sufferings, they pressed for some mark of respect towards the man who had made their town famous in the circles of high science. Dick was to have a public funeral. The announcement was made by the chief magistrate, and ended thus:

> . . . We accordingly invite all who wish to testify their respect for our departed friend to assemble at his house in Thurso on Thursday, the 27th current, at one o'clock p.m., to accompany his remains to the New Burial Ground of Thurso.[49]

Smiles continues with a sympathetic, indeed by his standards, emotional, account of the funeral. The town virtually shut down; there were two military bands leading a long cortege. 'It was one of the largest, most impressive, and remarkable funerals, that there had ever been in Thurso.' There, as in the chief magistrate's announcement, no mention is made of the Kirk.

A heading for *Robert Dick* (p. 431) reads 'Dick a religious man.' So he was. But we find that 'the "unco guid" said hard things of him. They drew a religious moral from the painfulness of his death.' Smiles goes on to describe him as one of those

> reverent natures which are essentially religious, though not cumbered about with forms or ceremonies or sectarian differences. Indeed one of the things which drove him from the church was the quarrels of those who were ministers in it.

If we may deduce from the evidence in *Robert Dick* that the theist hypothesis has some substance, we must yet look what religious views Smiles exhibits when he is giving advice. He was, after all, one of the most prolific advisors of his age. Like his biographies, his *Social Gospel* has little to say about religion, and, as mentioned above, much of it is based on premises which imply that organised religion has failed.

Nor, when Smiles sets out to write about specifically religious subjects, do we find any great difference of approach. One of his great enthusiasms was for the history of the Huguenots, on which he wrote two books and several articles, supported by references in other books. The story of *The Huguenots* is not, however, primarily concerned with their beliefs. There are two sides to it: the Huguenots have a long track record of self-improvement under circumstances varying from acute difficulty to brutal persecution, and praise and blame are allocated exactly as we might expect of Smiles. The second side is a lengthy explanation of how the British economy, and indeed the 'National Character', had been improved by the qualities brought to it by Huguenot immigrants. This latter theme is present throughout the book, but forms a major component of Chapters 1, 6, 14 and 15. Its message is simple and clear: the persecution of Huguenots was not only unjustifiable on humanitarian grounds, it was also a serious economic loss to the persecutors. The comparatively tolerant British people not only profited spiritually, but monetarily as well, and that at the expense mainly of the country with which they were most frequently at war, namely France. Conversely, for the French, a policy of religious intolerance was not only reprehensible, but downright stupid. As we shall see, it is an underlying theme of the *Self-Help* series and of *Lives of the Engineers* that good people, those who exhibit Smiles' secular virtues of thrift, hard work and cooperation with others, may well achieve financial as well as spiritual gain.

The supposed justification for such actions as the dragonnades after the revocation of the Edict of Nantes was that harming the bodies of heretics was a lesser evil than the harm their continued presence in this world would do to other men's souls. Smiles almost gloats over the consequences for France: 'The emigration gave a death-blow to several great branches of industry. Hundreds of manufactories were closed, whole villages were depopulated, many large towns became half-deserted and a large extent of land went entirely out of cultivation.'[50] He goes on to give specific examples, including that of Tours, where the number of looms in use fell from 8,000 to a mere 100 and of Lorraine where 346 out of 400 tanneries closed. There follows an explanation of how the Lyons silk industry had first come to prominence through 'civil and religious wars' in Sicily, Italy and Spain and that it had now been ruined by 'the same persecutions'. The perfectly clear assumption is that peace and prosperity, which some might interpret as the service of Mammon, was self-evidently better than the application of religious zeal to the saving of souls.

Next to Smiles' works on the Huguenots and his *History of Ireland*, the largest concentration of religious commentary is in the earlier part of *Duty*. At first it seems that he is advancing an orthodox Christian position, as he explains how ancient Rome was destroyed by its own 'corruption, profligacy and cruelty' upon which he enlarges before writing this:

> Then Christianity came, and revealed to men the true foundation of religion. St Paul carried it to Rome, as adequate to regenerate the world. It first took root among the enlightened poor. And why? Because religion is the explanation of human destiny, the poetry of our earthly existence and the consoling promise of a better futurity. . . .

He goes on to explain the beneficial consequences in exactly the sort of terms one would expect from a Victorian Anglican. But as we might guess from the false trails he laid in the account of Robert Dick's funeral, the euphoria is short-lived – less than a page elapses before: 'What a happy picture! Would that it had continued! Alas! the old Adam had not been effaced. The priesthood became the instruments of oppression. . . . What the pagans had done to the early Christians, the Christians did to their opponents.'[51]

This is the cue for a catalogue of misdeeds perpetrated in the name of Roman Catholicism, with occasional quotations like that from the free-thinker F.W. Newman: 'Strange how religion, in any form, should have generated cruelty.' The attacks on the Spanish Inquisition could easily come from a Cameronian, and Travers is the most credible of a number of writers who have thought they perceived an anti-Catholic bias, but Smiles broadens his attack, giving examples of Catholic martyrs as well as Presbyterian ones. Earlier, he had deplored the persecution of Jews and he now goes on to claim that the government of Spain was 'more liberal, more tolerant, more cultured' under Moorish than under Christian rule.[52] That was a fairly outrageous opinion, and certainly not what one would expect of an 'eminent and representative Victorian'. More typical would have been the view that Charles Martel's victory at Poitiers in 732 had, by turning the Muslims back from western Christendom, been the salvation of civilisation. The obvious examples of the Inquisition obstructing the advancement of knowledge – Copernicus, Kepler, Galileo, Dante – are mentioned, but that is only one aspect of the broader problem.

There follows a chapter which is given over almost entirely to the story of the persecution, torture and eventual execution of Savonarola. Smiles provides a detailed narrative in which it is made clear that he deplores the cruelty with which a man he regarded as both high-principled and harmless was treated. Again, he cannot resist going further, by pointing out that while Luther canonised Savonarola, the latter was in no sense a Protestant and was indeed 'more Catholic than the Catholics'. Luther, in other words, was making a cynical gesture to score off the Catholic Church, placing himself almost as far in the wrong as the actual perpetrators of the outrage.

If Smiles generally wrote of people he admired, and, subject to only a few exceptions that is true, then perhaps the most problematical of his more substantial works is *George Moore*. Moore's biography is the story of a man who made a great deal of money and, in Smiles' account, succeeded in giving a great deal of it away with such astuteness that he managed to avoid all the moral pitfalls awaiting the donor. He did not get 'suckered' by idle scroungers, he did not sap people's will to work by defying the self-help philosophy, he did not become proud or self-righteous about his own beneficence. He used his wealth and power for the benefit of the weak and deserving, and he did so largely because of his strong adherence to Christianity. But before we allow ourselves to believe that George Moore's goodness as presented by Smiles implies that Smiles shared Moore's beliefs, we should think a little longer. Aileen Smiles often remarks on what a happy man 'Granpa' was, and how he had a capacity to enjoy almost everything he did, but she recounts that he hated writing *George Moore*.[53] It was a commissioned work and he 'refused at first, not once but several times', before allowing himself to be persuaded to undertake it. Her evidence for this is sound: not only does his *Autobiography* mention his severe doubts about undertaking it, but a letter to 'Gingers' survives in which he describes what a burden he found the work.[54] It seems that, at this stage in his thinking, he did not relish the task of writing about an extremely rich man, and he pointedly remarks in the *Autobiography* that this was the first time he had written a biography whose subject was not of his own choosing. In short, it may be that not all that Smiles wrote in *George Moore* is entirely sincere; his dislike of the book may be the manifestation of a guilty conscience occasioned by writing what he was paid for. In fact, it seems possible that he did reluctantly come to view George Moore as a worthy man, for when he praises Moore's religious sincerity, he does so in a manner entirely compatible with the views suggested above: 'He found that Christianity required of him love, joy, peace, long-suffering, gentleness, goodness, faith, meekness, temperance, and, above all, charity.' Smiles also quotes Moore as writing:

All true Christians, whatever their denominational distinctions may be, are bound to each other by ties of the most sacred and enduring nature, and are conscious of a natural interest in each other's welfare, which gladdens this earthly-life and renders the prospect of a life to come more pleasing and blessed.[55]

There is not much there of the doctrine, dogma or intolerance which Smiles so disliked. He willingly admits that Christianity's ideals are of the highest and his account of Moore could be taken as an example of one of the exceptionally rare people who could actually live up to them. That would not be incompatible with a background view that organised religion was, on balance, more productive of intolerance, hatred and violence than of good. In fact, *George Moore* does not place any great difficulty in the way of the hypothesis that Smiles' religious views were not those of a supposed conventional middle-class England to which Hughes, Ritvo *et al.* have assigned him.

This has been a lengthy digression into a hitherto unexplored aspect of Smiles' life and thought. Smiles never hesitated to allow his feelings to govern what he wrote, and if we are to interpret his work, we must know what lay behind it, especially if we are using him as factual evidence. There is a more pressing reason, however. Smiles has been researched and written about by social historians, historians of education, less frequently by political historians and most frequently by engineering historians. Writers in each of these groups – and some others – have tended to see Smiles as one of their own, whether as the subject of their study or a forebear of it. Engineering historians have made little attempt to view Smiles as literature; educational historians have neglected engineering. Only Travers has tried to find a system of thought, or even a guiding theme, throughout his writings, and if the present attempt is to succeed, it must begin with a formative decision made at the tender age of thirteen – that he would not be a minister – which would affect everything he thought and wrote thereafter. The place of non-conventional religion in the nineteenth century is often underrated by those in quest of a 'Victorian frame of mind' or 'Victorian values'. There were people who did not fit neatly into categories such as Anglican, Roman Catholic, Dissenter, and not all of them were Bohemian artists and poets dividing their time between inspiration and opium-induced oblivion. Some – well, one at least – might be found among those considered to be both eminent and representative Victorians.

CHAPTER TWO

Smiles the Radical

Not every commentator on Smiles has observed that, earlier in life, he was of quite radical opinions. In some cases, such as that of L.T.C. Rolt in his introduction to *Lives of the Engineers*, the reasons are eminently understandable, if not entirely supportable. Rolt was an engineer writing about engineering: more specifically he was an engineering biographer writing about the effective founding father of the genre and a man who had, quite literally, been a source of personal and professional inspiration to him.[1] Smiles, for his part, introduced some obfuscation in one of the few passages where he writes about the political views of one of his subjects. He records that Telford read and was 'at once carried away by' Paine's *Rights of Man*,[2] and goes on to explain how such views were potentially professional suicide. Telford later realised how views such as Paine's led to the murderous brutality of the French Revolution and 'became wonderfully reconciled to the enjoyment of the substantial freedom which, after all, was secured to him by the English Constitution.'[3]

Smiles is being a little disingenuous here. The implication is that Telford became a bolshie, left-wing rebel and later grew out of it, coming round to what he, Smiles, allows us to picture as the right point of view. In fact, large numbers of British people sympathised, like Telford, with the aims of the French Revolution in its early idealistic stages and only recoiled from it later when the killing got out of hand and war with France brought issues of patriotism into frame. In telling us nothing new and nothing actually false, Smiles tempts us to form our own picture of his views, a technique at which he was particularly adroit. He might in this case be thought to go so far as to encourage us to mislead ourselves.

When Buchanan considers the political allegiance of some of Smiles' subjects he avoids questioning what Smiles' own ideas might be, and rests content merely to encapsulate him as 'physician turned journalist and publicist'.[4] The more one studies Smiles, the harder it becomes to encapsulate him. Some writers have made regrettable judgements of Smiles based, presumably, on a sketchy reading of *Self-Help*. Certainly Hobsbawm should have regretted his statement that Smiles 'hymned the virtues of capitalism' and Anthony's toes should have curled up at the mention of 'The Official Ideology' when, or if, either read Tyrrell – or any of the passages of Smiles cited in this chapter.[5]

It is no new discovery that Smiles was no more a typical middle-class gentleman (if such a creature ever existed) in politics than he was in religion. On the contrary, a succession of writers has drawn attention to his radicalism. Some, like Fielden, have done so comparatively briefly, in that Smiles' minor works are pretty sparingly cited, as indeed is anything he published before *The Life of George Stephenson.*[6] Anthony is more perfunctory, passing swiftly on to the main argument of a chapter entitled 'The Official Ideology: Laissez-faire and Self-help'. This is not the place to digress into the self-help question, which is the subject of a later section, but Anthony's study exhibits a severe truncation of source material. Only four writers, namely Travers, Tyrell, Fielden and Morris, seem to have paid any serious attention to what Smiles was writing early on in his literary career. Four might sound a lot, but when we consider the number of people such as Ritvo who feel they can refer to him in shorthand, it is not many.

The most curious such omission is that by Briggs: he has made much of the way in which *Self-Help* is derived from a tradition of 'success literature', which began before Smiles and continues to the present day.[7] It seems obvious that one place to look for the origins of *Self-Help* is not in the things Smiles *read* before he wrote it, but in the things that he *wrote*. Briggs does go back to a pamphlet *The Education of the Working Classes*, published in Leeds in 1845, but appears content there to let the matter rest. There is also, of course, the possibility that from an investigation of Smiles' early writings something interesting might emerge completely unconnected with *Self-Help*, or at least with our present perceptions of it.

Let us return to the young Smiles at Haddington. He describes how he trained at Edinburgh as a surgeon, and how, when he was there, he received a message that he must go home immediately as his father was 'ill of cholera'. By the time he got back his father was dead.

Cholera was very deadly in the town at that time. Many died in the front street, near where my father lived. The cause of the fatality was afterwards discovered – want of wholesome water and utter want of drainage. The defect was afterwards remedied after many years' delay.[8]

Over forty years later, in a passage which seems to have been more quoted than understood, the man whom Sir Keith Joseph told us was against collectivism[9] had this to say:

> Why, then, is not sanitary science universally adopted and enforced? We feel it is merely through indifference and laziness. The local authorities – municipalities and boards of guardians – are so many Mrs Maclartys in their way. Like the dirty matron, they 'canna be fashed.' To remove the materials of disease requires industry, constant attention and – what is far more serious – increased rates. The foul interests hold their ground, and bid defiance to the attacks made on them. Things did very well, they say, in 'the good old times' – why should they not do so now? When typhus or cholera breaks out, they tell us Nobody is to blame.[10]

That, of course, is *not* the passage which more than one commentator has borrowed from Briggs without having to undergo the tedium of reading volumes-full of Smiles. (Which is eminently forgivable: remember that the most affectionate student of Smiles, namely his granddaughter Aileen, did not deny that he was sometimes tedious.) It is the passage immediately preceding, which sets the context for the well-known bit, and which makes it abundantly clear that Smiles was not the man sometimes pictured. Anthony has the gall to place him in line of succession after Andrew Ure as toady-in-chief to the capitalist exploiters, while Joseph portrays him as opposed to state interference and wholly in favour of individual responsibility. Both explanations read persuasively, but have the disadvantage of coinciding only occasionally with what Smiles actually wrote. Continuing from the passage which Joseph, borrowing from Briggs, quotes, we find the bit he did not quote:

> The responsibility rests somewhere, and if we allow it to remain, it rests with us. We may not be able to cope with the evil as individuals, single-handed; but it becomes us to unite, and bring to bear upon the evil the joint moral power of society in the form of a law. A law is but the

expression of a combined will. . . . Laws may do too much; they may meddle with things which ought to be 'let alone'; but the abuse of a thing is no proper argument against its use, in cases where its employment is urgently called for.[11]

Here is the man we have been told was against public expenditure and against intrusive legislation, speaking derisively of people who wish to keep rates low or avoid legislation, condemning them as not merely idle, but harmful, morally reprehensible and indeed verging on homicidal. Particularly interesting is the statement that 'the responsibility lies somewhere . . .', introduced almost as a throw-away line. There is no shortage of writers who tell us that the very nature of an unjust government is that it is irresponsible; with an engaging simplicity Smiles points out that responsibility cannot be dematerialised: it cannot be nowhere, therefore it must be somewhere, attached to somebody. This was not a broadly accepted idea in the 1870s: some might have considered it a little radical. We may compare Joseph on Smiles (he 'was definitely in favour of economic *laissez-faire*') with Smiles on *laissez-faire*:

Nobody has a theory too – a dreadful theory. It is embodied in two words – *Laissez faire* – let alone. When people are poisoned by plaster of Paris mixed with flour, 'Let alone' is the remedy. When *Cocculus index* is used instead and men die prematurely, it is easy to say 'Nobody did it.' Let those who can, find out when they are cheated; *Caveat emptor.* When people live in foul dwellings, let them alone. Let wretchedness do its work; do not interfere with death.

Before leaving this sub-plot and returning to Smiles' formative experiences, it is worth pausing to consider another of the reasons why Smiles would, in Joseph's technicolour dream world, undoubtedly have voted for Margaret Thatcher.

Entrepreneurs in one form or another are the subject of many of Smiles' anecdotes, bringing new or improved products or services to market, pioneering new methods of production: opening up new means of linking producers and customers and new sources of supply. His entrepreneurs can be owners, risking their money in the venture, or managers. Their main motives may be the fulfilment of a dream, the making of a fortune, the desire to succeed, the joy of creating, sometimes a mixture.[12]

It is, of course, rather foolhardy to try and generalise about the people Smiles wrote about, because if we include everyone from the subjects of the major biographies down to the passing references (especially in *Life and Labour*) there are literally thousands of them. What Joseph says here is undoubtedly true of a significant number, probably a majority. However, among the major biographies, the only subject who could be considered purely entrepreneurial is George Moore, who is also unique in being the only subject Smiles did not choose for himself and, as we have seen, the only one he recorded that he disliked writing about. When asked to write the life of the railway contractor Thomas Brassey, he declined. When he wrote *The Life of George Stephenson* he concealed the financial expertise and entrepreurial 'fixing' which were key elements in the rise to prominence of his subject.[13] Among the subjects for whom the highest praise was reserved were Robert Dick (bankrupt baker), Thomas Edwards (failed cobbler) and Jasmin (penniless barber). All three were gross failures in amassing money and 'bettering themselves' socially but worthy exemplars of other kinds of success.

Foremost among those who opened up new means of 'linking producers and consumers or new sources of supply' were the railway engineers. They were dependent, however, on the larger entrepreneurs, namely the railway financiers who do not appear to have been among Smiles' favourite people; of the railway mania he writes,

Folly and knavery were, for a time, completely in the ascendant. The sharpers of society were let loose and jobbers and schemers became more and more plentiful . . . they rose like froth into the upper heights of society, and the flunkey FitzPlushe, by virtue of his supposed wealth, sat amongst peers and was idolised. Then was the harvest-time of schemeing lawyers, parliamentary agents, engineers, surveyors and traffic-takers, who were alike ready to take up any railway scheme however desperate, and to prove any amount of traffic even where none existed. The traffic in the credulity of their dupes was, however, the great fact that mainly concerned them, and of the profitable character of which there could be no doubt.

The alleged advocate of private enterprise was not done yet; having perhaps foreshadowed the yuppies of the 1980s' property boom, he went on to allege worse:

> Parliament, whose previous conduct in connection with railway legislation was so open to reprehension, interposed no check – attempted no remedy. On the contrary, it helped intensify the evils arising from this unseemly state of things. Many of its members were themselves involved in the mania, and as much interested in its continuance as the vulgar herd of money-grubbers.[14]

The hero of the story of the railways was, of course, George Stephenson. Recent research has suggested that he was at least as much a 'jobber and schemer' as he was an engineer, perhaps more. That is not the point: Smiles specifically denies any such involvement by George since involvement in the finances of railways would have demeaned a hero of the working classes as just another of the 'sharpers of society'; 'He himself never speculated in shares.'[15] It is important to remember that the man who coined those ringing condemnations was himself the secretary of a railway company at the time, and was thus taking a considerable risk when he wrote as he did. To suggest that he was an uncritical admirer of untrammelled capitalism and all its works is to sign one's name to a confession of not having read even a selection of Smiles' best-known books.

Back to the recently bereaved medical student. He had learned from his father's death a lesson for life, but there was more to be learned in Haddington. It may well be that the true origin of *Self-Help* is to be found in Haddington rather than Leeds, but the immediate lesson was that which he learned when he attempted to commence practising as a surgeon. The market was flooded by a 'peace dividend' of former army and navy surgeons. None of the established practitioners wished to employ him, and he had not the capital to set up on his own. All he could get was 'some remnants of practice, mostly among the poorer people'.[16] So among the poorer people he worked for a time. Generations of cutesy Arcadian literature on the one hand, and Parliamentary Enquiries backed up by land-interest funded propaganda on the other[17] (such as the bizarre memoirs of the so-called 'factory cripple' who was of dubious cripplehood

and had certainly never worked in a factory: he was a jobbing journalist)
have served largely to conceal what he learned there, namely that however
bad living standards in the towns of the industrial revolution might be,
those in the contemporary countryside were generally worse: on the skirts
of the ducal park

> skulk a party of poachers who have faced the cutting blast of the winter's
> wind, the toils and penalties of the law, and even the terrors of sudden
> death itself, [Smiles is referring to spring-guns] and all for the sake of a
> few birds, on the killing of which, it may be, the very lives of these men
> and their families depend. Follow these men to their huts and what do
> you find? Four bare walls, a shake-down on a clay floor, sometimes only
> of straw, on which the family, sometimes a very numerous one, lay
> themselves down to rest. The wind blows through the damp hut, through
> the window chinks, the ill-closed door, the badly-thatched roof and
> through the very walls themselves, while these poor peasants vainly press
> together for comfort.[18]

He then goes on to describe how labourers in full employment are little
better off and to invite the reader to imagine their condition:

> Will it [their family budget] do anything for their education? Will it
> clothe them properly? Will it even afford them sufficient food? Yet such
> is the case of a large proportion of the rural labouring classes of 'Merry
> England'! Alas! It is a dismal picture from the further delineation of
> which our hand shrinks.

The passage above was written after Smiles had moved to Leeds and
begun to mix in industrial and commercial circles. Was he, perhaps,
seeking to denigrate conditions in the countryside in order to 'build up'
the conditions in a city where his friends and fellow Anti-Corn Law
Leaguers included the prominent engineering manufacturer James Kitson
and the mill magnate Garth Marshall? If Smiles' involvement with the
Oddfellows was indeed part of what Morris styled a 'retreat to a petit-
bourgeois utopia' – of which more anon – then by 1850 it had not yet
changed his perception of the problems of industrial towns or his
willingness to express them forcefully:

> It [capital] sets the mills a-going, employs labour, feeds many mouths;
> but let a bleak wind blow, and capital suddenly disappears – the mills
> stand, the labourers are idle, and tens of thousands of mouths want food.
> Even in our most favourable periods of prosperity, such as this which we
> have indicated, what is the physical and moral state of our labouring
> population? Look into the streets in which they live and you will find
> discomfort, foulness, unhealthiness, disease and much slow dying. Want
> of drains, want of sewers, want of water! And then come the typhus and
> the cholera, sweeping away their thousands of victims. . . . We can no
> longer shut our eyes to the facts. They loom before us like some huge
> demon: they oppress our hearts like some hideous nightmare.

These are no more the words of a toady to the mill owners than they are
those of an anti-collectivist supporter of enterprise.

Despite these appalling urban conditions, one of the constant themes of
his writings on education, on savings banks and benefit clubs was that
industrial workers were comparatively well paid.

> Take the wages of skilled Mechanics for instance: they are from 26s. to
> 30s. a week, and in many cases above this; or from £70 to £80 a year. –
> equivalent to most of the working Curates of England and perhaps of
> most Dissenting Ministers. A good mechanic is better paid than an
> Ensign in a marching regiment, or than a lieutenant in the navy.[19]

The same principle applied at lower levels of pay:

> The condition of the female factory operative is by no means necessarily
> one of degradation; on the other hand, it is, as regards the remuneration
> given for work done, superior to most other kinds of female
> employment.

Smiles then goes on to explain that factory women earned far more than
dressmakers or milliners and roughly twice as much as school mistresses or
governesses.

It should, he thought, have been within the capabilities of industrial
workers to save a little in good times to tide themselves over in bad. Factory
owners, after all, had not sent press gangs into the countryside to recruit

people to exploit: they had no need to, for the comparatively high wages they offered were sufficient incentive. When Smiles gave up the unequal struggle in the country and moved to an industrial town he found poverty and exploitation, but his experience was already sufficient for him to know that the answer did not lie in turning back to an imaginary Arcadia, as did such highly improbable bed-fellows as Engels and Carlyle, both of whom thought their (profoundly different) solutions to the urban crisis could be found rooted in a rural past. It lay rather in moulding a new future in which contemporary problems would themselves form the solution to the 'Condition of England Question'.

That experience made him a wiser commentator than many of his contemporaries. The idea that the past was, at least in parts, better than the present, and that we should learn from it is not necessarily fallacious, but it has always been fatally easy to take the extra half-step which calls us not only to learn from the past but to try to return to it. The problem with the past is that it seems so easy and so appealing to pick the bits of it we like while neglecting the others, forgetting that the past, like the present, is one immensely complex entity. How nice it would be for present-day Britain to have the low crime levels of the 1950s. The price to be paid includes the return of pea-souper smogs and the damage done to the child population by diseases already half-forgotten – diphtheria, tuberculosis, polio.

From the end of the Napoleonic Wars until the early 1850s, there was a feeling of unease in government and among the upper middle classes about 'the workers'. We need not be surprised at this: in its earlier stages the French Revolution had found plenty of apologists in Britain. Smiles' ideas on education, and especially political education, are said to have owed a good deal to Rousseau. In later works, he exhibits a marked cooling towards Rousseau, apparently provoked by a disapproval of his life-style.[20]

William Cobbett's argument in *Cottage Economy* that tea-drinking is a 'degrading curse' which renders workers unfit to encounter hard labour, 'deducts from the means of replenishing the belly and covering the back', 'corrupts boys as soon as they are able to move from home' and sends girls to the 'gossip of the tea-table [which is] no bad preparatory school for the brothel'[21] invites us nowadays to see him as a likeable, quintessentially English, eccentric. The few of us who still live north of Watford are quite amused by his references to London as 'The Great Wen' and there is something rather engaging about his passion for mangelwurzels and *ruta baga*. We must not forget that he was a pretty fearsome rabble-rouser in his day, and his tragi-comic acquisition of the bones of Tom Paine should prompt us to question what use he wanted to make of the 'holy relics' of a man pretty generally loathed and feared by the political establishment.[22] The occasional governmental atrocities like Peterloo were founded not so much in casual brutality as in fear. Continuing troubles on mainland Europe did nothing to reduce the tension, and while the law did become a little more liberal, the fears remained in the background. The Chartists brought them to the fore.

The men who tried to understand what was going on, as distinct from merely giving us the benefit of their opinions, fairly soon identified the main source of the strength of such groups: '. . . the bitter discontent grown fierce and mad, the wrong condition therefore or the wrong disposition, of the working classes of England'.[23] This bitter discontent was manifest in a long-lasting wave of rural violence in which one might highlight the Swing riots of 1830 and the wave of arson which occurred in East Anglia in 1843–4. But these events, unpleasant though they might be, were widely separated in place and time: they posed no serious or coordinated threat to the state.

The case was quite different in industrial towns, with their high population density and rapid 'grapevine' communication: their population was much more threatening. The question was asked how it came about that as the country became nationally more and more prosperous the industrial workers suffered increasingly from environmental and occupational diseases. Higher wages might solve some of their problems, but by no means all of them – industrial wages were already relatively high. Leaving aside the reactionaries who believed that there was no social problem the military could not solve, there remained the two basic answers to the 'Condition of England' question: to look back to the age before the problem existed and seek to re-apply its secrets, or to look forward to an age after the problem had ended. The advocates of the former approach were numerous, and while they included such celebrated thinkers and persuasive writers as Thomas Carlyle, they were backed up by an entire neo-medievalism industry with interests not just in literature and publication but in art, design, architecture and music. We have already seen some evidence that Smiles was a definite forward-looker.

This did not mean that they could not agree: one of the great issues of the day was the price of bread, on which Smiles and Carlyle were in total agreement. Smiles, in 1842, spoke dismissively of the 'Bread-Tax Parliament', while Carlyle, reviewing the work of Ebenezer Elliott, 'The Corn Law Rhymer', wrote, in characteristically succinct style,

> Mournful enough that a white European Man must pray wistfully for what the horse he drives is sure of – That the strain of his whole faculties may not fail to earn him food and lodging. Mournful that a gallant manly spirit, with an eye to discern the world, a heart to reverence it, a hand cunning and willing to labour in it, must be haunted by such a fear. The grim end of it all, Beggary![24]

Smiles expressed exactly the same idea more simply: 'Men, who, by protracted and daily toil, are barely able to keep body and soul together, cannot in reason, be expected either to have very refined feelings or a highly cultivated mind.'[25]

While Smiles and Carlyle might differ on the remedy, they concurred on the nature and origins of the problem: the governing class was not fit to govern. It has often been remarked upon that Smiles, for a time, supported Chartism, but the emphatic manner of his support is not always made clear:

> I hail Chartism as one of the most notable steps in the march of modern civilisation. I cannot look upon it with the fear and trembling that some persons do; but consider it to be one of the most hopeful of all the signs of the times. [Another little dig at Carlyle, whose *Signs of the Times* were not very hopeful, perhaps?] It is the result of knowledge – political knowledge if you will – flowing in upon the minds of men who find themselves living in the midst of wealth and civilisation a degraded and an oppressed class.[26]

The less money an ordinary family had to spend, the higher the proportion of it which had to be spent on bread, and high bread prices therefore had a dire effect on the poor. (The description 'poor' is here used loosely, to mean those who suffered a pitiable standard of living, not in the technical sense of their being paupers.) The urban poor, who were unable to grow any food for themselves, might benefit from competition between shopkeepers, but high population density could also cause locally inflated prices. The price of bread was inflated by the duties paid under the Corn Laws, an import tariff imposed to protect home producers of corn. The effects of this inflation extended far beyond keeping country landowners in the manner to which they had become accustomed at the expense of those who had no political voice. However we may choose to define a subsistence wage in the towns, the inflated price of bread increased that wage and therefore increased manufacturing costs. For those who, temporarily or permanently, did not earn wages, the parish had to make Poor Law provision and the cost of that also increased with higher bread prices. Even before we allow of any possibility of humanitarian concern on the part of manufacturers in particular and the urban middle classes in general, it was clear to them that they were subsidising people of whom they did not particularly approve. Among those middle classes were some at least who were genuinely concerned for the state of the poor, and among them was Samuel Smiles.

Smiles' first book, *Physical Education; or the Nurture and Management of Children* (1838) is a rare but mostly unremarkable work such as might be written by any surgeon or physician.[27] Smiles suggested in his *Autobiography* that Dr Andrew Coombe wrote a rather better book (*Treatise on the Physiological and Moral Management of Infancy*) on the subject shortly afterwards, but in fact he mentions Coombe's book in the introduction to his own work. He was well aware of, and emphasised, the importance of cleanliness, good ventilation, and drainage and he made some hard-hitting remarks about the 'terrible and unnatural' rate of infant mortality. As Travers points out, the emphasis on 'unnatural' is important. 'That [excessive infant mortality] is not, however, the design of our Creator.'[28] There are, however, hints of what was to come in his later works, in that he identified poverty as a significant and avoidable cause of disease and death. One of the ways to break the circle of poverty and disease was cheaper bread, but the provision of cheaper bread did not lie within the competence of an obscure and unsuccessful country doctor.

For the editor of a radical newspaper in a large and populous industrial town things might be different. In a number of his short publications on the subject of education Smiles states quite clearly that one of the benefits of widespread education is the spread of the rudiments of literacy in order that people can read newspapers:

It is because of the peculiar and urgent interest which the study of politics possesses to all classes, that NEWSPAPERS [Smiles' capitals], the records of political movements, are at the present day the literature of the great bulk of the people. The newspaper is now-a-days what the preacher was some two or three hundred years ago. It is the guide, counsellor and friend. It is our best moral police. It watches with lynx-eye over the proceedings of legislatures; it stands in front of benches of magistrates and justices of peace [*sic*]; listens at the poor man's door, as well as prys into the doings of palaces. It exposes abuses, unmasks jobs, censures vice, lashes tyranny.[29]

The passage continues in this vein at some length. Among other points it makes is the value of newspaper correspondence columns as a means for the weak and the poor to have their grievances heard, and its coda tells us that the newspaper is the great agent of political education, the chief bulwark of liberty, and the most active pioneer of public intelligence. So now we know: country doctors might be able to watch with lynx-eye, but they did not get to lash tyranny. Nor did they get to publish the texts of public addresses which expressed, as this one did, a clear conviction that not only was the British government operating a legal and fiscal system which victimised the poorest members of society for the benefit of the richest, but also that the ground rules under which they did so were just as wrong as the results. So it was that when the poet Robert Nicoll was forced to give up the editorship of the *Leeds Times*, Smiles allowed himself to be head-hunted as his successor.[30]

There was another man who had felt the same a few decades before, and who had taken to publishing in a similar vein for a similar reason. Among all the possible writers who may have had an influence on Smiles, he seems scarcely to have been considered. To this writer it seems that the most interesting individual to single out for a 'compare and contrast' exercise is, by a long way, William Cobbett. That Smiles read Cobbett and admired what he read is easily established. In his well-known address to the Leeds Mutual Improvement Society, he says this: 'Let me here show, for your encouragement, how Cobbett, one of the purest and best of English writers, learned Grammar, and overcame the difficulties of composition. The description is given in his own words. . .',[31] and there follows a quotation from Cobbett's slightly self-pitying account of how he learned grammar as a private soldier, deprived of every possible aid – money, comfort, books, pens, paper, ink, even light – through his determination to master the subject. In another Smiles article we find: 'In William Cobbett – that strong-minded man of common sense, though of great English prejudices – we recognise one of the greatest Educators of the past century.'[32]

At first sight the differences between Smiles and Cobbett are great. The counterpoise to Cobbett's loathing of tea, mentioned above, was his ebullient exposition of the merits of home-brewed beer, which occupies no fewer than thirty-six pages of his *Cottage Economy*. Smiles, on the other hand, obviously disapproved of alcohol:

An investment in beer or tobacco is very profitless. A temporary pleasure may be produced, but invariably at the expense of a corresponding reaction and loss. There is a loss of health, a loss of money and a loss of home comfort, without any equivalent whatsoever in physical or moral or intellectual satisfaction.[33]

The difference between the two men here is entirely superficial, because we have strayed from the underlying point made by two different men writing in different places at different times. Cobbett is advocating the home-made beer of the countryside as cheap, hygienic and nutritious, attributes still commonly lacking in rural water supplies a century or more after he wrote. The beer Smiles denounced as profitless to the consumer was volume-produced, commonly at egregious profit to the brewer, in town breweries and similarly lacked all those desirable qualities. It was relatively costly, made from poor ingredients, commonly adulterated with harmful additives, and often kept and served in poor conditions (and condition). It served mainly as an alternative to gin as a way of avoiding life's numerous and persistent problems for a little while. To Cobbett, home-made beer did not help the drinker avoid the problems – it positively and beneficially diminished them.

Underlying the two men's different attitudes is a common purpose. Smiles spoke frequently and vehemently in favour of temperance, referring to drink as a great vice, but his support for temperance was not a matter of teetotal principle. His admitted liking, in later life, for his whisky toddy,[34] might be taken as evidence of hypocrisy in this respect, but is nothing of the kind. Smiles did not object to drink *per se*: he objected to people spending money on drink they could not easily afford and thereby depriving themselves and their familes of things they needed more. Among the urban workers, drink was the greatest single enemy of thrift: to Cobbett, among the rural workers, the enemy of thrift was not beer, but tea. We may think Cobbett's arithmetic crazy or we may shrink from Smiles' moralising: if we do either we miss the central point which the two men had in common.

Both of them opposed the Corn Laws, deplored the Game Laws, and thought that the traditional land-owning classes were a bunch of corrupt and insupportable drones. Both were strongly in favour of the 'dignity of labour' and both wanted to see far-reaching political changes which would reflect what they saw as the proper relationship between those who produced and those who only consumed. Neither was in favour of violent revolution. Above all, both came to the same conclusion as to one effectual engine of change: it was that the workers should achieve a measure of financial independence. In Cobbett's rural environment that meant that the worker should be able to produce the bare necessities of life for himself so that his pitiable wages could provide a few extremely modest luxuries and a small nest-egg. In Smiles' urban environment it meant that the worker – well paid by Cobbett's standards – should accumulate a bit of capital, so that when hard times came he was able to retain his self-reliant pride. Both writers, in short, recognised the vulnerability of the 'wage slave' and proposed a solution. In each case, we might think the proposals unrealistic, but both authors went so far as to provide detailed instructions for achieving the 'impossible'.

Smiles has earned a good deal of adverse criticism (and the approbation of Sir Keith Joseph) for his opposition to strikes. In 1861, he published *Workman's Earnings, Strikes and Savings*, which has allowed some commentators to assume that the former radical newspaper editor had moved a long way to the right and had his lynx-eye dimmed by his new position as a senior officer of a railway company. A slightly more leisurely perusal of this book reveals that much of it is a rehash of views voiced in a string of writings from 'What is doing for the People of Leeds?'[35] onwards. Smiles' objection to strikes is much the same as his objection to drink: they divert the workers' money from the key objective of finding that modest measure of financial independence. It is difficult to do justice to his argument without a rather lengthy quotation:

It was stated at a late public meeting of operatives at Preston, that in one strike of the cotton spinners at Manchester, which lasted four months, they spent £400,000 in loss of wages alone; and in two others they lost £600,000 . . . [and several other examples] made a total of *three millions sterling*, which to all intents and purposes had been spent in vain – as, in nine out of ten cases the strikes completely failed in their object. Just think of this amount of capital being expended on land, on buildings, on co-operative production establishments, or on the means of physical, moral and intellectual improvement, and what glorious results might not have been anticipated from it!

It may be true that on some issues the lynx changed his spots over the years, but this was not one of them. In *Thrift* (1875) Smiles still gives examples of what he considers huge wastage of workers' resources on pointless strikes and of ways in which that money could have been spent to produce a real improvement in their material condition, political influence and self-respect. Specifically mentioned are the application of workers' capital to cooperative ventures of the kind envisaged not only by moderate groups like the Rochdale Pioneers but also by the Chartists.[36]

Some of the attacks made on Smiles' political views are based on such transparent ignorance and prejudice as to deserve no comment. By far the most damaging attack, because it comes from one who has carefully researched local politics in Leeds, is that of R.J. Morris.[37] His central contention, well supported with references from Smiles' early writings, especially in the *Leeds Times*, is adequately summarised in the subtitle of his paper, 'The retreat to a *petit bourgeois* utopia'. He traces a process in which Smiles starts as a radical and is gradually driven by failures in the early 1840s to water down his position until he arrived at *Self-Help*, which does not offer any answers to the problems of the working class: it offers them methods of becoming *petit bourgeois*. This is a powerful and scholarly paper: it is based on a formidable knowledge of political and quasi-political bodies in Leeds, and, like the works of Smiles himself, it has a compellingly simple underlying story line: that of a political 'wild man' gradually drifting to the right as he grew older and richer.

This writer, however, would not be mentioning the paper in such complimentary terms (if at all!) did he not believe that it contains several serious flaws. The first of these is Morris' contention that the self-help doctrine is some kind of climb-down from a more radical earlier position. Smiles' Bradford Address of 1842 makes it quite clear that such was not the case. Although it contains some pretty fiery pro-Chartist stump oratory, Smiles did not argue there or in earlier writings that the remedy for the condition of England lay *solely* in the reform of a corrupt and incompetent government and later change his tune to claim that the remedy lay solely in the hand of the individual. On the contrary, he consistently argued over a long period that *both* needed to change and that the changes needed to coincide. Passages already cited from *Thrift* and *The Life of George Stephenson* suffice to illustrate that he continued to believe that effective state action was necessary. For the converse view, that state action alone was not sufficient, we find in the Bradford Address:

> For instance, a good Government can secure to every individual the fruits of his honest labour; but a Government, no matter how good, can do little or nothing towards making the idle and slovenly industrious, the improvident careful, the drunken sober, the lewd virtuous. No! These are reforms which must come from the people themselves; and are almost entirely beyond the reach of the most enlightened and philanthropic Government.[38]

This is nothing more or less than any experienced reader of Smiles should come to expect: simple commonsensical stuff which indicates that in 1842 as in 1875 he was aware that there were two sides to the question. Certainly the Bradford Address contains material more seditious than that for which Cobbett had been imprisoned, but that is not all it contains, and it seems unreasonable to claim such a partial view as the basis of an argument in favour of failure or climb-down by Smiles.

It is has long been a favourite sport to try and prove that Smiles' ideas were self-contradictory, and Morris would probably be less than human if he did not join in. The example he chooses, however, seems worse-founded than most: Smiles is a hard man to catch out. Morris argues that the British economy could only enable people to improve themselves through self-help if they disregarded the practice of thrift: otherwise there would be no-one to buy the fruits of self-help which emerged in the forms of an ever-growing GNP and an ocean of manufactured goods. Morris here fails to understand Smiles' view of the rest of the world, which was scarcely an unusual one at the time. Why did the Creator, having completed his supreme achievement, Great Britain, bother with the rest? There must have been some use for it.

Indeed there was, and it is not complex: the rest of the world was partly there to supply a few things such as silk which the Creator, in one of His little lapses of concentration, had failed to provide in Britain. Its real place in the scheme of creation, however, was as an export market. Few people in mid nineteenth-century Britain, and certainly no people as astute as Smiles, imagined that Britain could or should consume all it produced. That is why the Port of Liverpool, for example, engaged in a programme of dock building between 1825 and 1860 which quintupled its water area and resulted in a more than proportionate increase in tonnage handled.[39] British shipowners dominated world trade, and in the event of facilities at the far end of a trading link being inadequate, British civil engineers could be relied upon to export their services and solve the problem. Liverpool-trained dock engineers turn up all over the world.

The most serious problem with the Morris thesis, however, is the underlying one, which is that the (dubious) retreat was the result of failure. Middle-class radicals like Smiles may have failed in their objective of forming a symbiotic partnership with the Chartists where they provided money and respectability and the Chartists provided an impressive head-count. They may also have failed to change the fundamental class structure of central government. In other respects they emphatically did not fail. The Corn Laws *were* repealed. Municipalities *were* empowered to effect vital sanitary reforms, prompting a wave of improvements both in water supply and in sewage disposal. Municipal medical officers *were* appointed. Perhaps more significant in the long term, the Public Libraries Act was the first of a sequence of measures which marked the acceptance of a public duty to provide for the cultural needs of ordinary people. Needless to say, Smiles had been one of the witnesses before the Select Committee. The result was a gradual fading of the image of the worker as a dangerous, riotous, Chartist looney. In its place appeared a new archetype, possibly just as inaccurate in detail, but just as influential in its popular perception: the 'intelligent artisan'.

The part played by Smiles in building the image of the intelligent artisan is another phase of his career, which might be said to begin with his early offerings on *The life of George Stephenson* (1850–2), but which achieved maturity in *Lives of the Engineers*. This series and its lesser brethren were so influential in changing perceptions of the working class that it is tempting to suggest that the Morris thesis may be stood on its head: if Smiles changed his emphasis at all it was not because he had lost, but because he had won what he recognised was only Round 1 of a long contest. For Round 2, tactics would need to be different, for they had now to be addressed not only to the referee, but partly also to the beneficiaries of the success of Round 1. As he used to put it, 'Sensible men change for the better.' But the problem with the Morris thesis of retreat is more fundamental than that. How does anyone remain a lifelong radical? There are only two ways: by being a lifelong failure whose ideas are never taken up, or by being a lifelong capricious trouble-maker who ensures that the answer is never found by repeatedly changing the question. Lifelong radicals are not praiseworthy men who refuse to sell out their beliefs: they are losers, either born or self-created. Successful radicals are those who see old radical opinion become the new orthodoxy: that is what makes them winners. Smiles was a winner.

The final problem with the Morris thesis of a retreat is the difficulty of identifying exactly when Smiles had a particular idea or formed a particular line of thought. He had a habit of re-using or reworking material time and again over long periods: examples have already been cited above, and Travers' careful researches in identifying early magazine articles (especially in *Eliza Cook's Journal*) provide many more examples.

There is another often-neglected question about Smiles' works, which only Tyrell seems seriously to address.[40] It is very easy to assume that Smiles wrote for an upper working-class or petit-bourgeois audience, because these seem to be the people he is addressing. Why, after all, tell the story of how a common pit boy became the most distinguished engineer in the world to, say, chartered accountants? The stories must surely be told to the people who will benefit from them. If we believe that, then once again we underrate our man. It was possible to reach that market as editor of the *Odd-Fellows Magazine*, through the pages of the *People's Journal* and possibly through cheap printings of the texts of addresses like the one he gave at Bradford.

Smiles' books, however, were far from cheap. They were handsomely produced by a prestigious publisher at prices normally between five and seven shillings, which in the 1860s was almost a quarter of a week's pay for a well-paid skilled man. When they were getting past their first flush of popularity, Murray suggested producing cheap editions, and Smiles would have none of it. 'Cheap books will not do', he wrote to John Murray, and no cheap editions appeared until the 1890s. The familiar uniform cheap editions, of which thousands were given to reluctant recipients as school prizes, and which may nowadays be had for only a hundred or so times their original price of 3*s*. 6*d*., did not appear until 1905, when Smiles was safely dead and buried.[41] Presumably his family either thought his works deserved a revival – which these editions gave them – or they wanted the money.

But at whom, then, were the books aimed? Whoever it was, the aim was astute, for most ran through multiple printings and the more successful ran through dozens. Several were produced in more than one foreign language: overall, Smiles was among the best-selling authors of the second half of the century. Travers has produced an estimate of the sales of *Self-Help*,[42] and the range of printings of Smiles' major works can be gained from the *British Library Catalogue* and the *National Union Catalogue*. The *Self-Help* series alone ran to over 200 printings in English and several dozen in other languages. There were, and are, three basic types of book-buyer: those who want to own the book themselves, those who buy it to give to other people, and librarians. It is perfectly clear that Smiles' works, or at least the more successful ones, appealed powerfully to all three. While that may account for the commercial success of his work, it still does not clearly explain who he was addressing or why he chose latterly to address them through the medium of relatively expensive books. Had he drifted to the right or had he not?

If, as suggested above, Smiles and his like had emerged relatively victorious from the ruins of Chartism, there were still two important objectives outstanding which were likely to prove more problematical to attain than the repeal of the Corn Laws or the move to win public libraries. These were universal education and universal suffrage. Now, we already know from Smiles' Bradford Address, his more famous discourse to the Leeds Mutual Improvement Society, his address on industrial education and his open letter to Edward Baines on national education, as well as a host of minor offerings in, for example, *Eliza Cook's Journal* (5 July 1851), that he regarded education as extremely important. He also made clear his opinion that the inadequacy of existing provision was both qualitative and quantitative, and was incapable of reform under the existing system.

In recent decades it has become part of the stock-in-trade of political debate to accuse opponents of using schoolchildren as political pawns, implying that the real issues of education are subordinated to political dogma. It is always tempting to believe this of whichever side it is with which one disagrees, but education was certainly an intensely political issue by Smiles' time, if not long before. Specifically, it was linked with the suffrage question, for the people who argued that there was no benefit in educating children above their station tended to be the same people who argued against widened suffrage on the grounds that one could not have elections determined by a load of uneducated peasants voting on issues they could not understand. It therefore became almost inevitable that those who wanted universal suffrage had to argue for universal primary education.

Fear of 'the mob' was fairly widespread during the earlier decades of Victoria's reign, and is certainly a consistent theme in Smiles' writings. To a man who deplored force, there had to be an alternative to repetitions of Peterloo, and there was. The behaviour of a mob was, he thought, determined by a small number of troublemakers backed up by a lot of really quite harmless people who were easily led astray. Modern political rhetoric on the theme of 'rent-a-mob' perpetuates his views. The reason that harmless people were easily led astray was, of course, that they had not been properly educated, for educated people would not behave like that, or so Smiles thought. He was able to point to the fact that, then as now, the majority of convicted criminals were notable for their poor standard of education. From that position, he neglected the possibility that only ill-educated criminals were thick enough to get caught, while the educated did not, and assumed that education disposed people against crime. He did not, however, make the common mistake of assuming that crime was necessarily perpetrated by the 'lower orders': he held strong and not universally palatable views on the subject of white-collar crime.[43]

That was not the only connection between education and politics: another one which was potentially just as dangerous to the victors in the Corn Laws debate was the question of the other effects of free trade. If it was free trade to export manufactured goods all over the world it had to be recognised that those manufactured goods included tools and machinery which would increasingly enable overseas competitors to close the technological gap Britain had opened up. Free trade was a two-edged sword, and Smiles was not slow to recognise this: he argued that improved technical education was necessary if Britain was to retain her industrial primacy. There was no point trying to give a technical education to young people who could not read or write. Therefore Britain's position in the world would soon come, if it had not already, to depend on universal high-quality primary education.

It may here be objected that Smiles was inconsistent, and so, to a degree, he was. In the late 1840s his view of educational improvement hinged on two main points: the diminution of the 'wide and growing gulph [*sic*] of separation which divides the educated upper and the uneducated lower classes of society',[44] and the need to do away with sectarian and ideological education:

> The Church does little, and what it does, is done with the view mainly of inculcating its own creed. The great class interests in the State do nothing; and perhaps it is better that they should do nothing, as unprejudiced help is scarcely to be expected from them. . . . To enslave a nation, it is not necessary merely to impose despotism upon the people and compel them to submit to it by a huge standing army. There is a far more wily and effective method; which is, to get hold of the minds of the young and imbue them early with slavish ideas.[45]

Neither state of affairs was acceptable, yet each was, according to Smiles, widespread. The limited public funds available for grants to schools were allocated on the basis that they were matched 2:1 by local funding. This meant, of course, that those rural areas where landlords had no interest in educating the workers – or indeed were positively against it – attracted no funds. The money went to those places, urban or rural, where people were already improving the system, further widening the 'gulph'. Amid a string of examples of tight-fisted landowners we find that

> The colleges at Cambridge are the principal owners of land in another parish, and these also refuse to subscribe a farthing towards local schools of any kind. The dean and chapter of a cathedral possess 800 acres of land in another parish, and they too, though repeatedly applied to, will not contribute anything towards the schools.[46]

By contrast, the people who were conspicuously in favour of popular education were the members of the working classes themselves:

Lovett, Vincent, Collins and others of the same class; men known for the intensely political cast of their opinions and who, in fact, owe to politics (as is the case with the most of our intelligent artisans and mechanics) almost all of the education they possess.[47]

The apparent inconsistency lies between his strong advocacy on the one hand of what we may loosely term DIY educational organisations such as mutual improvement societies and on the other of the various self-taught heroes of *Lives of the Engineers*. What place was there for spoon-fed public-sector education when so much good came from the exercise of personal qualities? Were not the achievements of self-educated geniuses such as James Brindley and George Stephenson as good an argument as any Cambridge college might want for avoiding spending money on its peasantry?

As is often the case with Smiles, the difficulty is only superficial. His view is actually quite clear: he did indeed believe that life was a race in which those who did not try hard enough were the losers, and for those who competed and lost he had relatively little sympathy. *Thrift* is rich in the denunciations of the idle, the thriftless and the drunkards, strictures which found such repeated favour with those who objected to paying poor rates. But unlike most producers of such denunciations, he believed that everyone had a birthright to a place on the starting line of life's great race. Hand-outs might often debilitate the recipient, but that did not exonerate society from accepting some responsibility: 'The duty of helping the helpless speaks trumpet-tongued.'[48] Their birthright imposed duties on society as a whole, to provide a wholesome environment, the means of bare subsistence, and a basic education. Otherwise, the winners of the race were predetermined, and that was not only bad for the losers in the race, but for its organisers as well. What, he had once asked, would the consequences be if medical qualifications were, like the ownership of land, hereditary?[49]

Smiles' biographies and their messages form the subject of a later chapter, so they must be passed over quite briefly here. Most of the best-known subjects are consciously and admittedly produced as exemplars of the way in which intelligent and energetic members of the working classes could become not only rich and famous but also significant benefactors to all mankind through achievements of truly epoch-making importance. This is one of the points at which Smiles really is ambivalent: while we may choose to believe that his exemplars are exceptional men, he is often at pains to point out that they did not possess any inborn genius and to emphasise their ordinariness. As we read through their lives, we may suspect that here, too, is the doctrine of the starting line, but there is no doubt that in some cases he overshot his own mark: if Brindley and Stephenson could do what they did while remaining only semi-literate, who needed an educational system?

In 1867, he squared the circle in a little-noticed speech at the annual soirée of the Huddersfield Mechanics' Institute on the subject of industrial education of working men.[50] After clear statements of the dangers which accompanied the benefits of free trade, there follows a sequence of invidious comparisons between the way in which the intelligent artisan is educated in Britain and, for example, Saxony, France, the United States, Austria and Switzerland. Next comes a selection of *obiter dicta* from such luminaries as Lyon Playfair and William Fowler on the inadequacy of the British system. As he winds up to the conclusion, he quotes from a letter addressed to Lord Taunton:

> of what use is an industrial scientific education to our working men if they have not had a good elementary education to begin with. . . . Let this national elementary education once be established throughout the country and you have a fine nucleus for scientific industrial schools. . . .[51]

Then comes the resolution of the central problem:

> There is, perhaps, no nation in the world that can show so many brilliant instances as ours does of men sprung from the ranks of the working class, who, in the face of difficulties apparently insurmountable, have raised themselves to the highest positions as inventors, discoverers and leaders of industry. But it must be acknowledged that these are exceptional cases. . . .
>
> But with the great mass of the people, who stand outside the domain of knowledge, the case is very different indeed. They must be helped to help themselves; and this can only be done after a well-devised plan and system, which it is the business of society, acting through its organised instrument, the Government, to arrange and settle. . . . That the poor boy should be started on the road of life with his poverty, is burden and calamity enough; but that he should be started also with ignorance, is a still heavier burden and a still greater calamity.

It may be worth digressing briefly here to remind the reader that the year in which Smiles was first sounding his warning about the technical education of artisans was the year of the Great Exhibition, wherein the excellence and dominance of British industry and technology were displayed to an admiring world: it was a year of euphoria in which Britain rolled about hugging itself at the spectacle of its own greatness. More sober observers knew that the technology on display had, by the act of displaying it, become international public property. By 1867 the message had become one of urgency as Smiles pointed out the comparative effectiveness of educational systems elsewhere in Europe.

Many years later, in *Thrift*, he would again describe a good education as the equivalent of possessing capital: it was an asset for life, and in his description of the educational attributes of Haddington in his *Autobiography* he repeated exactly the same argument. This represents a shift from his position in earlier writings, when he backed the teaching of political economy to the working classes as a means of stabilising society. Again, as in his alleged 'retreat' into self-help, we may feel that Smiles moved to the right as he grew older: in fact the reason for the change in emphasis is once again not failure but success. The fears of revolution which beset English society with varying intensity from the end of the Napoleonic Wars largely disappeared during the 1850s and, long before *Thrift* was written, the intelligent artisan was a well-known stereotype. Shortly before *Thrift* was written, Gladstone's reforms, beloved of generations of O Level and GCSE history examiners, had left Smiles with few political objectives to seek. In education, as in self-help, he had not retreated. He had seen his once rather outrageous views become first policy and then law.

Objectives in technical education were a different matter, and one on which Smiles often fails to display the optimism which is characteristic of his writing on most other subjects. His concern seems to have been almost entirely with the lower echelons: the problems which were becoming increasingly obvious at the sharp end of engineering development largely passed him by. This is evident in the peculiarity of his selection of biographical subjects: as Buchanan has remarked, nearly all Smiles' heroes were dead by 1860. We search in vain for the men who were making the technological running during the period when Smiles was at the height of his success as an author. Particularly puzzling is the absence of W.J.M. Rankine. His teaching at Glasgow, and his production of a succession of engineering textbooks which remained current for generations, placed Rankine among the most influential figures in the entire history of engineering education.[52] But there are numerous other equally puzzling omissions: almost any engineer who made any great contribution either to engineering theory or to the merging of theory with practice is likely to be absent. William Armstrong, whose company made important steps in scientific testing, recording and development of products (in hydraulic engineering and in armaments manufacture) raises no enthusiasm. Froude, who played a major part in turning naval architecture from a craft mysterie into a science is absent.[53] There are no electrical engineers at all, and no industrial chemists unless one counts the likes of Wedgwood.

These seem like serious shortfalls in Smiles' interest in education, but they only seem so if we cannot accept the suggestion made above, that Smiles' concern was in getting people to the starting line of the race. His view, and it is one for which he has suffered a good deal of both contemporary and posthumous mockery, was that once a young man had a fair start, he could win. Smiles has been especially castigated by those of a sensitive and artistic disposition for suggesting that even great artists could achieve their greatness by application and hard work rather than by inspiration, a bizarre taste in clothing and excessive ingestion of various harmful substances in garrets.[54] It may well be that Smiles did not fully understand matters of high art, but Sir Joshua Reynolds, from whose *Discourses* Smiles lifted the idea, has generally been reckoned sufficiently handy with a paint brush to be qualified to comment.[55] That position too is compatible with the starting line explanation. Getting young Reynolds to the starting line was all that was necessary: his ability and perseverance would do the rest. Similarly, young engineers could do as their fathers had done, and make their own way.

This raises a further ideological problem in Smiles' view of the role of education. If young men in the 1860s or '70s did not owe a sufficient debt of gratitude to, say, Rankine to justify his appearance in a small eulogy by Smiles, then we must assume that previous generations of engineers – the great men who were dead by 1860 – had not needed to learn from books either. But this is not the case: by the early years of the nineteenth century, the better libraries in cities such as Newcastle, Liverpool or Manchester, where much engineering was going on, stocked not only the latest works in 'natural philosophy', but also the works of leading French theorists from

Belidor to Carnot. Thomas Telford may have been a stonemason by training, but his books, which he left to the Institution of Civil Engineers, are the collection of a man familiar with theory as well as practice.[56] Smiles nowhere denies this, but he allows the reader to form an inaccurate impression, because that is what his ideology tempts him to do.

Easily the most 'theoretical' of the subjects of Smiles' major biographies is James Watt. Cardwell argues the case for Watt as virtually the father of thermodynamics,[57] but one does not have to go nearly so far as that to call Smiles' view into question. He concedes that 'it was probably because Watt was a great theorist that he was a great inventor' and again that 'new theories suggested new arrangements'.[58] Yet the book closes with an account of a visit to the preserved 'garret workshop' in which Watt reputedly spent most of his retirement hiding from an over-houseproud wife, and the final sentence of the book begins 'But though the great *workman* [my italics] has gone to his rest, with all his griefs and cares . . .'.[59]

It is quite impossible that Smiles was unaware that Watt was something more than a 'great workman': one chapter of the book is, after all, devoted to the famous Lunar Society and relates in some detail the relationships which Watt enjoyed with some of the leading scientists of his age.[60] In Chapter 4, Smiles writes of Watt's contacts with Robison and Black and, perhaps most telling of all, mentions that Watt read the works of Desaguliers and others.[61] Yet the overall impression which readers derive from Smiles, that he saw great engineers as not much involved with theory, is soundly based, for the emphatic bits, the memorable bits of the narratives and the summaries of the characters of the engineers drive home the message that these men are not scientists or theoreticians but great workmen. Who, after all, could forget Brindley's dying words 'Then puddle it again – and again'?

A misleading message? Of course it was, and as time went by the more theoretical engineering became and hence the degree of misleading that was going on increased. It does indeed seem that engineering 'stopped' for Smiles around 1860. But in terms of engineering education, what he was writing was ideology, encouragement to the young men who used the libraries he had advocated, to take up engineering, to educate and improve themselves. If we are to dismiss what he wrote as wrong-headed, we should do so in terms of those objectives: what, to use modern jargon, were Smiles' Output Performance Measurement Indicators? The continuing growth of the profession, and the domination of the world-wide market for civil engineering services by British engineers, suggest that his books had a clear educational target and that they hit it. His Huddersfield speech suggests that his educational ideas had a clear political target, and he hit that too.

Obviously it is difficult to tell exactly how much influence Smiles' writings had. It seems clear, however, that he had strong and fairly consistent views on politics and education from the late 1830s until at least the early '80s. There were shifts in emphasis from time to time – it would be a pretty poor political writer who did not recognise the need to move with the times, and Smiles was a political writer with an uncommonly long writing life. The fact remains that he lived to see legislation enacted which fulfilled virtually all his programme. It was not just a matter of corn laws and votes: his wider concerns – responsibility for such things as preventing the adulteration of food, the elimination of unhygienic living conditions, the provision of public libraries, ensuring the security of the savings of the working man – were accepted as obligations on society at large and provided or enabled through the agency of national or local government. Of course others had trod the same path, and it is not a matter of logical inevitability that they, or Smiles, could go only that way. But they did, and it worked in the sense that changes brought about peacefully were comparable in extent and far greater in durability than most of those resulting from the minor revolutions on mainland Europe.

It would be going too far to claim that Smiles was a great or original political theorist. It seems reasonable, however, to suggest that he was more sophisticated, more consistent and above all more successful than has hitherto been recognised.

CHAPTER THREE

The Self-Help *Series*

If the suggestion in the previous chapter, that Smiles had a consistent politico-educational programme which extends through most of his writings, has any substance, then the need arises to look again at our approach to *Selp-Help*, Smiles' most famous and successful book. It is the work by which he is most generally remembered, the one which has never been out of print, the one which is considered to contain the essentials of 'The Smiles Philosophy', the one which has attracted the most comment at every level of competence.

We may begin by discounting the comments and the passing references of those who portray Smiles as the apostle of *laissez-faire*, as an advocate of the establishment or as an icon for mid-Victorianism. There has been no credible attempt to rehabilitate such a view of Smiles since the publication of Asa Briggs' thorough and interesting introduction to the centenary edition of *Self-Help* promoted a more sympathetic approach. Nor, as he pointed out, was he the first: he cites the spirited defence of Smiles given – rather unexpectedly – by Robert Blatchford in *The Clarion*. Smiles was not in favour of socialism, but Blatchford, after quoting the opinion that *Self-Help* was 'a brutal book: it ought to be burned by the common hangman' went on to describe *Self-Help* thus:

> 'Self-Help' is one of the most delightful and invigorating books it has been my happy fortune to meet with. It has done me nothing but good, nor can I conceive how it should do harm to any. So far from signing its death-warrant, I would advise its adoption as a reading-book in our schools, and would recommend it to the youth of these islands as a safe and efficaceous mental tonic.[1]

He then goes on to refute a number of other charges commonly levelled against Smiles, notably that he was a Philistine concerned only with success, measured mainly in monetary terms, that he fostered snobbery and selfishness. Such accusations could, according to Blatchford, only be made by people who had not read Smiles, a view in which most later commentators, and this writer, concur.

It would be unwise, however, to underestimate the strength, tenacity or extent of opinion based on the diligent non-reading of Smiles. The writer possesses a referee's comments on his first effort at a paper on Smiles which include the question of whether Smiles' ideology related to social Darwinism. It rather depends on what one means by a relationship: Smiles has a chronological relationship in that *Self-Help* was published ten years before Galton's first offering.[2] Its assumptions about life and achievement are related as well, in the same way that the north and south poles of a magnet are related. Where Galton suggested that achievement arose from inherited characteristics Smiles insisted at repetitive and boring length that achievement did not even require any unusual degree of talent: it required honest hard work and perseverance. Smiles, it is true, regarded race as a factor: he enthused, for example, about the energy and capacity for work of the Jutes – qualities inherited both by the then inhabitants of Jutland and by the English.[3] This is, however, a misleading line of argument, for Smiles' enthusiasm for race seems to have been greatest around 1870, just the time when he was also working on his two books, and several articles, on the Huguenots. They, too, were good, hard-working people, but they were not of any specific racial extraction. Where Galton imagined the possibility of 'breeding' out social problems, Smiles described how they could be worked out.

Galton provides an association of ideas which forbids the commentator on Smiles, however much he might wish to do so, to shirk the comparison with another Lowland Scot, husband of Haddington's famous detractor, Sage of Ecclefechan and proto-Nazi, Thomas Carlyle.

Carlyle was, of course, no more a forebear of Nazism than was Galton, Wagner or Jesus: it was simply their shared misfortune that their writings or *obiter dicta* could be fitted or twisted into the amazing hotch-potch of ideas which became *Mein Kampf*. That said, it is true that Carlyle clearly stated in a number of places, most notably in 'The Hero as King',[4] that what the proletariat needed was simply that the best and most able person in the land should rule as monarch. This simplified political theory in the most delightful manner: just as the books on medieval chivalry said, they owed obedience to him, he owed protection to them and that was about all there was to it. As soon as more than one ruler was involved, then some form of organisation became necessary, which represented the human counterpart of the 'mechanism' which Carlyle deplored loud and very long in *Past and Present*. The simpler, the better. There was the slight problem that mistakenly giving absolute power to an '*un*able man' was a 'diabolic wrong'.

This stance was so obviously at variance with the views which Smiles held in the early 1840s that it seems, approaching Carlyle from that angle, that they could have little or nothing in common. In fact, Carlyle was at least as many-faceted as Smiles, and his paper 'On Chartism' would need only to be translated from its characteristic bombast into the commonsensical language of Smiles to be eminently mistakable for the work of the latter. Both Blatchford and Briggs make the comparison, and it behoves us to take it seriously.

Carlyle, like Smiles, believed in the dignity of work.[5] Briggs states that neither of them made the distinction he attributes to Ruskin and Morris between useful work and pointless toil, but this seems rather to fail to take account of the implicit prejudices of Smiles and Carlyle: when we observe Carlyle's frequent use of the word 'work' in *Past and Present*, and his assertion that 'All work, even cotton-spinning, is noble',[6] we are tempted to forget that Carlyle did not regard all forms of employment as 'work'. We find the answer in his incandescent diatribe *On Hudson's Statue*: his view of people who worked in financial services was, or at least became, even more jaundiced than that indicated by the extracts from Smiles on the subject of the railway mania given in Chapter 2, above.[7] Carlyle does not seem to have committed himself to print on the sanctity of the work of the gamekeeper, but we may deduce it. When he repeats *laborare est orare*, which he translates as 'Work is Worship', it is perfectly clear that, as in most other cases, he is to be believed only in so far as the statement is compatible with his own implicit as well as explicit views.

To Smiles, the idea of work as worship undoubtedly complied with his rather vague religious tenets as discussed in Chapter 1. When, however, Carlyle moves on to the idea of Gurth, born thrall of Cedric the Saxon, being happy in his brass collar of serfdom because he knew where he stood – exchanging obedience for protection – the idea of Smiles concurring becomes laughable.[8] The entire and abiding message of Smiles is that people should not be content with where they stand. Cobbett's remark, that he despised the man who was poor and contented,[9] is far closer to Smiles' idea of what the work ethic was about: work was not good *per se*: work was good because it improved the state of the individual, the community or the nation. In most of the biographical examples he gives, work achieved at least two, often all three, of these objectives. To Cobbett as to Smiles, the successful worker was the one who could earn for himself a little independence. To Carlyle, that would be toil in the mere pursuit of money, for what benefit was there in being independent from such a nice man as Cedric? Whatever he might say about all work being sacred, he clearly regarded the results of a great deal of it as comprehensively despicable: his introduction to the ambience of twelfth-century Britain explains how the Ribble and the Aire are 'unpolluted by dyers' chemistry . . . no steam-demon has yet risen smoking into being . . . [the future site of Liverpool] . . . clangorous with sea-fowl . . . no monstrous, pitchy city'.[10]

Carlyle fulminated on behalf of the poor, especially in relation to the Corn Laws and the new Poor Law. References to workhouses as 'Poor Law Bastilles' were surely intended to be not only graphic, but, coming from the historian of the French Revolution, threatening. The threat was directed at a class perceived to be made up of useless, idle, rural landowners, for whom Smiles had no time either. When, however, Carlyle went on to urge this former governing class to pull its collective finger out and govern properly again, Smiles' toes must have curled into clove hitches. In his scheme of things, the only landowners who deserved a living were those such as the Duke of Bridgewater or Lord Dudley who bankrolled industrial developments or those ennobled on the strength of well-earned industrial fortunes. He would probably have approved of Lord Leverhulme as much as Lord Leverhulme approved of him. That is speculation, but his views of Carlyle are in print:

We must admit, however, that the revolutionary and destructive genius is stronger in Carlyle than the conservative and constructive. He is emphatically a puller-down, not a builder-up. He never wields his giant's club with greater delight than when he is assailing some cherished idol of society; his humour is then almost savage, and his sneers sarcastic, bitter and full of gall.

Further down the same page, we find that if Carlyle really respected all work, then Smiles had certainly not perceived him as doing so:

> Kings and Priests, self-chosen, he calls on to get out of the way; all professors of cant, of shams, of trickeries, quackeries, frauds of all kinds . . . nay, he would even do battle against humane and true workers, because they do not, like him, wield the club of steel and whip of fire. We have seen how he could fall foul of the humane treatment of prisoners. . . . He has no sympathy for such notions of making men better. . . he is down upon the 'humanity-mongers' with all his might. Carlyle never cares how or where his strokes tell. The bullet shot by him may kill a general or a private soldier; it matters nothing to him.[11]

Although Smiles has not generally been regarded as a polemicist in the same league as Carlyle, he was capable of landing the occasional telling blow when roused, and some of Carlyle's ideas clearly aroused him considerably. Blatchford, looking for extracts from Smiles which fitted his socialist viewpoint, provides the following: 'Caesarism is human idolatry in its worst form – a worship of mere power, as degrading in its effects as the worship of mere wealth would be. . . .'[12]

Smiles, in his usual homely manner, cites Napoleon III – an example carefully chosen to arose suspicion and hostility – in support of despotism and then enlarges on the parallel he alleges between Carlyle's 'worship of power' and one of his favourite *bêtes noires*, 'mammonism'. Self-help will destroy Caesarism, for 'the two principles are directly antagonistic'.[13]

It is suggested in a later chapter that he came to regard other of Carlyle's ideas, despite the points on which they agreed, as equally harmful, and that he built up what one might dignify with the description of a philosophical structure, intended to enlarge upon the idea that Carlyle was essentially self-contradictory. As suggested above, Smiles and Carlyle were actually moving in opposite directions, and the fact that, in passing, they lighted briefly upon a few of the same subjects and agreed on them does not alter the fact that their starting and finishing points were entirely different. For the present, we may pause with, and consider further, the Smiles assertion that self-help is the key to the overthrow of 'Caesarism' and hence to the upholding of successful democratic government.

The question is the nature of the outcome of successful application of

Self-Help. Certainly the consequences for the individual might include serious wealth: among the first of the cameo biographies in *Self-Help*, we find Joshua Heilman, inventor of a number of useful devices for the textile industry, most notably the combing machine. Years of toil, persevering in the face of repeated failure and reducing himself to poverty, eventually resulted in his receipt of unspecified sums well over £50,000 for the use of his patent. Unfortunately,

> . . . he did not live to enjoy it. Scarcely had his long labours been crowned by success than he died, and his son, who had shared in his privations, shortly followed him. It is at the price of lives such as these that the wonders of civilisation are achieved.[14]

The next chapter is occupied with the life stories of three potters: Palissy, Böttgher and Wedgwood. Of these, the first died in prison (for his religious beliefs) and the second died at the age of only thirty-five from a combination of over-work and excessive drinking; only Wedgwood became rich and successful. What self-help had achieved for all of them was that they were all 'fairly entitled to take rank as the Industrial Heroes of the civilised world', and their entitlement was based on their refusal to accept failure and the beneficial results for others of what they had achieved.

If the reference to 'Industrial Heroes' is, as seems likely, a sly dig at Carlyle's ideas of the role and nature of the hero, or his attacks on 'mechanism', Smiles was not the man to be vindictive: among a number of examples of people who overcame crushing setbacks we find the anecdote of the destruction of Carlyle's manuscript of Volume 1 of his monumental work on the French Revolution, and Smiles' admiration of the way in which he 'set resolutely to work to re-write the book', a task of 'pain and anguish almost beyond belief', seems as sincere a description as it is unqualified.[15] A high proportion of the anecdotes relate to the overcoming of difficulties rather than the acquisition of money.

Clearly some of the men who successfully practised self-help did become very rich, notably some of those who went on to figure at greater length in *Lives of the Engineers*, such as Watt and the Stephensons, but their riches are not mentioned in *Self-Help*. They are included, along with strings of others, as examples of the benefits of application and perseverance. Their reward does not need, in those circumstances, to be stated: it was simply that the reader knew who they were.

The characterisation of Smiles' stories as exhibiting 'luck and pluck' begins to look increasingly absurd as he piles on example after example of people whose success had nothing whatever to do with luck. Among the relatively few stories whose central subject is described as acquiring large sums of money, we find an account of William Phipps. Phipps found some £300,000 worth of treasure aboard a sunken Spanish vessel, and his share of the salvage amounted to some £20,000. He did not, however, gain it by luck: he gained it by such patient searching for the wreck that his crew twice mutinied, in the belief it would never be found.[16] His success is no less a success of perseverance than is that of the other persevering worthies. It is, however, expressed in monetary terms, so we should move on to consider the Smiles view of money. This is scarcely difficult, since Chapter 10 of *Self-Help* is titled 'The Use and Abuse of Money'.

The sequence of treatment of the subject is slightly odd, in that we might expect Smiles to begin with warnings of the dangers of 'mammonism', when in fact that is the theme of the end of the chapter. He pulls few punches: 'The power of money is on the whole over-estimated. The greatest things which have been done for the world have not been accomplished by rich men, nor by subscription lists, but by men generally of small pecuniary means.'[17] At the time Smiles wrote this, he was the secretary of a railway company: he knew very well what the power of subscription lists was. But their power did not extend to the things he proceeds to put forward as the ones that really matter: the greatest thinkers, discoverers, inventors and artists have been men of moderate wealth, many of them 'little raised above the condition of manual labourers in point of worldly circumstances'. A little further on we find that 'riches are oftener an impediment than a stimulus to action' and the situation is summed up by stating that intelligence, public spirit and moral virtue are greater and nobler powers than that of money.

To those who seek to establish Smiles as the ideological prop of mid-nineteenth-century capitalist exploitation, such statements would seem to offer plentiful meat and drink – they savour rather of the servant who 'makes drudgery divine', and the whole burden of the last chapter of the book is that 'The True Gentleman' earns that title not by money but by character. One of the examples of true gentlemanliness given is of two English navvies in Paris who followed the coffin of a complete stranger to the graveyard, because no one else was following it. Similarly, people with money frequently squander it on useless trappings of respectability and, indeed, run into debt in the quest of yet more of them. 'We must be "respectable", though only in the meanest sense – in mere vulgar outward show.'[18] The message seems to be that is possible to be poor, happy and virtuous, so let the rich people have their riches, which are only bad for them really, and await your reward in heaven.

That is not, however, the real burden of the chapter. The biblical distinction between reasonable seeking of money and the quest for money for its own sake is clearly drawn, as is that between thrift and miserliness. The practitioner of self-help can perfectly well look to earn more money, and it is for the reason mentioned in Chapter 2, above: '. . . the man who is always hovering on the verge of want is not far removed from slavery. He is in no sense his own master. . . .'[19] The point of this has been missed by a variety of commentators, though few have missed it so comprehensively as de Maré, who averred that 'Smiles had a host of eager listeners who aspired to middle-class status'. If they did, they were reading the wrong book. Smiles, we are told, was 'misleading himself and his million readers', and as time went on there were ever fewer opportunities for the kind of dramatic rise that George Stephenson had enjoyed.[20] Self-help and its benefits simply were not available to ordinary struggling men. The self-deception is, however, de Maré's, for he has completely failed to understand what Smiles meant by the rewards of self-help, and even what the nature of self-help was. He pours scorn on Smiles, questioning how a man with little or no education, with a family to support, compelled to work all hours for £1 a week could 'escape from his thraldom'. This supposed appeal to common sense is in fact empty rhetoric based on an inaccurate general impression of the period: Smiles, on the other hand, was there, living at the time, and he, not de Maré, is to be trusted.

In this author's specialism of port history, it is worth noting that an unskilled dock labourer in Liverpool at the time earned 6d. per hour; even in that notoriously badly-paid job one had to work not 'all' but 40 hours to earn £1. Skilled men earned about £2 per week, and elite groups such as corn porters about £3. The suggestion that self-improvement (within de Maré's misunderstanding of the meaning of the term) 'grew even less possible even for those of outstanding gifts' might be modified by perusal of the career of Miles Kirk Burton. He began work as an office boy and retired as Secretary and General Manager of the Mersey Docks & Harbour

Board – probably the most powerful man in the entire port services industry at the time. Sir Alfred Jones rose from humble beginnings as a cabin boy to the ownership of a major shipping line and almost complete control of the entire trade between Britain and West Africa. The Vestey brothers were the sons of a small-time butcher: they ended up as peers of the realm, controllers of a world-wide meat trading empire. Thomas Royden was apprenticed as a shipwright and ended up in the 1890s controlling 1 per cent of the entire British shipbuilding output, which, of course, dominated world production. William Lever's soap, vegetable oils and chemical empire was built up by the son of a small grocer who read, and acknowledged his debt to, *Self-Help*. Not one of these men, as de Maré insists, 'inevitably came from healthy rural stock'. The odds against a rise from rags to riches may be difficult to quantify, but it always had been possible, it continued to be possible, and it is still possible today. Smiles was not 'presenting a dream', though he does seem unwittingly to have presented themes upon which historians have composed the freest of variations.

But we have not plumbed the full depths of de Maré's misunderstanding. He was writing in the 1970s, when the fruits of success were external and visible. Smiles' statement that 'what some men are, all without difficulty might be. Employ the same means and the same results will follow,'[21] can indeed sound absurd. But 'what some men are' is not rich and famous: the condition to which the average workman may aspire by the practice of self-help is to be 'useful, honourable, respectable and happy'. His views of what de Maré, as a child of his time, interpreted as success, are clear. The Victorian equivalents of the owner-occupied detached suburban house, the smart motor car, the dinner parties and the skiing holiday get short shrift: 'There is a dreadful ambition abroad for being "genteel". We keep up appearances, too often at the expense of honesty; and, though we may not be rich, yet we must seem so.'[22]

As the passage continues, it is explained in uncompromising terms that social display leads at best to unhappiness, at worst to misery and crime. The message is simple, though often overlooked: that the benefits of self-help are not external, but internal. Furthermore, he practised what he preached: in later life he lived in some quite expensive houses, threw some parties and went on continental holidays. He went to the opera and the races, but he did so only when he was well able to afford it. During the later part of his life, his income often exceeded his expenditure by four digits per year.[23] That was independence. Manly independence, even.

It has been conceded that Smiles can sometimes be dreary, repetitive and long-winded. This does not alter the fact that he often writes pleasant, easy-to-read passages which express themselves with remarkable economy. For example, the following could not readily be shortened without loss of meaning:

> Rightly earned, it [money] is the representative of patient industry and untiring effort, of temptation resisted, and hope rewarded; and rightly used, it affords indications of prudence, fore-thought and self-denial – the true basis of manly character. Though money represents a crowd of objects without any real worth or utility, it also represents many things of great value; not only food, clothing and household satisfaction, but personal self-respect and independence.[24]

The key to the economy of this passage, which practically encapsulates a code of behaviour for everyday life, is the implicit cross-references to other parts of the book in which it abounds. It tells us that money which is *rightly earned* is an indication not of greed or miserliness but of virtue, and, by implication, that money earned without the exercise of virtues expounded here and elsewhere is not rightly earned. 'Manly character' is among the two or three highest forms of praise in Smiles' writings, sometimes elevated to 'a truly noble and manly character' and rivalled (possibly) only by 'truly sterling worth'. Here, the award of the near-ultimate accolade depends on the ways in which money is both earned and spent. The key words, as so often in Smiles, are those like 'rightly' and 'truly', which remind us that he is using commonplace expressions such as 'work', 'earn', 'manly' and 'respectable' in a highly idiosyncratic way.

SMILES AND WOMEN

The mention of 'manly character' may perhaps serve as the prompt for a brief digression into Smiles' view of women. There are comparatively few passages of his work in which they play much part as individuals, and virtually none of his well-known works has much more to say of individual women than to retail a few well-known yarns of Florence Nightingale,

Grace Darling and the like. *Lives of the Engineers* is notable for its almost complete failure to mention wives, mothers, sisters or daughters of engineers, and one cannot help but suspect that some of the few occasions where they do appear are merely prompts for the incorporation of stock literary components to flesh out the story a bit, of which more in following chapters. Not all engineers, of course, behaved in an exemplary manner with, or towards, women, which accounts for the absence of any mention of the women in the lives of, for example, James Brindley or Robert Stephenson. The former was an ancestor of Arnold Bennett, by virtue (if the reader will pardon the expression) of seducing the daughter of the millwright to whom he was apprenticed, while the latter was marginally responsible for the Scout movement through his relationship with one Henrietta Powell.[25] Civil engineers were itinerant high earners in a glamorous profession (how things have changed) and it is only to be expected that some of them would succeed in getting their evil way with impressionable young women. By the time Smiles was writing *Lives of the Engineers* the engineering world had been scandalised by the seduction of Harriet Hartley, wife of the distinguished dock engineer John Bernard Hartley, by James Thompson, Engineer to the Liverpool & Bury Railway Company.[26] If one wanted to use engineers as social exemplars, perhaps it was better not to say too much about their treatment of women.

We are set, then, to identify Smiles as somehow 'typically Victorian', whatever that means, in his desire to keep women out of the story, out of the way, safely engaged in pointless pursuits such as needlework and not troubling their pretty little heads about real life for fear of suffering attacks of the vapours. In Haddington as a youth, his education had been completed after the death of his father only by virtue of his mother's hard work and astute domestic management. However sexist he may sound at times, he never forgot this debt.

Sexist he certainly was, and at the time he lived it would have been extremely odd had he not been. His treatment of the suggestion that men and women were indistinguishable equals is little short of derisory. He was against the idea of women going out to work, and saw them as the essential element in the stability of home life. It was the constant example of selfless motherhood exhibited to her child, especially in the early years of childhood, which formed character.[27] While this may sound uncomfortably close to the 'pregnant, barefoot and in the kitchen' approach, it was not all that close, and it formed a unifying theme for most of Smiles' ideas on the subject of women. If we choose to trade in aphorisms, he showed much greater enthusiasm for 'the hand that rocks the cradle rules the world'. In one sense he followed the fairly orthodox Victorian view of 'separate spheres', but in another his views were broader, perhaps at times to the extent of being unclear.

The achievements of some Victorian heroines depended on their having behaved like men. Florence Nightingale may have been compassionate when attending to wounded soldiers, but the key to her success, and her fame, lay in her tigerish assaults on bureaucracy and the military hierarchy. That side of her does not figure prominently in Smiles' account, but he does remark on the improbability of a woman being able to 'undertake to nurse soldiers in time of war'. What was remarkable about Grace Darling was not so much what she did as that she was a girl doing the job of a macho lifeboatman.[28] It may be significant that Smiles devotes as much space to Sarah Martin, a comparatively little-known prison visitor and honorary prison chaplain (presumably Quaker, though this is not specified). Both she and Grace Darling exhibited great courage, but Sarah Martin typified Smiles' ideal female: instead of courage, physical strength and skill in rowing a boat, she showed compassion, loyalty, perseverance and the willingness to provide a good example in the most trying circumstances.[29] Those were the qualities required in the average mother of a family in, say, Oldham or Stockport, where the lifeboat was called out only infrequently.

It is always for the 'average' family that Smiles appears to be writing, and he really could be very clever in the way he approached them: his scornful denunciation of 'etiquette' (his scare quotation marks), for example, was an effective and reliable device for unifying a readership which neither knew nor cared when one should leave a single calling card and when one should leave two.[30] To this readership he addressed a fairly simple message. Men and women are different, and the consequences of their trying to be interchangeable are not usually happy ones. Men who exhibited feminine (not effeminate; Smiles did not write of such indelicate subjects) characteristics were likely to fail at work through lack of strength and aggression. Women who worked, whether in factories or in commerce, were likely to be hardened and corrupted by their experience. It all sounds rather like a development of the probably prurient speculation so prevalent when debating the iniquities of partly or wholly naked women working down mines in close proximity to similarly unclad men back in the 1840s, on canal boats, in agricultural gangs and in West Midlands chainwright's shops. (One suspects that if the men had to work nearly as hard, and drank nearly as hard, as we are told they did, they would not have had the strength to get up to anything very naughty anyway.)[31] There remains the possibility that some people did sincerely believe that some forms of work were unsuitable for women. This particular jaded old cynic has his doubts.

This, however, is not the Smiles message. He is mainly a gentle and didactic writer, and when he writes of working-class problems and failings he generally does so in a sympathetic manner. He may disapprove of working-class thriftlessness, of strikes or of general sluttishness. The denunciations which exhibit real malice on his part are those which relate to dissipated aesthetes such as Byron, who is a favourite villain, decadent aristocrats, but, above all, rapacious businessmen. Smiles hated the share-dealers, the 'middlemen', the manufacturers of shoddy goods, the adulterators of food. This, rather than the mills or the mines, was the world from which he wished to exclude mothers on moral grounds, not because they would do dirty things in some corner of the workplace but because they would absorb and pass on to their children values which Smiles thought had no place in the most civilised country in the world.[32]

There was another aspect to women's employment. When women went out to work in order to increase the family income, they almost invariably worked for less money than men. So far did this lower men's wages that the agricultural workers' union was reduced actually to subsidising its members to emigrate, in the hope that the reduced supply of labour would force the payment of reasonable wages to those who remained. Smiles was obviously not averse to that idea, as he praised 'the late Mrs Chisholm's efforts to help young women to emigrate'.[33] Broadly speaking, it is true that the areas in which women were most successful in finding employment in the late nineteenth century not only became, but have remained to this day, low-paid. These were large consequences to arise from the desire of women to increase the family budget, and we would rightly expect Smiles to question whether it was necessary. He does not disappoint us: a woman's place is, in most circumstances, in the home.

In the home, she could not only act as a constant benign influence on her children, uncorrupted by the world of business: she could act as a wise

manager of the family budget and a prudent and thrifty provider. That may
be the essence of some of Smiles' argument, but it is by no means all of it.
He rightly questioned how a woman could manage a household, however
modest, if as a girl she had attended a school where arithmetic was for boys.
On educational matters he stood four-square with the feminists of the day.
Further, he argues that women are unfit to bring up children if they have
no knowledge of physiology, and to sustain a family if they have never been
taught the rudiments of nutritional science – or even of cookery.[34] As usual,
his apparently unsophisticated commonsensical approach offers achievable
solutions to serious problems. How did a young mother know what was
wrong with a bawling infant? Was it hungry, in a bad temper, or ill? In
ignorance, the usual recourse was to alcohol and/or opiates, which
produced peace and quiet, and almost certainly contributed to the
deplorable rate of childhood mortality on which Smiles repeatedly
remarked. It seems genuinely to have mystified Smiles that the rearing of
children, which he regarded as requiring considerable knowledge and skill,
was left to chance in the hands of completely untrained and ill-educated
girls. Perhaps it was just pique occasioned by the fact that his *Physical
Education; or the Nurture and Management of Children* (1838) had not sold at
all well.

Cookery might not be a matter of life and death, but incompetent
cookery wasted money on ingredients and fuel, and provided meals which,
on a good day, might aspire to marginal edibility. The unhappy results
extended beyond the lack of a frugally priced yet nutritionally sound diet:
it drove men out to the alehouse, where cheese sandwiches or their like
made good the deficiency. The result was that the man paid twice over for
the food he needed, he wasted money on beer, he neglected his family and
those who did not go to the alehouse with him remained undernourished.
While this was undoubtedly the result of his human weaknesses, he had
been severely tempted, and Smiles' condemnation of his fall is pretty
mild.[35]

It would be easy to assume that the other side of the coin was
condemnation of the stupid feckless sluts these unfortunate chaps were
sufficiently ill-advised to marry. It has to be admitted that Smiles veers a
little in that direction when giving us the benefit of his opinion on the
subject of marriages originating in the combination of male lust and
female pulchritude, but as we should by now expect, his real feelings lie

elsewhere. Motherhood is not only a skilled job, it is among the most important jobs there are: a man serves an apprenticeship to learn to make unimportant things; a woman is expected to take charge of her little share of the future of the human race on the basis of a few words of advice from her mother, who has been 'educated' in an equally ineffective manner. Ignorance thus became hereditary, and major changes in the education of, and attitudes to, women were needed.

So much, briefly, for the role of the wife at the subsistence level. What was the role of women who did not have to struggle just to attain the basics? As remarked above, Smiles had no time for females who divided their time between needlework and hostess-ship: 'It is still too much the practice to cultivate the weakness of woman rather than her strength.'[36] The good middle- to upper middle-class woman could be meritorious in her own right if single, or could be a 'help-mate' to her husband. This latter term is one which has caused a good deal of confusion, and is commonly taken to patronise women. In a sense, the controversy which lies behind that view is of quite recent origin, because nineteenth-century feminists do not seem to have worried too much about the minutiae of the words we use. Smiles used two different terms interchangeably, simply because although it was a potentially controversial subject, he did not feel it necessary to pay constant and careful attention to exact shades of meaning. The two terms are 'help-mate' and 'help-meet', and their exact meanings were different then and are different now.[37] Both come from Middle English, the former meaning a trusty comrade, with undertones of subordination, as in the mate of a ship. The latter derives from 'mete', meaning fitting. A help-meet was someone who supplied the deficiencies of their partner, so that two individually inadequate people made, together, a team capable of great achievement. Reduced to its simplest, Smiles' message on marriage was that its whole was greater than the sum of its parts, scarcely a position of breathtaking originality.

Smiles gives many examples of this phenomenon. Some are, to be blunt, little above the level of great men sustained by wives who cosseted them while they worked, but others illustrate genuine contributions by women, such as were made by the wives of Galvani, Lavoisier and Buckland. His choicest example is the naturalist Huber, who was blind from the age of seventeen but who succeeded in continuing a highly visual form of research, literally through the eyes of his wife. An outstanding example

Smiles does not quote, for its significance only became clear after his death, may help to clarify matters. This writer, when told by his help-meet that it is his turn to empty the kitchen bin (usually when a force 9 is driving the rain against the back door), has been known to quote to her the words of Lady Elgar: 'Is not the nurture of a genius a sufficient life's work for any woman?' Lady Elgar, however, did more than empty the bin: all but one of Elgar's mature works before he lapsed into an unhappy mixture of arid neo-classicalism and nostalgic pot-boiling were written during his comparatively brief marriage to Alice. From a sequence of turgid quasi-Wagnerian works in his early years, there is suddenly released the genius who wrote *Enigma Variations, Gerontius, The Apostles, The Kingdom,* the two symphonies, the violin concerto, *Coronation Ode* and *Falstaff.* Just seventeen years of Elgar's long life produced all but one of his great works, and those seventeen years were during his marriage. The last great work, his cello concerto, is the exception which proves the rule, for it was Alice's requiem. After that, there would not be another 'great beautiful tune', as she described the 'doodling' on the piano which she heard, and which became the motto theme of the first symphony.[38] Was Lady Elgar a down-trodden spouse? It depends on how one defines terms like 'nurture' – and 'help-meet'. Some might say that she corrected a failing in Elgar, namely his inability to recognise which of the innumerable ideas he had were truly great and which merely competent. We need not agree with Smiles' view of the help-meet, but it is possible to recognise that it had at least some substance.

Smiles provides a few passages which allow us to gain an impression of his view of 'free-standing' women. There are numerous passing references, sadly of little substance, to literary figures such as Madame de Stael or the rather dreadful Mrs Schimmelpenninck. In 1847, he had published an article on the supposedly scandalous George Sand, and in the following year he wrote of her associate Felicité Lamennais: in the same volume of *Howitt's Journal* he produced the actress 'Mademoiselle Rachel' as an exemplar of self-help. Clearly he did not disapprove of talented and independent women. It is in *Brief Biographies,* however, that we find a passage which seems neatly to sum up Smiles' attitude to the independent woman, if not to women in general:

Miss [Harriet] Martineau is a woman with a manly heart and head. In saying this, we neither desire to cast a reflection on the sex to which she belongs, nor upon herself. It would be better for women generally did they cultivate as she has the spirit of self-help and self-reliance. We believe it would tend to their greater usefulness as well as happiness and render them more efficient co-operators with men in all the relations of life.[39]

So it was for women as for men: education and self-help were the entrée to usefulness and happiness, via the low-key but constantly reiterated avenue of cooperation, which was no less useful a solution to social problems when occurring between the sexes than between the classes. We should remember that Harriet Martineau is generally well regarded in present-day feminist circles: when Smiles wrote about her she was considered a bit 'dangerous'.

In what we now call gender relations, Smiles proffered the same solutions as he did elsewhere, summarised as the need to exhibit a manly character, whether the exhibitor was male or female. Taken as he meant them, such solutions were capable of a great deal of amelioration of the lot of down-trodden women, as of down-trodden workers. He saw no point in preaching equality, but his message as a leveller is clear. He no more believed or pretended that women and men were the same than that Quaker and Catholic were, but in both cases he resolutely avoided any suggestion that one was better or worse than the other. Men and women were different physically, pyschologically and socially, but they were help-meets, possessed of complementary qualities. Just as the perpetuation of the human race required the proper exploitation of their physical differences (which Smiles was, naturally, too genteel to mention) so the fulfilment of mankind required their coming together in harmonious cooperation. In short, he broadly complied with the doctrine of separate spheres, but characteristically modified it by the application of his ideas of character, truth and cooperation, all summed up in his willingness to accord to a woman the accolade of manliness.

WHAT WAS THE PURPOSE OF SELF-HELP?

Smiles produced a sequence of lecture texts, pamphlets, magazine articles and books on this theme over a period of almost fifty years. We know from his other works that he was capable of writing on a number of other themes, yet nearly all his output refers back in one way or another to *Self-Help* or its antecedents. As suggested in Chapter 2, Smiles viewed self-help as nothing less than the key to the central problem of the Industrial Revolution, famously named by Carlyle as 'the "Condition of England" Question'. If it was true that changes which created wealth on a scale unprecedented in world history also created squalor, disease and misery, then the solution of that problem was the most important question facing the inhabitants of Britain and the other countries following her pattern of industrialisation on this side of the Last Judgement. If the suggestion in Chapter 1, that Smiles was not an orthodox Christian and may therefore have had a less-than-complete faith in that Judgement, be correct, then the solution of the 'Condition of England Question' simply became the most important issue facing mankind at the time. The seriousness with which he addressed the problem in *Lives of the Engineers* suggests that that was exactly the way in which he saw it, and that he was turning the self-help philosophy into nothing less than a complete and unified secular religion.

CHAPTER FOUR

Lives of the Engineers

In 1848, George Stephenson, the man reputed to be the founding father of the British, and hence the world, railway industry died. According to Smiles, the prominent Leeds locomotive manufacturer James Kitson suggested to him that he, Smiles, ought to write a biography of George Stephenson. As related in Chapter 1, the two men had been acquaintances for some years, and there is no reason to disbelieve Smiles on this point. Other cries went up for a biography of the great man, most notably from John Scott Russell, who wrote the Institution of Mechanical Engineers' obituary of their first president.[1] Smiles, despite or perhaps because of his already considerable experience as a writer, was not immediately convinced that anyone would buy, or even publish, such a book. As he more tactfully put it, 'the preparation of such a work involved too much labour to be lightly undertaken'.

His preface to the 1862 edition then chronicles further pressures for a biography of George Stephenson, including 'a very suggestive and able article in the *Athenaeum* of December 8, 1849, urging the claims of the subject of railway enterprise and its early history upon the attention of literary men'. Suggestive though the article may have been, it did not, according to Smiles, arouse much passion in literary breasts, for although John Francis' *History of the English Railway* had its merits, it 'failed in the main point of biographic interest' and Hyde Clark's articles on the life and works of George Stephenson were also deficient: 'though valuable as a collection of facts and dates, it was not a biography'.[2] *The life of George Stephenson* 'remained to be written'.

Smiles met Robert Stephenson to discuss the subject in March 1851, and received little encouragement: Stephenson could not see that such a biography would be of much interest to people, but he agreed to help if Smiles decided that he wished to proceed. So began the preliminary research survey, and the results were discouraging, suggesting that it would be necessary to spend a good deal of time seeking out people who had known and worked with the subject in order to make good the deficiencies of the written records. This Smiles decided he had not the time to do, but three years later his work required him to spend the summer in Newcastle, which allowed him to pass his evenings in 'fieldwork' among those who remembered George Stephenson. He met and spoke to members of all strata from Edward Pease to lowly pitmen, and decided that the 'Life' must be written.[3] Reporting back to Robert Stephenson, Smiles was now given every reasonable assistance, including introductions to a plethora of engineers, great and small, who had worked with or for the great man. There was also the offer of some money towards the costs of publication, which Smiles declined on the grounds that if the proposed book could not be published on a normal commercial basis, it was not worth publishing.[4]

When *The Life of George Stephenson* was eventually published by John Murray in 1857, it went through four printings (totalling 20,000 copies) in its first year, suggesting that Smiles' account, summarised above, of how it came into being may not be entirely a case of conventional authorial modesty: it may well be that he was as genuinely surprised by its success as were John Murray and Robert Stephenson. Smiles had a good track record as a journalist and writer of short articles, but his only full-length works to date were the unsuccessful *Physical Education*, the unremarkable *History of Ireland and the Irish People under the Government of England* and *Self-Help* – which at this date remained unpublished, having been rejected by Routledge. He could justly feel surprise along with the gratification when *George Stephenson* became an instant success.

Tangye is reported to have said of the use of his hydraulic jacks to coax the reluctant *Great Eastern* down the launching ways that 'we launched the *Great Eastern* and the *Great Eastern* launched us'.[5] The initial temptation is to apply the remark to Smiles and Stephenson: it would make a nice analogy. Sadly, it will not work, for George Stephenson's reputation was well afloat before Smiles arrived on the scene. But the idea of expanding the successful work into a series was immediately tempting to Murray and to Smiles alike. In this, Smiles was encouraged by Robert Stephenson, who now recognised his mistake in assuming that the biography of his father would be of limited interest. Thus was born the idea of *Lives of the Engineers*, which began with two volumes in 1861, and in 1862 produced a third, which was a reworked and updated version of *The Life of George Stephenson*, incorporating an account of Robert Stephenson, who had died in 1859. In 1865 the lives of Boulton and Watt were added, first as a separate work and then as Volume 4, and in 1874 the *magnum opus* was re-edited and extensively updated to emerge in its final five-volume form.

It makes a nice tidy story, but the question arises of whether Smiles could actually have done it like that. He had first worked on George Stephenson for an article in *Eliza Cook's Journal* in 1849 and had been gradually collecting bits of evidence, both documentary and anecdotal, ever since. He supposedly started work in earnest on the book in 1854, and it took him three years. The suggestion is that within another four years he was able to write nearly a thousand printed pages, of the order of 300,000 words, on the general history of civil engineering and the lives of several engineers. Although there were existing accounts of the lives of Telford, Brindley and Watt to form a starting point, a considerable amount of what he wrote was the result of 'coal face research'. During the same four years he also prepared the rejected text of *Self-Help* for its successful publication by Murray in 1859, wrote a number of articles for Murray's *Quarterly Review* and published the important *Brief Biographies* in America.[6]

Now there is no doubt that Smiles practised what he preached in terms of hard work and perseverance, and he was probably truthful in stating that his writing was recreation after coming home from a job which he did not have his heart in. Even so, it would be quite impossible for him to have done all these things in the time available, so we are driven to the conclusion that he had actually had the idea of *Lives of the Engineers* at the back of his mind for some time. The writer, despite the exhibition of a character of truly sterling worth (and being employed as a full-time research historian helps), makes no pretence that this book could have been researched and written at the same time as his other publications nominally of this year: notes on and references to Smiles have been accumulating since 1987, when the intention of one day writing a book on Smiles first arose. With due deference to historians who quite properly distrust the expression 'must have', it is submitted that Smiles must have nurtured a long-term intention to write biographies of more engineers than just George Stephenson.

The reasons why such a project might have occurred to him are fairly straightforward. George Stephenson was, or could be turned into, as good an example of the application of self-help as one could possibly wish to find. As portrayed by Smiles, he was born into a poor working-class family, he started work as a pit boy and by a combination of innate talent, honesty, perseverance and hard work, he attained the position of enginewright. His father was blinded in an accident, which meant that much of George's enhanced income had to go towards supporting his parents. When he produced innovative ideas in steam locomotion he had to fight against ignorance and prejudice, but he overcame every obstacle and was, by the time his Liverpool & Manchester Railway opened in 1830, by far the most accomplished and successful railway engineer in the country. He did not allow fame to turn his head, and still thoroughly enjoyed meeting up with old workmates and acquaintances from his early days in the north-east. His railways were of enormous value to ordinary people, allowing them to travel more quickly, cheaply and safely and providing them with cheaper domestic fuel, better and more varied goods.

If George Stephenson was a good example, others were scarcely less so. Brindley, like Stephenson, was a semi-literate, practical man who broke new engineering ground in the face of extreme difficulty. Like Stephenson, he was mocked and opposed by those who thought his ideas would never work. Like Stephenson, too, he was responsible for significant innovations which benefited the economy and the general well-being of the country to a considerable extent. So we could go on: the treatment of almost every one of Smiles' subjects is formulaic, and the formula is made to dance to the tune of *Self-Help*.

There is, however, far more to Smiles' interest in engineering than that; the basic idea of *Self-Help* was quite old, and his mind had not been at rest since the early 1840s: he had moved on and developed self-help much further. The medium for this development ought, logically, to have been the later books of the *Self-Help* series, but there is a case for viewing those more as mere expansions of *Self-Help* (and the reworking of material previously gathered for other publications) than as genuine development of the idea. Certainly, *Lives of the Engineers* shows some remarkable developments of his thoughts, but to identify them, we have to try to unravel the various messages which Smiles wrote into it.

The Idea of Progress

After the publication in 1931 of Butterfield's pivotal *The Whig Interpretation of History* it became a favourite sport for lesser historians, swimming bravely and strongly downstream behind Butterfield, to apply his ideas outside the arena of political history in which they were formed. That process was not necessarily harmful in itself, even when the authority of Butterfield was claimed for work of a less original and more tendentious nature than his. The problems arose when writers began to deride the idea of progress itself as 'Whiggish' and therefore summarily dismissible. At a philosophical level this raises the interesting question whether anti-Whig historians are not themselves guilty of Whiggery by assuming that their historical methods are axiomatically better than any of those which have gone before – why, after all, should historians themselves be exempt from the rules they seek to impose on others? There is no particular reason for assuming that modern methods of writing history are better than those used by Smiles unless we can prove it. When we set out to do so, we might embark on a quick nibble of humble pie before attacking the writings of a man who made a larger contribution to the history of technology than anyone had done before – and few afterwards can compete either.

The problem in trying to dismiss Smiles' idea of progress is that it was not, like Whiggery in its original habitat of political history, a construct of nineteenth-century politics anomalously applied to, say, the events of the Norman Conquest, and therefore cannot be so easily disposed of. It was rooted in the recent past and extended itself naturally into the present: as such it was hard to argue against then, and it is little easier now. Which among us can honestly say that the London water supply was better when it was largely made up of dilute sewage extracted from the river by private companies than it was after the sanitarians eventually triumphed? The improvement was, and remains, obvious. The ability to move people and goods around the country with greater speed and safety at the same time as lower price is a benefit which was sought long before the contributions of Smiles' engineers and we are still seeking further improvements now. Many, if not most, of the achievements of the engineers were perceived as genuine progress by the vast majority of their contemporaries and immediate successors. Those perceptions were not, like the concept of 'The Norman Yoke', laid on afterwards by historians.

We, of course, may disagree. The availability of cheap soap, generally regarded as important in matters of health and hygiene, depended on a cheap and plentiful supply of sodium carbonate, which was manufactured by the excruciatingly filthy and polluting Leblanc process. The price of removing sewage from the courts and back-houses was often putting it in the rivers. Domestic heating and lighting involved large amounts of coal, either directly or through the medium of coal gas, and hence poisonous substances in the atmosphere. Sitting smug in the late twentieth century, where only the really poor know what it is to wake up in the morning feeling very, very cold or to have no means of cleaning either their persons or their possessions, it is easy for us to deplore late Victorian pollution. When we do so, we commit the underlying cardinal sin of Whiggery, which is to impose our views on a past age. To the inhabitants of that age, the price was known and regretted, but it was worth paying: the changes which allowed cheap travel, soap, heat and shelter were progress. Only we in our century like to think we can have – or deserve – motor cars without traffic accidents or power stations without pollution. The nineteenth-century attitude was that you can't make an omelette without breaking eggs.

Whiggery, however, has another underlying cardinal sin, one of which Smiles may not be innocent, which is writing history backwards. The temptation is that when the historian knows the effect it is all too easy to misinterpret, or even completely invent, the cause. Smiles knew, for example, that although there had been several spasms of activity in locomotive design around 1804–5, 1810–12 and 1814–15, between 1815 and 1823 only George and Robert Stephenson continued any sort of systematic work. The combination of his preconceptions of the merits of perseverance and his knowledge that Robert's *Rocket* would eventually become the prototype of the 'modern' locomotive, tempted him to interpret the abandonment of other projects and designs as 'failure' brought about by a lack of perseverance.[7] Happy with that explanation, he failed to consider the relationship between the cost of buying and feeding horses and the willingness to invest in expensive and rather speculative research and development in steam locomotives. As we now know, there is a correlation close enough to suggest that experiments with prime movers were taken up when muscle power was expensive, and dropped again when its price came down. There really is no mystery in the hiatus in locomotive development after 1815: the end of the Napoleonic Wars produced a labour, and horse, surplus, and as Carnot pointed out, the thermal efficiency of muscles was much higher than that of steam engines.[8]

In certain aspects of Victorian society and technology, Smiles had almost boundless confidence. Telford's roads in the Scottish Highlands, for example, were far more than just a means of transporting people and goods. Before their construction, Highlanders were not only poor, but dirty, lazy and as morally reprehensible as only a Lowland Scot could think them. After the roads, the Highlanders learned better ways from the more civilised people with whom they were brought into contact: not only were they better dressed at less cost in the products of the mills of Glasgow, but they learned the work ethic as well.

> Sloth and idleness disappeared before the energy, activity, and industry which were called into life by the improved communications . . . the pigs and cattle were treated to a separate table . . . the dunghill was turned to the outside of the house. . . . But not less remarkable were the effects of the road-making upon the industrial habits of the people . . . the moral habits of the great masses of the working classes are changed . . .[9]

This is entirely consistent with the rewards of self-help as discussed above: those rewards were not merely financial but qualitative – one might even say spiritual – as well. The improvement in the moral and physical condition of the Highlanders results from the work of an engineer who, born in humble circumstances, trained as a stonemason and showed indomitable perseverance in rising to the very top of his profession. His reward was not just being rich and famous, which he was, but in being of demonstrable service in the progress of mankind.

In this case as in others we might differ with Smiles and view Telford's roads as just another attack on Highland culture, albeit a peaceful one compared with some. We would do well to remember that to most people at the time Highland culture meant one of two things: the grinding poverty of some rather primitive people living in a nasty, infertile place or the romanticised view, verging on the notion of the 'noble savage', which derived from the novels of Sir Walter Scott, spurious pseudo-historical tartans and the possibly spurious poems of Ossian. Smiles specifically remarks that they were previously dressed in 'tartan tatters' which 'gave place to the produce of Manchester and Glasgow looms'.[10]

The words 'rather primitive people' should serve as a prompt to remind us that a number of new extensions of western man's knowledge of the world had greatly reinforced not only the idea that time was linear and irreversible, but that movement through that linear and irreversible time proceeded according to some principle or other. One key development lay in the discoveries of remains of Neolithic and Palaeolithic men: it was not necessary to read, understand or agree with Darwinian theory to recognise that the 'primitive' peoples encountered by explorers and colonists were surviving pockets of the genuinely primitive. It can be argued that such a view is positively anti-Darwinian, in that it was used as a powerful support for the idea of linearity and progress. Some would suggest that evolutionary theory, with its 'branching model' of development, works in exactly the opposite direction.[11] Be that as it may, Victorian archaeologists and anthropologists between them evolved an agreed hierarchy of skills in the making and use of tools. This was a linear development in time:

> Civilisation began with tools, and every step in advance has been accomplished through their improvement. Handicraft in bone, stone, or wood was the first stage in the development of man's power; and tools or machines in iron or steel are the last and most efficient method of economising it, and enabling him intelligently to direct the active and inert forces of nature.[12]

How far behind western Europe the aborigines were said to be naturally depended on whether the writer accepted the notion of geological time, or was still working on the date of creation 'calculated' from the Old Testament, but either way the answer was that the Victorians had before them the living proof of the means of mankind's progress. From that position it was necessary to garble and simplify Darwin only very slightly to start off the great hunt for 'The Missing Link' – the conjectured transitional creature between a monkey and, say, an Aborigine.

MAN AND NATURE

The Charter of the Institution of Civil Engineers refers to 'harnessing the great sources of power in Nature to the use and convenience of Man'. Smiles' view of nature seems ambivalent: according to Travers, Smiles saw nature as being governed by laws which were essentially benign.[13] But in other ways, to Smiles as to his engineer subjects, nature was not a sunny place provided by the Creator as an agreeable habitat for Romantic poets.

Nature offered man a cold, wet, miserable and probably short existence, fraught with danger. She also offered the basis of the answers to the questions she posed, but they were only potential answers, which needed to be found and fulfilled by the application of certain qualities which should not, by now, need enumerating again. The task of the engineer was to transform: 'Thus, in the hands of the Engineer, water, instead of being a tyrant, became a servant; instead of being a destroyer it became a useful labourer and a general civiliser.'[14] Nature provided raw materials such as coal, metal ores and suitable stone for masonry work, but these had to be found and won through ingenuity, hard work and the acceptance of financial risk and physical danger. They had to be applied to useful purpose by engineering knowledge, manual skill and more plain hard work. Only then could a splendid structure like the Menai suspension bridge arise to benefit the local community and the travelling public at large, and only when it did that did it reflect credit upon its designer.

If nature was the enemy, from whose tightly clenched and unwilling hand any gain in the material well-being of man had to be either snatched or wheedled, then clearly the idea of conserving nature would be alien to Smiles. From his point of view it was precisely the need to live with, rather than overcome, nature, which had distinguished, and continued to distinguish, primitive man as primitive. The idea that aborigines could exist happily without umbrellas or grand pianos would have been hard for him to come to terms with. Before we laugh too loudly, we should remember that as recently as twenty years or so ago, plenty of very well-meaning buffoons thought they could solve famine problems in Africa by spending a lot of money on sending Africans tractors and artificial fertilisers. The idea of inevitable linear technological progress in overcoming nature has died hard – and recently.

Among the most virtuous of the early achievements of civil engineering was land reclamation work, including notably the drainage of fenland in Lincolnshire and East Anglia. The displacement of the previous occupants (at times by military force) is dismissed by Smiles' enclosing of 'the valuable race of Fenmen' in mocking quotation marks. The Fenmen are portrayed not merely as primitive and backward-looking, but as thugs. The Fens were not just useless, but 'lurking places of disease', and the result of the work of the engineers was that

Dreary swamps are supplanted by pleasant pastures, and the haunts of pike and wild-fowl have become the habitations of industrious farmers and husbandmen. Even Whittlesea Mere and Ramsay Mere, – the only two lakes, as we were told in the geography books of our younger days, to be found in the south of England, – have been blotted out of the map, for they have been drained by the engineer, and are now covered with smiling farms and pleasant homesteads.[15]

It behoves us to remember, before we pillory Smiles for praising the destruction of what we would now designate as a Site of Special Scientific Interest, that in the eighteenth and early nineteenth centuries malaria was common in Lincolnshire, as indeed it was in the Somerset Levels. There were very sound, simple reasons for draining fens, and persuading mid-Victorians of the desirability of preserving the habitat of sundry harmful members of the genus *Anopheles* would have required rhetoric of a very high order.[16] Exactly the same reasoning applied when he praised the achievements of earlier reclamation engineers like St Guthlac or Vermuyden.

As we read of the industrial achievements of Boulton and Watt, we look in vain for any mention of the undesirable side-effects of the industrial expansion said to have arisen from their work. Boulton's brass-working activities would inevitably have resulted in spent vitriol going into the canal or the nearest river, though such was the increasing population density of Birmingham that this might prove to be a blessing in disguise, in that it would make the sewage therein stink less. Perhaps the outstanding example of Smiles ignoring any possible claim for nature is his approbation of William Murdock's invention of gas lighting. Gas lighting was not developed in order that thrifty housewives could mend clothing during hours of darkness, or that self-improving factory workers could read technical or scientific works from the Mechanics' Institute library during the evening. It was intended to enable mills and factories to work at night, and thus keep up their spoliation of the environment twenty-four hours a day. Until around 1850, when the tars and liquors began to serve as raw materials for other branches of the chemical industry, only the gas and the coke were of much use. Gas works were among the foulest of polluters, not just through their smoke, smell and dust released into the atmosphere and their waste liquids released into rivers, but also through their ubiquity: by 1850 just about every industrial town had one.

In some areas, mining activity alone was sufficient to cause serious pollution of waterways as mine adits or pumping shafts set up unnatural waterflows, bringing dissolved inorganic salts out of the ground in large quantities.[17] Examples clearly visible to this day are stretches of the Bridgewater, Coventry and Trent & Mersey Canals which were each colloquially known to boatmen in working days as 'Cocoa River' since their waters varied from the colour of a cup of cocoa through to a fierce terra cotta red. Canals in urban industrial areas were not the fingers of peace and quiet we now know, but rivers of filth. George Smith, 'The Boatman's Friend', is known to have exaggerated his case, but even after allowing for that, the canals of 1875 sound less than idyllic:

The water was inky black, and the stench was intolerable. Large bubbles of gas were continually rising to the surface, being unmistakable proof of decomposing animal and vegetable matter. This will refer to all our canals passing through or close to our large towns: so thick in many places are dead animals floating on the surface that the 'boat gauger' has to push them out of the way before he can gauge the boat.[18]

It is unlikely that such a scene would be conjured from this passage summarising the effects of the construction of the Bridgewater Canal:

Manchester men of this day may possibly be surprised that they owe so much to a Duke, or that the old blood has helped the new so materially in the development of England's modern industry. . . . The cutting of the canal from Worsley to Manchester conferred upon that town the immediate benefit of a cheap and abundant supply of coal; and when Watt's steam-engine became the great motive power in manufactures, such supply became absolutely essential to its existence.[19]

Now it might be thought that there was no reason at all why Smiles should identify or disapprove of pollution problems, which have only become a major political issue over the last couple of decades. This is not so, and we do not have to rely upon the evidence of 'literary Luddites' such as Wordsworth or neo-medievalists such as Carlyle or Ruskin to establish it. Air and water pollution became a political issue well before the last edition of *Lives of the Engineers* was published, yet virtually the only mention Smiles makes of pollution is in the context of sewage in waterways as being both unhealthy (he remained an adherent of the unscientific but empirically sound 'filth theory' of disease) and wasteful in that nightsoil should be used as fertiliser, not thrown in rivers: 'It is calculated that the manure which yearly flows into the Thames in London alone is competent to the production of food for not less than a million of population.'[20]

The fact is that the Alkali Act of 1863 and the Rivers (Prevention of Pollution) Act of 1876 were based on extensive investigations by, respectively, a Select Committee and a Royal Commission in which specialists and ordinary citizens alike condemned the status quo. The legislation was rendered largely ineffective by the feeble enforcement provisions of the latter Act: the apparently impressive initial success of the Alkali Inspectorate in doing away with clouds of hydrochloric acid gas depended on manufacturers dissolving it in water and then pouring the acid solution into waterways. This is not material: there remained poisonous manufacturers, and there remained magistrates who were in the manufacturers' pockets, but there was also a body of opinion in favour of attempting to diminish the damage to nature. In most of Smiles' works there is no variation in the position that nature is in need of subjugation to man's ends. His tendency to empathise with the subjects of his biographies should lead us to expect that there would be exceptions to be found in the lives of Thomas Edwards and, more particularly, Robert Dick. So there are, but what is a little surprising is that instead of merely making statements about how Dick loved the countryside, or quoting passages such as that in Chapter 1 above, Smiles enthuses about it for himself, albeit in a modest kind of way:

> The lofty range of the Ochils is a prominent feature in the scenery of the Devon [valley]. The hills are soft, green and pastoral. Their sunward slopes are here and there varied with magnificent wooded glades, intermingled with copse and whins, which in their golden colour are supremely beautiful. The burns and streamlets come down in cascades. . . .[21]

This is lyrical stuff indeed for the urban and prosaic Smiles, but we must remember that the main source he employed for the writing of *Robert Dick* was a number of collections of letters lent to him by Dick's academic correspondents. He would have been a hard man indeed had Dick's

Samuel Smiles, date unknown, perhaps mid-1880s. An ogre of laissez-faire and apologist for exploitative capitalism? Looks quite a kind old man. (Illustration from the Autobiography)

Grace Darling: hero, yes; female, yes; heroine of Smilesian womanhood, doubtful. (From Duty*)*

The astonishing beauty of the Pont-cysylltau aqueduct is a triumph of art over Nature: it was not difficult to believe that its designer was somehow different from ordinary men. (From LofE, *1874)*

The Ochils from the Devon Valley (see p. 80). (From Robert Dick*)*

George Stephenson. The ultimate Smilesian hero. (From LofE, *1874)*

Robert Stephenson: is it just this author that detects a hint of Ozymandias' 'frown, and wrinkled lip, and sneer of cold command'? (From LofE, *1874)*

True or false? A Nasmyth steam hammer in action . . .

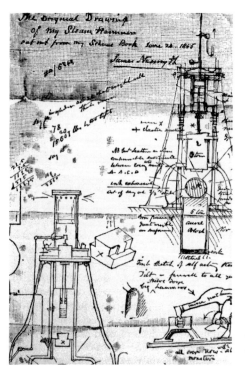

. . . and a detail from the drawing (published by Smiles) which Cantrell uses as evidence that Nasmyth stole the idea from Schneider. (Both from James Nasmyth, Engineer, An Autobiography)

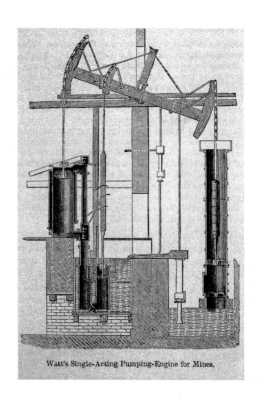

Watt's Single-Acting Pumping-Engine for Mines.

One of the seminal machines: James Watt's pumping engine.

'The type of the modern locomotive'? The Killingworth Locomotive. (Both from LofE, *1874)*

A refuge from hen-pecking or a holy shrine, depending on one's viewpoint: James Watt's garret workshop. (From LofE, *1874)*

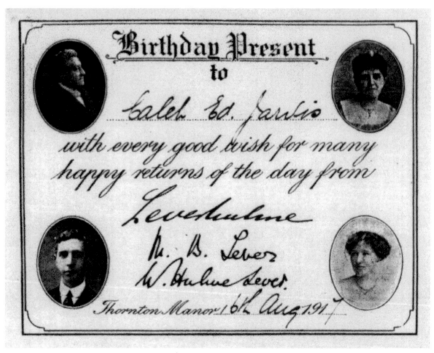

Bookplate from a copy of Thrift *given to the author's father. There is a copy of* Duty *as well. But Lord Leverhulme practised what Smiles preached: my father, as a 'village boy' in Port Sunlight, was given his place on life's starting line. In 1926 he graduated as the youngest Mus. Doc. in the country.*

passionate love of nature never got through to him. Even so, a line or two on from the above quotation we find that the charming burns and streamlets are 'turned to use in many mills along the valley'.

There is indeed a difference between Smiles' treatment of nature in his works on Dick and Edwards and his treatment of it elsewhere, and it is readily reconcilable when we refer back to the principles of *Self-Help*. The value of an achievement is not determined only by the end result, but partly also by the degree of difficulty confronted and overcome. To Edwards and Dick the difficulties lay in humdrum matters like making a living to enable them to continue their work in natural history. To the engineers, nature herself was always among the difficulties; commonly she was the principal one.

THE RELIABILITY OF *LIVES OF THE ENGINEERS*

The two preceding sections have identified reasons why Smiles' *Lives of the Engineers* might be rendered seriously inaccurate by the emotional overburden of *Self-Help*. The next chapter will argue that it is not nearly as simple as that, but this is the point at which to try to evaluate the historical accuracy of the work. Clearly it is not possible to investigate in detail the entire work, which eventually achieved some 1,500 pages, so a few of the most famous of Smiles' engineers will be chosen and considered, the rest neglected.

Smiles was a diligent gatherer of information, and his prefaces often give a reasonable idea of the sources he used. Although he did not provide references to what would nowadays be considered a scholarly standard, there are occasional footnotes, sometimes relating the processes whereby he acquired the information. It is clear that he stored bits of information long in advance of actually using them: some material he used in *Robert Dick* (1878) was originally gathered for *Self-Help* and material used in *James Nasmyth* (1885) had been gathered for *Industrial Biography* over twenty years earlier. The question arises of how critical and selective he was in the acceptance of the evidence which he used.

In the first place, it is clear that he was perfectly happy to accept as authentic information which people provided about themselves. *James Nasmyth*, which is admittedly not technically part of *Lives of the Engineers*, is the clearest example, in that Smiles seems to have done little more than edit memoirs provided by Nasmyth. As Cantrell has shown, Nasmyth may well have been responsible for the claim that Schneider attempted to pirate the steam hammer from him, when in fact the exact opposite was true.[22] Much the same appears to have been the case with Telford: Smiles was clearly heavily influenced by Telford's own autobiographical notes, subsequently written up and published by Rickman. Hadfield's detailed textual comparisons of parts of these seem clearly to establish that there was a definite reputation-building exercise in hand, whose products Smiles seems to have willingly believed. Whether this was because he failed to recognise what was going on or because the falsification suited his other purposes is immaterial: the result was that Smiles accepted as true some highly suspect information. James Watt and James Watt Jnr have been attacked by John Griffiths and Hugh Torrens for deliberate and dishonest building-up of Watt Snr's reputation at the expense of, respectively, William Murdock and Jonathan Hornblower.[23]

While the degree of duplicity alleged by Hadfield might be unusual, it would be strange indeed if autobiographical or family information of this kind were not partial. Furthermore, at the time when most of *Lives of the Engineers* first appeared in print, Smiles was, as we have seen, working at a phenomenal rate, so it is perhaps forgivable if he did not always check his sources with the thoroughness we might expect in a new scholarly biography today. He did, however, have access to a fair amount of reliable documentary material, and it is clear that he used it. Furthermore, the production of the 1874 five-volume edition provided the opportunity to update the work.

In the case of Volume 1, on Brindley and the early engineers, the erroneous impression conveyed to the reader by earlier editions that Brindley practically invented canals was corrected by the addition of an appendix on Pierre-Paul Riquet and his Grand Canal du Languedoc. Similarly the volume on George and Robert Stephenson was subject to a host of minor modifications over the years, of which a few were of genuine importance to the overall interpretive story line. In particular, the role of Trevithick in the early development of the locomotive receives reasonable recognition in later editions. Even as early as 1864, substantial differences are noticeable from the 1857 version, particularly in the assessment of the importance of the Killingworth locomotive.[24]

These alterations show us that Smiles was not a man to stand by an error simply on grounds of obstinacy or authorial dignity. Nor did he give up research interest in a topic once he had his book in print: there is a wealth of informative footnotes in the 1874 edition, providing extra material he had come across since the production of the appropriate previous edition. The notes are obvious, but changes within the main text much less so: large chunks of text are re-used verbatim, so that skim-reading would reveal them only to an experienced Smiles-watcher with an elephantine memory. Normally it is necessary to do what this author does, and read two editions carefully in parallel.

The most complex of Smiles' subjects to study in this way is, by a large margin, George Stephenson. The book on him more than any other aroused a great deal of interest and hostile comment, the latter especially from E.M.S. Paine and O.D. Hedley.[25] The first significant alteration, however, making a significant change in interpretation, occurred in the year of publication, before either Hedley or Paine was in print. In a much-quoted passage, Smiles had extended the opprobrium resulting from the collapse of the railway mania and the ruin of George Hudson to include some engineers as well. The first edition contains these somewhat intemperate words:

> This boundless speculation of course gave abundant employment to the engineers. They were found ready to attach their names to the most daring and foolish projects. . . . No scheme was so mad that it did not find an engineer, so called, ready to endorse it.[26]

If we consider, and it has never been seriously denied, that *The Life of George Stephenson* was intended at least in part to immortalise an exemplar of *Self-Help*, Smiles needed passages like this in the book. The railway industry had earned for itself a highly unsavoury reputation for financial impropriety and it was therefore necessary to establish a clear division between great men such as George Stephenson, whose integrity was beyond reproach, and the lesser men who would take money for putting their names to a prospectus whose only real purpose was the creation of scrip. Thrift was, as we have seen, an essential component of the proper use of money, which was in turn essential to the successful application of self-help. Railway speculators, and those members of the professions who provided them with their plans, their traffic surveys and their parliamentary petitions, were much worse than just profiteers or thieves. They were undermining the solution of the 'Condition of England Question'.

The engineering profession saw matters differently. Despite the collapse of railway construction after the mania, railway work remained the largest single source of income for civil engineers, and it was for that underlying reason that the council of the Institution of Civil Engineers asked the president, two vice-presidents and the secretary to contact Smiles with a view to the removal of the offending passage. They could hardly have appointed a higher-powered delegation than Locke, Bidder, Hawkshaw and Manby, so we may assume that the council felt very strongly about the matter. It is probable that ex-president Robert Stephenson was pulling strings in the background.[27] Be that as it may, Smiles did back down and remove the passage, but the passages quoted on pp. 28–9 above, with the same general message, remained in various other editions. That passage would cause no great anguish in the Institution, but only a few lines further on, we find specific mention of 'scheming . . . engineers'.[28]

That was only marginally less offensive than the passage which Smiles, under pressure, had agreed to remove. The pressure was formidable, because Locke and the others could have dried up Smiles' sources of verbal information for future publications and probably caused him severe problems in his employment as well. That he resisted fairly stoutly, and when he did give in made only the minimum of changes, suggests that he felt deeply about his message and was not willing to apply the whitewash brush to please other people.[29] Obstinacy is another possible reason: he had been irritated by some editorial changes to *George Stephenson* by an advisor to John Murray. Once the book was selling he promptly re-inserted some anecdotes which had been cut, including the account of how George made cucumbers grow straight and the story of the 'Crowdie Nights', both absent in 1857 and present in 1862.[30] Trivial though these anecdotes seemed to Murray and may seem to us now, they can be seen as part of a careful and detailed characterisation of the subject, and as such a part of the underlying plan of the book.

Smiles recorded that he found it best to write 'full-hearted': may we take this to mean that he would not publish anything in which he did not entirely believe? It is permissible, if dangerous, to speculate that this was the reason he refused a lucrative commission to write the life of Brassey, the railway contractor. The 'Life' as eventually written, on Smiles' recommendation, by Arthur Helps gave a very inflated impression indeed of the works, and indeed the importance, of its subject.

The present writer is probably the most sympathetic commentator on Smiles since his granddaughter, but that is taking speculation too far. It is a curious fact that previous readers of Smiles have neglected his American publications, which are not mere reprints of English ones, and have therefore failed to observe that there are numerous discrepancies, some of them quite significant. In side-by-side readings of the 1868 Harper edition of *The Life of George Stephenson* with the English editions of (late) 1857 and 1874, more than a hundred discrepancies were noted. Since, as in other comparisons, it was possible to find passages of several consecutive pages which were reproduced verbatim it seems reasonable to assume that the changes were made for some definite purpose.

A number of the differences relate to the achievements of George Stephenson. While English editions, for example, give the distinct impression, without actually stating it as fact, that the Stockton & Darlington locomotive *Locomotion No. 1* was constructed at the Robert Stephenson & Co. works under George's control and to his design, in *Brief Biographies* it is made clear that *Locomotion* was in fact the *Active*, designed and mostly built by Robert before he went to South America. All that had happened since his departure was the completion of the job, and the provision of a new nameplate. While Robert was away, George wrote to him urging him to return as 'the fate of the locomotive hung upon the issue' – a different view from that in English publications which state that George fought the battle for the locomotive single-handed. In England, the Killingworth locomotive 'may in fact be regarded as the type of the present locomotive engine' and that was in response to the fact that 'An efficient and economical working locomotive engine, therefore, still remained to be invented; and to accomplish this work Mr Stephenson now applied himself.'[31]

This may well be thought to sell Trevithick short, who had invented or applied all the essential components of the Killingworth locomotive eleven years earlier, and thrown in the steam blast (which the Killingworth loco did not have) for good measure. In America, Trevithick is accorded a 21-page 'Memoir' in which Smiles gives him full credit for his amazing inventiveness. In England, the lofty 1857 claims for Stephenson were moderated from 1864; the locomotive was 'not the invention of one man'.

But also in 1857, it was 'remarkable how little Trevethick [*sic*] achieved'. In the Harper edition (1868) it was not Stephenson but Trevithick who 'may be fairly regarded as the inventor of the steam locomotive, if any single individual may be entitled to that appellation'.[32]

Smiles was quite plainly playing games with his readers, and in the light of later research we can see that it is the American version which is nearer the truth. But it was not a case of Smiles getting better through the benefit of continued research: the examples cited above are not incorporated into the 1874 edition. This poses the question of why Smiles should falsely and deliberately credit to George Stephenson achievements he knew were properly those of other engineers, notably Richard Trevithick and Robert Stephenson. The answer cannot be as simple as the obvious wish to build up his exemplar of self-help.

We may reasonably assume that he was to some extent misled, in the same way he would soon be by Rickman, Muirhead and Nasmyth when he came to write the lives of Telford, Watt and Nasmyth. Robert Stephenson found himself in an extremely difficult position: for all his working life a number of his key achievements had been popularly and wrongly attributed to his father. He could scarcely come out after his father's death and lay claim to that which he had not claimed when his father was alive. In some cases, such as the adoption of the blast-pipe/multi-tubular boiler ensemble to produce a lightweight, high-speed locomotive and indeed the abolition of the winding engine at inclines, the developments attributed to George had not only belonged to Robert, but had been achieved by him in the face of the resolute opposition of their supposed inventor. It had become, in short, a very tangled web.

It was a web in which the financial stakes were high. As Edward Pease wrote in his diary, it was a 'kindness' that George died when he did. Indeed it was, for had the full extent of the connections between George Hudson and George Stephenson become known, the plight of the railway industry and all who sought to make a living from it would have been dire indeed.[33] It was essential to Robert that George could be presented in the manner he was: the bluff, blunt, practical man with no time for stock-jobbery, foppery, fine wines or, indeed, anything except engineering. We now know that George was at least as important as a 'fixer' as he was as an engineer, and we know that much of his substantial wealth came not from engineering but from successful speculation in mining. That had to be concealed: in the first surge of railway construction, one of George's most successful ideas was turning himself into a brand name through assiduous promotion both of himself and of the two companies, George Stephenson & Son and Robert Stephenson & Co., dealing respectively with civil and mechanical engineering. Now, in the drive to repair the damage done to the industry by Hudson's collapse, that brand name must be pressed into service again, as the mark of honest good value. Despite his success, and his wealth, Robert Stephenson knew what it was to live dangerously: he had come close to ruin both with the financial collapse of the Stanhope & Tyne Railway in the winter of 1839–40 and the structural collapse of the Dee Bridge in 1847. It is scarcely likely that he would lightly risk a collapse of at least equal magnitude by telling Smiles the whole truth and nothing but the truth.[34]

So it proved to be: in contrast to Telford appropriating credit, we find Robert Stephenson busily shedding it. After the furore caused by the 1857 edition, Smiles published 'Robert Stephenson's Narrative of his Father's Inventions etc' as an appendix to the 1862 edition. It is not an overstatement to suggest that it is a string of falsehoods. Within the first page we find the complete exclusion of Trevithick 'When my father commenced upon his improvements upon the locomotive engine' there had been only two comparatively successful previous attempts, by Blenkinsop and by Blackett. Now, Robert Stephenson was not only fully aware of Trevithick's work, but had seen the Gateshead locomotive working. Next, we find the statement that Blenkinsop adopted the rack-rail because he held 'the conviction (then prevalent in the minds of all engineers) that the adhesion between a smooth wheel and a smooth rail' would be insufficient for the machine to pull any load. Robert Stephenson was an engineer of very high ability, and he knew perfectly well that the reason that Blenkinsop adopted rack-rail traction was to diminish the adhesive weight needed: the objective was not to gain traction but to avoid the rail breakages which were an inevitable consequence of greater weight. These are not mistakes: they are falsehoods, and we read on through statements that 'my Father' invented and did practically everything. It has taken a long time to disentangle the truth, since the spurious version came from an apparently unimpeachable source which stated, for example, that George not only designed the *Rocket* but oversaw its construction as well. The latter suggestion is of demonstrable absurdity, since George was not in

Newcastle at the right time. When, of course, Robert was answering questions before Select Committees in Parliament as to his experience as an engineer, a different story emerged, as indeed it does from the Hartree Papers, where Robert says of the construction of *Rocket:* 'I had charge personally of the engine. . . . Whatever was done to the engine was done under my own eye and direction' – which is a very different version from that in his own *Narrative* as published by Smiles. In another place, the mask slipped again when he responded to the suggestion that the idea of the blast-pipe might have come from Hackworth: 'I utterly deny it – it was quite unnecessary for my father to talk to Hackworth about the form of his blast pipe because I knew what it was exactly, and I preferred my own arrangement at the time.'[35] There are two key words in this quotation, both in the last clause: they are 'I' and 'my'. Those are words absent-mindedly used by a man in control, who had momentarily forgotten that he was supposed to be playing the role of the dutiful and admiring son.

As a tentative explanation, it is suggested that Smiles at first believed the material thus deviously fed to him by Robert, but that as he continued his investigations he found increasing difficulties with the interpretation foisted upon him. Once Robert was dead, he could, and did, progressively water down the attribution of absolutely everything to George. The achievement of such a volte-face as attributing *Locomotion* to Robert or admitting that the locomotive works could not work without Robert was going a little too far: Robert and Joseph Locke might be dead, but Bidder and George Robert Stephenson were still very much alive. Away from their influence, and perhaps from others, in America the truth could be told. It seems it was.

There are various possible objections to this suggestion. The first is that Smiles would not have wished to do anything to weaken the image of George as the engineer and the exponent of self-help *par excellence.* The fact is, whether he welcomed the need for changes or not, he made them. It would actually be possible significantly to reduce the claims of most of Smiles' engineers and still have them appear as exemplars of self-help. If, as Hadfield argues, Telford was not in charge of the Caledonian Canal until Jessop died, there remained to him more than adequate achievements, notably his roadbuilding, to establish his position in the Smilesian scheme of things. It would be possible to drop about half the discoveries or improvements attributed to George Stephenson and still end up with the formulaic story line of hard times to begin with, the rise to prosperity through hard work and perseverance, the consideration for others and humility in greatness, to say nothing of being kind to animals. At a less cynical level, both Telford and Stephenson would have had easily sufficient 'residual' achievements fully to deserve recognition as great engineers.

The second objection is this: if Smiles was obstinate enough to meet the Institution of Civil Engineers only about halfway when Robert Stephenson was alive, would he take a blind bit of notice of them when Robert was dead? It is quite possible he would not, but it must be remembered that in his 1862 edition, he had mounted a robust defence of the 'Robert Stephenson version' in two appendices. As time went by, new adversaries appeared in the shape of descendants of the numerous engineers with whom George Stephenson had fallen out, or whose achievements he had claimed. These later arrivals included Vignoles Jnr, Trevithick Jnr and Gurney Jnr.[38] Smiles may have been a reasonably brave controversialist, but if he had been forced to admit that his *Life of George Stephenson* was deeply flawed by false information from Robert Stephenson he would not only have incurred the wrath of the Institution, he would have been joyfully shredded by these and other opponents. Francis Conder, self-appointed maverick and gossip columnist to the engineering profession, would no doubt have enjoyed himself as well. A gentle, steady back-pedal must have seemed to Smiles the only sensible compromise between dishonesty and the speedy disappearance of his long-sought and hard-won reputation as an author.

Robert Stephenson was by no means the only source of false information lapped up, readily or otherwise, by Smiles. Another was the speeches, and reports of speeches, made at the openings of railways. It was in one such speech that George was first described as the 'inventor of the first locomotive'.[39] These speeches need to be treated with the greatest possible suspicion, if not outright disbelief. At the functions at which they were delivered, enormous quantities of drink were consumed, and it would be a temperate guest who left after a few hours having consumed only two or three bottles of wine. Quite apart from that which accompanied the meal, there were rarely fewer than a dozen toasts on the programme, each of which represented not a token sip but a full glass – that is a total of a couple of bottles per head. Extra toasts were not uncommon, nor was the replacement of a chairman who had become perpendicularly challenged. At the famous dinner at Dunchurch, for example, George assumed the chair after some eight and half hours, becoming a wheelbarrow case himself around 4.00 a.m. The credibility of utterances made in such circumstances is low, even before due allowance is made for them being reprocessed a few hours later by newspaper reporters probably no less inebriated than the speakers.

According to Smiles, George had a more-or-less standard speech for these occasions. Lambert rather unkindly implies that this was in order that he could remember it when paralytic drunk.[39] It involved, among other things, 'the difficulties he had early encountered in the promotion of the railway system, and in establishing the superiority of the locomotive'.

These are themes which Smiles drives home with great gusto, apparently without a second thought. Yet he was the secretary of a railway company, and he had been a newspaper editor. Although by no means a teetotaller, he had absolutely no time for immoderate drinking: is it possible that he was unaware of what went on at railway openings, or that the reports emerging from them (often a day or two later) might be unreliable? He simply cannot have been: it has to be an instance of the evidence suiting his case when writing 'full-hearted'. There was worse to come. Leifchild, who wrote a cameo biography of George Stephenson, tells us how 'it was always a subject of boasting amongst the Newcastle miners, that their trams and their mechanisms furnished the thoughts and plans for railways, and this principally through Geordie [Stephenson]'.[40]

We begin by querying where Newcastle miners obtained the information on which their boasting was based, and have to assume that it was most likely either the reports of drunken speeches written by hung-over reporters from the local newspaper, or second-hand oral summaries of them. Next, we consider where their boasting was done, and we are driven to the conclusion that some of it just might have been on licensed premises. Finally, we query the nature of a boasting session, which is simple and well known: it is that every story told must be 'capped' by a better one. In this process, truth had been an early casualty, existing some time before the speech that begat the report that begat the anecdote. Boasting is a folk entertainment eminently more virtuous than watching pornographic videos, but no more valuable as a source of historical information. Into this whirlpool of fiction strode our eminent oral historian. Perhaps he bought them beer, perhaps he did not: either way, they told him what he wanted to hear and he should have known (and in his heart of hearts did know)[40] better than to believe them.

From similar beginnings we can see obvious origins of other inaccuracies. Smiles deliberately sought out old men who knew, or claimed to have known, 'Geordie' before he was rich and famous. Now imagine, dear reader, that you knew the present author long before he became immensely rich and famous, and a crew from Anglia Television came to interview you about his early life. Would you admit that you couldn't stand him and never spoke to him, or that he thought you a hateful, acned squit? Or would you succumb to the temptation to spin a good yarn for the television about how humble, accessible and overwhelmingly nice he was, but that it had always been clear that under his ordinary exterior there lay unfulfilled greatness?

Oral history is a well-established, reputable and scholarly discipline, always provided, of course, that it is conducted in a scholarly way. It is perfectly clear that Smiles was not in the least scholarly in this respect, for reasons considered in the next chapter. It would, in any case, be wrong to expect that he should be, for he was a man of his time and such treatment of oral evidence still lay nearly a century in the future.

Malet described Smiles as 'biased and inaccurate', a statement with which it is difficult to disagree. It is, however, about as helpful as the explanation that it is usually possible to determine which way is up by releasing a heavy object from the hand and observing which way it falls. Of course Smiles is biased and inaccurate: every historical source and every secondary work is. Nothing, whether written or spoken, is entirely accurate. It would have been nice to see in Malet some flickering recognition of the fact that the business of the historian is not to cast about until one finds a supposedly unbiased and accurate source and then crib it down verbatim, but to weigh and assemble evidence of varying content and reliability from many different sources. Smiles did that: his problem seems to have been that he failed sufficiently to heed the advice of the psalmist: 'The children of men are deceitful upon the weights; they are altogether lighter than vanity itself.'

CHAPTER FIVE

The Communion of Saints

Many writers have half-jokingly referred to 'The Gospel of Self-Help' or to 'Samuel Smiles' Communion of Engineering Saints'. These are not, as might at first appear, just cheap jibes at Smiles' expense: they are perfectly reasonable remarks on the spirit in which *Lives of the Engineers* and some of the other biographies were written. They may deserve to be taken more seriously than perhaps their authors intended. Here, as in other cases, Smiles' writings have suffered by being viewed in isolation. *Lives of the Engineers* has been considered almost solely by engineering historians: only Simon Dentith has viewed Smiles as a halfway serious literary figure. The thoroughness with which literary critics have ignored Smiles is remarkable: Garraty's *The Nature of Biography* has a chapter on the nineteenth century which succeeds in avoiding even the mention of the name of the man who wrote more of them than most people and turned down more proposed commissions when he was in his seventies than most biographers would be offered in a lifetime. Cockshut informs us that his time would be too precious to waste on reading Smiles were it not for the other influences of Smiles. It depends on one's ideas of the relationship between literature and history, or, indeed, the preciousness of one's time.[1]

Biography is a strange form which perpetually lingers somewhere between history and literature. It is supposedly factual, yet it frequently relies heavily on highly unreliable oral sources such as those mentioned in the previous chapter. Just as it may be vitiated on the one hand by filial piety, obsequious gratitude or rapacious adhesion to reflected glory, so it may be assailed on the other by spurious claims of precedence and the boundless comfort afforded to authors by the knowledge that dead men cannot sue. Yet, placed in the context of nineteenth-century engineering – and literature – how can it possibly be literary? Can some tedious fellow like Froude, who did a lot of hard sums to reduce the art of naval architecture to a prosaic, if useful, applied science, provide a life story to stand alongside the *Idylls of the King* in the library, or, more importantly, sell alongside it in the bookshop? That was precisely the challenge which Smiles rose to meet, and while he may have ducked the extreme case of Froude, the sales figures show that the challenges he did accept he met successfully.

We already have some idea of why he attempted to do this, from the elementary argument that his subjects were the saints of the secular religion of self-help. This is not a complete or satisfactory explanation, as the next chapter seeks to show, but it has sufficed for others and it will suffice for a start here.

If we view biography as a form in its own right, then the earliest examples we can find, such as Plutarch's *Parallel Lives*, are clearly quite as ideological as they are historical: they offer templates of good and evil behaviour against which the reader is supposed to measure his or her self, and they were so perceived by Smiles.[2] Moving rapidly forward to work written in England, Bede (generally regarded as Britain's first critical historian) is perfectly blunt about the purpose of writing about the lives of saints or sinners: it is that

if history records good things of good men the thoughtful hearer is encouraged to imitate what is good: or if it records evil of wicked men, the good, religious, listener or reader is encouraged to avoid all that is sinful and perverse and to follow what he knows to be good and pleasing to God.[3]

For them to do that, it was necessary for Bede to tell the reader quite clearly which were the good men and which the bad. He did so in a manner no more ambiguous than the 'villains wear black hats' convention in Westerns. Any idea of a judicious and impartial biography is completely anomalous, because biographies were not there to provide an impartial and balanced account of what happened or why it did. They were there to deliver an account of what a person did and how it related to the working-out of God's purpose in the world.

Let us leap, rather athletically, through many centuries. Perhaps Samuel Smiles really had developed a secular quasi-religion in which the end result was not an abstract heaven but simply a vaguely theist, utilitarian heaven-on-earth in which everyone strove to earn, and those who strove well enough were not disappointed. Earning, of course, did not refer only to earning money: Smilesian success was at least as much a matter of earning (and not just gaining) the gratitude or respect of one's fellow men. If that was so, then the basic message of a Bede-style history would be appropriate to his intentions. The temptation, though it seems at first a far-fetched one, is to consider whether Smiles' biographies might not be more closely identifiable with the gospel of work and an associated canon of saints than has previously been recognised. If true, then this is more than an exercise in comparing literary styles: it becomes the clue to an ideological content of wider importance than merely the presentation of exemplars of self-help.

That ideological content, if proven, must be assumed to be a dominant influence, for an ideology is by definition the most important thing in the world to the person advancing it. As the late Bill Shankly (a football manager probably unknown to the learned readers of this book) famously put it, 'Football is not a matter of life and death: it's much more important than that.' It may lead us to believe that Smiles, the man who was 'no thinker', was in fact making a fair attempt at a philosophical synthesis aimed at resolving what he saw as the fundamental problems of nineteenth-century Britain. L.T.C. Rolt has remarked that *Lives of the Engineers* is so extreme in its praise of its subjects, rendering them completely without blemish, as to damage its own credibility and thus, indirectly, the reputations of the engineers.[4] It is true that, with very few exceptions, the engineers were portrayed as not just good and great but perfect. This is particularly strange, since Rolt was doing no more than echo Smiles' own view expressed in *Character.*

> Then as to foibles, the greatest of men are not usually symmetrical. Each has his defect, his twist, his craze; and it is by his faults that the great man reveals his common humanity. We may, at a distance, admire him as a demigod; but as we come nearer to him, we find that he is but a fallible man, and our brother.[5]

Sound, sensible stuff, yet Rolt is right: we search in vain for indications of fallibility and are treated instead to an endless barrage of references to the need for perseverance in support of the idea that what one has done, all might do. Of all the subjects, only Watt could be said, from Smiles' account, to exhibit any significant failings in character.

There is naturally a temptation to view Smiles as an archetypal respectable Victorian gentleman who would cling tenaciously to the principle of *de mortuis nihil nisi bonum* (literally, 'about the dead, nothing unless good'). This principle was not so universally embraced as is generally imagined: in 1813, for example, James Stanfield published his *Essay on the Study and Composition of Biography* in which he emphasised this need:

> To have the independence of spirit, not only to abstain from direct falsehood, but to possess the noble confidence of declaring the *whole truth* is the indispensable test required from the writer who engages in the composition of personal history [italics in original].[6]

According to Stanfield, biographers had both a right and a duty to sit in moral judgement on their subjects, but they must consider the values and morals of the subjects' lifetime as well as of their own. There is nothing new in relativism. Similarly, in 1881, George Bentley published a polemic in favour of 'warts and all treatment'. In between, Smiles himself had published a distinctly unkind brief biography of the late Edgar Allan Poe.[7] It was perfectly possible for biographers, including Smiles, to write ill of the dead, and the question is why Smiles felt it necessary to render his engineer subjects so comprehensively wart-free.

It has long been a favourite sport among historians of nineteenth-century Britain to portray the country as divided into two camps by just one great controversial issue. There are plenty of choices: we may have an individualist camp and a collectivist camp in the Keith Joseph mould; we may have, also discussed briefly above, forward-lookers and backward-lookers; there are paternalists and cooperators. No doubt such portrayals form an interesting framework for a book, but they are oversimplifications. One might recall the naive surprise expressed when supposedly left-wing London dockers supported the supposedly right-wing views of Enoch Powell on immigration, as though it was inconceivable that any issue, or attitude, could bridge the infinite – and imaginary – chasm between Left and Right.

Any attempt to place Smiles on one side or the other of a 'great controversy' like that is doomed to failure, as we have seen in the case of Sir Keith Joseph's misbegotten attempt to place Smiles firmly in the supposed 'anti-collectivist' camp. In his *Lives of the Engineers* Smiles may have performed a fence-straddling exercise of great ingenuity and epic proportion. His treatment of the engineers is formulaic, and there seems a reasonable case for identifying that formula not just as a vague notion of the lives of a communion of secular saints of self-help, but as an adaptation of the genre and conventions of the saint's life itself.

For the reader to whom such a suggestion sounds immediately preposterous, the starting point must be to seek an answer to the question 'why not?', and that answer lies in the flourishing neo-medievalism industry of which we can find some beginnings in the late eighteenth century and which really took off in the early nineteenth century. It has to be admitted that it is probably only in retrospect that the connection between the first stirrings of Gothic architecture at Strawberry Hill and the first Gothic novel, Walpole's *The Castle of Otranto*, become clear: there was no reason why people at the time should have seen such a connection. But while distance may lend not just enchantment but also the temptation to make false connections between real effects and imagined causes, along with its dangers it brings the benefit of a wider perspective. The early developments in 'Gothic' were soon followed by the remarkably rapid revival in interest in King Arthur, as evidenced by the availability of Malory's *Morte d'Arthur*: after being out of print since 1634, there were three printings of Southey's new edition in 1816–17. The first printing since the sixteenth century of Geoffrey of Monmouth's *The History of the Kings of Britain* appeared in 1811. Those, in turn, may reasonably be seen as paving the way for Kenelm Digby's extraordinary book, *The Broadstone of Honour*, first published in 1823.[8]

The first noteworthy characteristic of Digby is his complete lack of any sense of the linearity of time. He takes Malory as being the authentic word on Arthur and his times with, apparently, no realisation that Malory was nearer in time to Digby than to the historical Arthur by almost half a millennium. Much less did he recognise Malory as a bulky superstructure of fiction, loosely based in a long tradition of myth and embellishment, teetering about like a sumo wrestler in stiletto heels on a tiny (some might say non-existent) historical foundation. With such an historical sense as that we need not find it surprising that he could subtitle his work 'or Rules for the Gentlemen of England' with a blithe indifference as to whether these 'rules' dated from the age of Arthur or whether they stemmed from neo-Arthurian romantic fiction of the twelfth or fifteenth century, or, indeed, from neo-Arthurian romantic fiction of 1823. Digby was proposing nothing less than that imagined values derived from highly stylised fiction should form a real everyday code of life in the early nineteenth century. Girouard's suggestion that Digby's writings were influential might initially arouse some scepticism, but Morris provides a pretty impressive list of personal contacts of Digby, including Newman, Acton, Faber, Wordsworth, Pugin, Disraeli, Fitzgerald, Burne-Jones, Morris and Ruskin. Obviously one cannot quantify Digby's influence, but we must accept at least the possibility that his ideas influenced leading figures in literature, art and architecture. Furthermore, although the Young England movement in which Disraeli more famously and Faber more committedly were involved was not a great success in terms of its original objectives, yet it carried some at least of Digby's ideas from the realm of the opinion-formers into that of the decision-makers.[9]

Some of the qualities Digby admired would later find their counterpart in *Self-Help*: 'Effeminate delicacy and the love of luxurious ease, may be consistent with persons of base profession, whose only spirit is in insolence, but with the temper and courtesy of a gentleman they are incompatible.'[10] From what we have seen of Smiles' tolerant and cooperative views in matters of religious or class divisions we might imagine him taking a different view from Digby, who was – to repeat the incredible – offering a code of ethics for nineteenth century life at this point: 'A knight should render no other reason to the infidel than six inches of his falchion thrust into his bowels.'[11] The present author has previously aphorised turn-of-the-nineteenth-century criminal law in the expression 'if it disagrees with you, kill it', which is precisely the Digby viewpoint, provided that 'it' is not a gentleman within the terms of your definition. Such an attitude would not appeal as a matter of principle to a man such as Smiles. In matters of degree, Digby must have seemed appalling. Smiles' linear, non-reversible view of progress tempted him to see the Spanish as has-beens, rulers of an empire which collapsed in the face of industrialism. Digby has this to say of Spanish literature: '. . . the same literature which is distinguished from that of all the Germanic Nations by a spirit of dissimulation and treachery, selfishness and impiety and upon an open disavowal of the common principles of truth and virtue'.[12]

The reader might well wonder what hideous crimes against humanity the Spaniards had committed to merit this attack. It was all quite simple: they had the damnable cheek to live in the same country which had once nurtured Cervantes, who had not merely been incapable of understanding chivalry but had presumed to mock it. One wonders why Britain, which had spawned the loathsome Smollett, whose *Adventures of Sir Launcelot Greaves* was just as treacherous, impious, etc., should rise any higher in his affections.

If your aim is to be a popular author, there is a limit to the extent to which you can kick against the pricks and still find a publisher. By the time that Smiles was seeking to publish his engineering biographies, neo-medievalism was well established in literature, painting, sculpture and architecture. Music is a problematical art for such purposes, but it is at least arguable that the high-tech, steam-driven concert organs which were appearing in civic halls opened the way for the Gothic sombreness of works such as Liszt's *Weinen, Klagen, Sorgen, Zagen* and later to Reubke's *Sonata on the 94th Psalm.* While Wagner may reasonably be seen as the final fusion between romantic fiction and music, he had his forebears whose contribution is less obvious only because they did not use words. The basic assumptions and texts of neo-medievalism were well enough known by 1840 to admit of their being successfully satirised in Barham's *The Ingoldsby Legends,* which ran to a second edition in 1843. Works of satire will only succeed where the target is not merely well known, but held in some respect. You cannot ridicule the already ridiculous, nor can you make irreverent fun of something which is not revered.

It has been suggested above that Smiles was quite astute in matching his writing to his target buyers. If his expensive books – and *Lives of the Engineers* was expensive – were going to sell and to propagate his message, they were probably going to have to sell to a middle-class public already influenced by, or at least familiar with, one or more of the many forms of neo-medievalism. Smiles was well read in medieval history, so he had, to borrow the parlance of the detective novel, both the motive and the opportunity for adopting the close connection with saints' lives which is here suggested.

'Thou seemest pale, Molesworth, is ort the matter? Come, youth, impart wot ails thee. (Note: Hist masters always talk like ivanhoe, blak arow ect.)'[13] No doubt we may accept the learned authority of Willans and Searle. But if 'Hist masters always talk like ivanhoe', who taught 'ivanhoe ect' to talk like that?

Obviously Sir Walter Scott did, but if we ask who taught him, we will wait a long time for an answer. Scott did not just invent a novelistic genre, he consolidated a literary leaning to the past and did not hesitate to invent *de novo* an entire neo-medieval language, a sort of bastardised Middle English, for his characters to speak. This is not a concordance of Scott, but it is worthy of passing note that from the hundred or so words offered by Roget's *Thesaurus* for a horse, almost every occurrence in Scott's chivalric offerings is of the handful which, like steed, destrier and palfrey, are of Middle English origin. Scott's novels sold in large numbers for many decades and were clearly influential in such matters as the publication by John Sobrieski Stuart, in 1842, of *Vestiarum Scoticum*, an allegedly sixteenth-century document on the designs of tartan which costume historians nowadays view as being less authentic than the poems of Ossian. Scott had possibly an even greater influence by virtue of being the author of the entry for 'Chivalry' in the 1818 edition of *Encyclopaedia Britannica*. It might not have sold many copies compared with *Ivanhoe*, but how many people consulted it over the years and believed it?

It would be easy to press this line of argument too far. In the first place, the interest in neo-medievalism may have been encouraged by some leading figures in the arts, but it was by no means universal. In the fields of architecture and historical painting, Renaissance and classical themes were plundered with almost equal enthusiasm, suggesting a more general historical eclecticism. In literature there were some eccentric souls such as Barham, Dickens and Thackeray who took up the mantle of Smollett. In the second, there were some components of medievalism which provided perfectly reasonable support for the paternalist school of industrialists, who thought they had found the answer to the 'Condition of England' question. They were willing to be like Cedric: awfully kind and decent to Gurth so long as he knew his place and didn't complain about wearing his serf's collar.

Clearly ideas like that would not appeal to Smiles, but other neo-chivalric tenets were not so unpalatable. Intellectualism was something Digby could do without: 'O the vain pride of mere intellectual ability, how contemptible when contrasted with the riches of the past, with "the feeling soul's divinest glow!"' Smiles may not have gone in directly for divinest glows, but he persistently claimed that the greatest engineering achievements depended on diligence and hard work rather than intellectualism, and we recall that he had pounced with delight on Sir Joshua Reynolds' suggestion that even the painting of works of art was more a matter of application than inspiration.

But there were limits. Just as Smiles could approve some of Rousseau's ideas of human equality without subscribing to any of what he saw as the 'noble savage' nonsense, so Digby (and other neo-medievalists) could plumb unacceptable depths of anti-intellectualism. There is the same degree of self-contradiction as well: Rousseau seems generally to have failed to take account of the fact that noble savages lacked printing presses for publishing the works of philosophers, and probably ate more music teachers than they kept in paid employment. So Digby tells us that

> I, for one, would rather err with such men as Sir Lancelot . . . destitute of human wisdom, unacquainted with the discoveries of science, knowing nothing of the historians or the moralists of any age and yet taught by God's word in all essential truth.[14]

Even by Digby's standards, this is extraordinary. Had he read Malory? It was Lancelot's affair with Guinevere that destroyed not only both of them, but Arthur, the Round Table and the whole of Camelot as well. It was the ultimate betrayal. The real contradiction is not that: it is that Digby professes that he would prefer to be unacquainted with the works of historians; had his request been granted, he would never have heard of Lancelot. Like Scott, who enthused on paper about the Middle Ages in a house lit by gas, he wanted to have his cake, to eat it and then to pretend that cake is evil.

These were powerful influences on the literary market, and they were adapted, particularly by Carlyle, to purposes of controversial analysis of contemporary society. It is here suggested that Smiles deliberately set out to steal the neo-medieval clothing of the anti-industrial lobby, which looked to an Arcadian past, and apply it to his consistent advocacy of cooperation, his solution to the 'Condition of England Question'.

This is a radical suggestion. Opinions on Smiles' biographies have varied, but generally only in the sense that later writers have agreed or disagreed with them. To some they have been 'authoritative', to others 'biased and inaccurate'. Most of the more observant commentators have seen the subjects as exemplars of self-help. An exemplar is an ideological vehicle, and Dentith has gone further than most in recognising the breadth and variety of the ideological content of Smiles. This writer argues for going a stage further: in addition to the standard literary devices which Dentith has identified in Smiles,[15] there are others from a much earlier period.

One of the tropes to which Dentith draws attention is that of the engineer pictured as child prodigy. This was undoubtedly a popular component in any good biographical yarn, to the extent that, as he points out, Dickens wrote what could have been a parody of Smiles' engineering biographies before Smiles had actually written them.

> He took, when he was a schoolboy, to constructing steam-engines out of saucepans, and setting birds to draw their own water, with the least possible amount of labour; so assisting them with artful contrivance of hydraulic pressure, that a thirsty canary had only, in a literal sense, to put his shoulder to the wheels, and the job was done.[16]

This is paralleled with the story of Watt's early manifestation of mechanical talents, but could equally apply to several others, notably Rennie and his fleet of model ships. Dickens was no engineer, but here as in a few other instances he was a very well-informed and up-to-date observer. When *Bleak House* was first published (1851–2) hydraulic technology was pretty recent stuff.

The use of such literary conventions was hardly surprising. Those rich and famous parents who expected their children to become rich and famous and inherit the family estate kept family documents: others did not, which meant that the biographers of those who were not hereditarily rich and famous were faced with a choice between making do with doubtful oral information, and making it up. Making it up from a hotch-potch of conventions may well have been the less inaccurate course. Other well-known conventions occur, notably the one which insists on hugely successful men having been complete duffers at school because their teachers were such blockheads as to be unable to recognise their talents. This was a long-term Smilesian theme (see Chapter 1) but it remained popular long afterwards. Sir Winston Churchill, for example, claimed to have been unsuccessful at school, when in fact the record merely shows that he was sometimes difficult and lazy. This is not uncommon among intelligent children, and in his case might be suggested to have manifested itself at some stages in later life as well.

A slightly different emphasis appears in the 'Life' of James Brindley. He was not a child prodigy, but while he was apprenticed to an incompetent and drunken millwright he was able to bring to bear talents which solved all the problems of the business, and to be put in charge of qualified men.[17] We know that Smiles would raid contemporary biographical conventions and he would, as we shall see, even raid fairy tales for a good story line. Had he raided the Bible for the story of the young Christ teaching in the Temple and used it to illustrate the talents of the young Brindley? If he had, there is no reason why we should assume that it was an original idea or even that he had done it directly, for what we may loosely term biblical plagiarism had a very long history, and one phase of its history may be thought to provide both a precedent for that breach of divine copyright and some other ingredients of his biographies as well.

In the period roughly between AD 900 and 1100, when England was popularly supposed to have developed into the recognisable forebear of nineteenth-century Britain (Welsh, Scots and similar defeated minorities only counted after they became Anglicised), by far the most widely available form of literature was hagiography – lives of saints. There were other forms available, including such blockbusters as Geoffrey of Monmouth's *History of the Kings of England,* over two hundred manuscript copies of which have survived the ravages of rats, fire, flood and goldbeaters to this day. Clearly many hundreds more did not. In general terms, though, we have to consider the means of production and who controlled it. Because printing had yet to be invented, the vast majority of books necessarily emerged from the places which had plentiful supplies of people who could write and had organised bodies of scribes. It is important to remember that these were *published* works: publication did not begin with printing. Before the growth of universities, virtually all the people who produced books worked in religious houses, with the result that most of what was published reflected monastic views of what was good for people. Universities were themselves a form of religious establishment, in that even the humblest student was technically a 'clerk in minor orders'. It is possible that stationers (who were producing copies for sale of such things as town chronicles) were also in the business of histories and saints' lives, either by direct production or by renting out exemplar copies, a quire at a time, for customers to have copied. Be that as it may, production and distribution was mainly under religious (in the non-technical sense) control.

The hagiographers developed a formula, perhaps comparable with the Mills & Boon formula of more recent times, which allowed a great deal of apparent variation while basically telling the same story with the same message every time. Some of the ingredients were obligatory, others optional. Absolutely fundamental to gaining approval by the monastic publication committee was the exhibition of a life which could appear in general terms to be dedicated to the service of God. If we transfer that idea into Smiles' terms, where God is an abstraction of good and good is almost entirely synonymous with progress, it is clear that engineers could, and often did, fill the bill – if one wanted them to. 'Good' could include improved material wealth (provided one did not seek it so avidly as to be a mammonist), the saving of life from natural hazards or disease, the spreading of perceived values of civilisation. Above all it involved the general improvement of society, in which the above were among the most important, but not the only, factors. The end result of the efforts of the engineers is demonstrable progress towards the almost utopian state of human relationships described in the later chapters of *Self-Help*. What, then, were the components of the formula which Smiles allegedly adopted? We may begin with the qualifications which made a saint.

Martyrdom was not essential, but it certainly helped. Many and picturesque were the forms of death inflicted on the saints whose lives – and deaths – were popular reading in twelfth-century England. None of Smiles' engineers was flayed alive, dismembered or fed to lions, but Brindley died prematurely (at the age of fifty-six) through 'the far more trying condition of the engineer's vocation – irregular living, exposure in all weathers, long fasting and then, perhaps, heavy feeding when the nervous system was exhausted, together with habitual disregard of the ordinary conditions of physical health.'[18] Other engineers, including Smeaton and Rennie, certainly had their ends hastened by it. Smiles clearly stated that the death of Brindley in particular resulted from his entire devotion to duty. But we need not consider this to be stretching a point, or that Smiles was merely implying martyrdom, for in *Self-Help* we find specific references to the 'martyrs of science', among whom was nearly numbered M. Jacquard, inventor of the digitally controlled loom. He narrowly escaped being drowned by a bunch of French Luddites who had correctly identified one of the ultimate implements of de-skilling and foreseen its likely effects on their income. When Boulton took in hand the matter of dealing with the Cornish patent pirates, he saved Watt from a mental strain which would otherwise have 'added another to the list of martyr-inventors'.[19]

For those saints who died in their beds of natural causes, the failure to achieve martyrdom made it important to come up with something instructive in the way of helpful pronouncements from the deathbed. Again Smiles does not disappoint us and again Brindley is perhaps the best example, with his inimitable dying words to a supplicant whose canal bed was leaking. Asked if he had puddled it thoroughly, he replied in the affirmative, whereupon the great man told him 'Then puddle it again – and again' and expired soon afterwards. Rennie, too, continued to work on his deathbed, providing a continuing benefit to others when his own bodily powers were spent.

George Stephenson lacks a poignant deathbed scene, but the approaches of supplicants during his retirement are broadly analogous. Particularly noteworthy is the enquiry made by a young man who wished to become an engineer and turned up in his best clothes and carrying a gold-headed cane – a perfectly reasonable thing for a young man to do when going to meet someone so rich and famous at his rather splendid country house – and was brusquely told: 'Put by that stick, my man, and then I will speak to you.'[20] Humility was required in these situations, and Smiles went to a great deal of trouble to provide anecdotes which illustrated George Stephenson's humility in greatness and lasting simplicity of taste. The occasional unguarded remark may cause us to view such stories with some suspicion: in American editions we learn that early in his professional life, George had been rather embarrassed when the offerings of the small wine merchant 'with whom he usually dealt' failed to provide a port to satisfy the refined tastes of Joseph Sandars. Later he 'lived to be able to treat Mr Sandars to a better article at Tapton House'.[21]

In recent times, accounts of miracles have frequently been a barrier to acceptance of the historical accuracy of medieval saints' lives. This is readily understandable, since medieval miracles contained two particular formulae which arouse suspicion in the modern mind. The first is the biblical plagiarism (in which the saint re-performs miracles of Christ or the Apostles) and the second is the physically outrageous, like the re-attachment of the severed head of St Winefride. Our inability, in the late twentieth century, to take stories of this kind entirely seriously, may miss the point. The purpose of a miracle story was twofold. In the first place, it demonstrated that God, who had invented the laws of nature, could, when He so chose, set them aside for the time being. Second, it demonstrated that there were men on earth of such exceptional quality that God was prepared to delegate to them, at least on an occasional basis, that particular facet of His omnipotence.

The engineers did indeed perform miracles. The most comprehensive example is Telford's construction of Highland roads, whose consequences, as mentioned above, stretched far beyond mundane considerations of travel and transport. The moral deprivation the Highlanders had been suffering resulted from there being no gainful work to do and no identifiable means of self-improvement. Telford's roads enabled the Highlanders to find work, to find markets for their produce and to import manufactured goods which cost less, thus freeing their efforts and their savings to be applied to more gainful things. Self-help required that people have a place on the starting line of life's great race, and Telford gave that place to, as Smiles portrays it, virtually the entire population of the Highlands, so that people who had previously been dirty, idle and depraved became good, decent and hardworking. In Smilesian values this was at least as great a miracle as converting a Saxon tribe to Christianity.

It might be objected that such an idea is directly contradicted by the arguments advanced in Chapter 1 and that traditional saints were about the last thing a secular religion needed. Smiles did not hesitate to make connections between conventional religion and engineering either directly or indirectly. As an example of the former we may take the story of St Guthlac and the building of Croyland Abbey: Guthlac was a saint according to canon law for his spiritual achievements, but he gained Smiles' approbation for the work he did in reclaiming fenland and building on it.[22] It is also clear from Smiles' account of Guthlac that he had not read Ingulph's *Chronicle of Croyland,* but he undoubtedly had read all three of the medieval 'Lives' of Guthlac. He knew his stuff.

As an example of indirect connection we may take a passing remark towards the end of his account of Smeaton's Eddystone Light. It was not just that generations of sailors had cause to be thankful for Smeaton's light, but that one might almost think that the Almighty had formed the rock for the specific purpose of placing a light on it. That, surely, puts Smeaton into precisely the category of men so favoured as to be allowed delegated powers to vary the laws of nature, which in this case stated that if you sailed near the Eddystone Rock in the dark or in poor visibility you were likely to die. Now, sailors positively looked for the rock, for it had been transformed from an agency of destruction into the means of safety:

> Many a heart has lept with gladness at the cry of 'The Eddystone in sight!' sung out from the maintop. Homeward bound ships, from far-off ports, no longer avoid the dreaded rock, but eagerly run for its light as the harbinger of safety. It might even seem as if Providence had placed the reef so far out to sea as the foundation for a beacon such as this, leaving it to man's skill and labour to finish His work.[23]

Perhaps the man to whom it was left to finish the divine task is seen as a rather special man.

There were certain conventions of structure as well as content in the writing of saints' 'Lives'. To make a more varied narrative, for example, direct speech was included. There was no likelihood that the actual form of words was accurate or even approximately correct: it is generally acknowledged that such 'quotations' were simply the hagiographer's impressions of what a man such as he knew the saint to be would have been guided by God to say in the particular situation. There was no intention to deceive anyone by pretending that these were the exact and actual words. It is clear that Smiles took the same view, though he did not openly admit it. There is, for example, one story of which he was very fond, so fond that he told it twice. It is the story of the young William Murdock seeking employment with Matthew Boulton. The world and his dog wanted a job with Boulton and Watt, and Boulton was about to send the young man packing when he noticed his 'curious' hat. The story shifts into dialogue, in which it emerges that the hat is made of wood and that Murdock made it himself on an oval turning lathe of his own design and construction. Boulton is impressed and hires the man who would later become an engineer and inventor of some importance. A splendid tale and well told: the problem is that the wording of the dialogue is different in each version. It is, in fact, a representation by Smiles of what he, as a man learned in the subject, thought the man and the youth *might* or perhaps *should* have said to each other.[24] Neither more, nor less. As such, both the accuracy and the intention are directly comparable to those of invented dialogue in saints' 'Lives'. This is not to suggest that invented dialogue was a convention peculiar to Smiles and to medieval saints' 'Lives', but it forms another piece of the jigsaw.

The idea of what was true and accurate has further and more serious ramifications: ideas of truth can vary in more than the mere exactness of a form of words. As a trifling example we may take Smiles' statement, in favour of his defence of the nobility of physical work, that all the Apostles worked with their hands. It is inconceivable that a man with Smiles' breadth of reading was unaware of the previous occupation of St Matthew and highly unlikely that he would assume such ignorance on the part of his readers. We seem to be faced, therefore, with a statement which Smiles knew to be untrue and which he knew his readers would know to be untrue, but which is nonetheless presented as fact. The obvious reason is that it was a simple mistake, an oversight, but where Smiles is involved, obvious reasons have a habit of being wrong.

The suggestion was made in a similar case of apparently conscious inaccuracy cited at the end of the last chapter that Smiles was writing 'full-hearted', that is to say scribbling busily away, preoccupied with the message rather than the medium. Present-day authors can use their word-processors to refine out little mistakes like those.

This author has previously suggested that even if Smiles had been able to indulge in the promiscuous redrafting which is commonplace nowadays, he would not necessarily have changed statements like that. He had read many medieval documents and publications: in addition to the 'Lives' of Guthlac, he knew all four of the 'Lives' of St Swithun and had certainly referred to the gargantuan *Acta Sanctorum*.[25] One of the recent documents he must have used (though he did not cite it) was Scott Russell's *Memoir* of George Stephenson, read to the Institution of Mechanical Engineers in 1848. This contains statements exactly comparable to Smiles' statement about the artisan Apostles. Scott Russell wrote, for example, that future historians would record that the steam locomotive had originated around the middle of the nineteenth century.[26] This was not a contentious matter about which there was any argument, and he had no discernible interest in publishing a falsehood, yet both he and his audience were perfectly well aware that what he said was not true. Even if their chronology might be a little vague, they knew that there were rudimentary locomotives wheezing around in the first decade of the century.

This statement, like Smiles' apparent gaffe over St Matthew, seems to be made recklessly, using that term with its legal meaning of complete unconcern as to whether it was true or not, or for any consequences of its truth or falsehood. There was, however, another contributor on the subject at the meeting of the Institution at which Scott Russell read his *Memoir*. A Mr Geach proposed a motion that the Institution's regret at the demise of its first president be formally minuted, and his speech contains a passage which has barely credible implications:

> He [Mr Geach] would quite allow that his [George Stephenson's] manners were sometimes rough; he would quite allow that there were peculiarities in his character, which had to be considered as peculiarities: but he was quite sure that those who knew him best considered that these very peculiarities gave him a greater claim on their regard. He was willing to allow that he had seen in Mr Stephenson what in other men might subject them to criticism; but when it came from Mr Stephenson it came from a privileged person.

We know some of the 'peculiarities'. George Stephenson had been involved in all manner of crooked dealings in railway bubble schemes, in mineral speculations and in plagiarism of the ideas of others. Whatever his achievements, he was in some respects an eminently dislikeable man and had fallen out with a small biographical dictionary-full of people. Geach knew this, yet was claiming that, because they 'came from a privileged person', George's disagreeable traits served positively to give him a greater, not a lesser, claim upon their regard. According to what we perceive as normal mid-nineteenth-century ideas of truth or logic as applied by engineers or scientists, the man was apparently talking drivel.

It was not so. We use different forms of logic in different circumstances: our approach to the Inland Revenue may be numerical, to the credit card company legalistic; to unwilling children we may offer exhortation or bribery; to doorstep missionaries, a pretence of profound deafness. There is no universal system of persuasion. Neither, despite what scientists have been trying to tell us since they first understood what Newton was on about, is there any universal system of truth. Smiles and Scott Russell alike perceived different forms of truth in different circumstances and at different levels. We do not have to look very far to find the prototype for the view of truth which allowed the deliberate perpetration of what was at a superficial level false, but which was actually a truth at a deeper and more spiritual level. It is, once again, evidenced in the writing of saints' 'Lives': 'I have nowhere read this, but so many reputable men assert that it happened that I believe it would be a great impudence not to believe it.'[27] The meaning of this passage is clear and simple: ideas of objective truth are not relevant in these circumstances. One says what it is *proper* to say of the subject. Geach and Eadmer might be separated by over 700 years, but they had at least one shared value. For all we know they may both have preferred goose to chicken as well.

Smiles generally chose to write biographies only of people he deemed worthy of the saintly treatment,[28] and the major subjects of *Lives of the Engineers* are without exception quasi-saintly. Those engineers who were not, or who did not appear to Smiles to be so, were simply left out. Trevithick, it will be recalled, gets only a modest *Memoir* in the 1874 edition, and a much fuller – and kinder – one in the 1868 American edition of *The Life of George Stephenson*. In the 1857 edition Smiles remarks dismissively on how little he achieved. The fact is that Trevithick did not fit the saintly template. He was an erratic genius, markedly short on dogged perseverance, and most of whose best ideas only really came to fruition in the hands of others. Financially, Trevithick was a chaotic individual who clearly did not practise that careful domestic management exemplified by the saints. Above all, he was involved with the Cornish engineers stigmatised by Smiles as patent pirates. That was a sin close to Smiles' heart: Trevithick and his kind attempted to deny to James Watt the due reward of his industry and perseverance,[29] and Smiles himself had suffered at the hands of copyright pirates. If Trevithick were portrayed as having succeeded, his success would foul up the entire message of the biography of Watt, which was that if you want to be like James Watt, rich, famous and a benefactor of mankind, all you have to do is work hard like he did. (Though being a genius might offer some marginal advantage.)

The Smilesian selection process follows the distinctively circular logic of the medieval hagiographer. A subject is chosen because he or she is saintly: once that selection is made, the saintliness is axiomatic, and the content of the narrative is single-mindedly directed to the illustration of that saintliness. People who perform saintly works are saints, and works performed by saints are saintly. Once the process is begun, any investigation or appraisal of either the subject or the actions would be, at the least, 'impudent'. That is exactly what Mr Geach, in his secular way, was explaining. For 'privileged person' read 'saint' and the difficulties about ideas of truth melt away. We recognise that we are no longer dealing with logic or proof, but with faith and dogma. That suppression of the critical faculties is probably what Smiles really meant by writing 'full-hearted'.

All the best stories have a villain, and saints' 'Lives' do not disappoint us. They may be obvious material villains mutilating or murdering virgin saints like St Agnes, or they may be the incorporeal demons attacking the soul of St Guthlac.[30] The Smilesian parallel here is perhaps less than totally conclusive, but there is certainly no shortage of villains. All that is open to question is whether they can be considered genuinely demonic.

The group about whom Smiles probably felt most strongly at a personal level was made up of people we might represent as fallen angels, namely engineers who worked against the forces of progress. There were various ways in which they might do this, but the commonest was by acting on behalf of objectors to new schemes. It is submitted that, bearing in mind his position as a railway employee and his need to maintain good relations with the engineering profession, Smiles went as far as he dared, in the passages on the railway mania quoted above. The manner in which Smiles treats the proceedings of the Select Committee on the 1825 Liverpool & Manchester Railway Bill is quite different. The engineers who testified against the soundness of George Stephenson's plans and survey are selectively quoted or alluded to in the adroit manner one might expect from an experienced controversialist such as Smiles. Comments and value judgements are rendered superfluous by astute reference to opinions which had been proved wrong by the passage of time, so that Palmer, Cubitt and Giles, for example, are held up to italicised ridicule for their statements against the practicality of Stephenson's scheme for crossing Chat Moss: Smiles does not need to tell his readers that the line across Chat Moss was successfully built and was still in use when he wrote.[31] What Smiles almost certainly could have revealed, but chose not to, is that the method of construction which succeeded on Chat Moss was adopted not *by* Stephenson but despite him. His usually clear narrative style becomes confused to the point where one needs to read the passage through carefully two or three times before realising that Smiles is (probably deliberately) concealing the truth.[32]

What could not be concealed was that the fundamental reason the first Bill for the Liverpool & Manchester Railway was lost was that the survey had been incompetent. Smiles passes on Stephenson's suggestion that Auty, one of his survey team, had been 'fee'd by some of the canal proprietors to make a botch of the job' and implied that Hugh Steele's suicide resulted from the fact that he and Elijah Galloway 'seem to have made some grievous blunder in the levels on Chat Moss'. Thus appears one of the groups of demons, the corrupt and insidious canal proprietors who were not only responsible for placing obstructions in the way of progress, but indirectly had the blood of poor Hugh Steele on their hands as well. Another group, of course, was the traditional landowners, who allegedly indulged in all manner of violence and skulduggery to prevent the surveying of the route and the acquisition of the land.[33] The worst action perpetrated by these groups was the hiring of the lawyers who destroyed George Stephenson's evidence. Alderson, the most destructive of them, is portrayed as a silver-tongued bully, driving the great engineer into purely verbal corners. The technique of showing that what was said to be impossible was subsequently readily and profitably achieved is again employed.

A quick perusal of the committee proceedings confirms that George Stephenson did indeed have a very rough time, and that Alderson in particular was a ferocious assailant. He may, for all we know, have been a very nasty man as well, but that does not make him a demon. Two other factors do. The first is that, like their clients, the opposition lawyers stood in the way of progress, and progress is the Way, the Truth and the Life in Smiles' philosophy. The second is that we may compare the temporary pain and humiliation of George Stephenson in 1825 with that of an abused saint: the saint's reward came in heaven, George's in the somewhat nearer future when the railway succeeded and he became rich, famous and powerful without even losing the humility which was an essential component of his true greatness – and of self-help.

The case of George Stephenson may provide the clearest and most detailed example, but opponents of other saints of progress are characterised by Smiles as stupid, evil or both. The Fenmen were thoroughly nasty people; Brindley was mocked by intellectual cretins when he proposed the Barton aqueduct; Hugh Middleton's construction of the New River to supply water to London was severely hindered by a combination of ignorance and selfishness on the part of opponents. Perhaps the clearest illustration of Smiles' attitude is when he recounts the destruction of the Albion Mill (erected by Rennie) by fire. It made a profit and it lowered the price of flour, so there was no more to be said.[34] If its destruction was indeed the work of incendiarists, Smiles' readers have been provided with information which will allow them to come to only one conclusion about the moral issues involved.

We can find various other strands of evidence to support a parallel between *Lives of the Engineers* and saints' 'Lives'. Smiles' description of the way in which he researched George Stephenson finds parallels in the sometimes strident assertions of authenticity which characterise some saints' 'Lives'. Again, it could be suggested that Smiles' description of Smeaton's tools lying neglected after his death parallels the cult of saintly relics, or that the abandoned garret workshop of James Watt was a shrine to engineering progress. These are marginal considerations which, having established some case in favour of the parallel, we may pass over en route to the central connection.

Anyone who has researched the work of an engineer for whom there is no existing published biography will be entirely familiar with the problem of finding out any details of the private or family life of the subject, in many cases even of finding out what sort of person the subject was. It is exactly the problem Smiles encountered when he first started work on George Stephenson, and which, in that case, he was able to solve by talking to people who had known and worked with the great man. Many of his subjects had died too long ago for him to be able to do that, and in some cases he was not even able to find direct descendants. The sources to which he had then to resort, such as reports, parliamentary enquiries, company documents, engineers' correspondence, all share the same weakness of relating only to the subject's work and actions. They do not tell us what he liked for breakfast.

The hagiographer had exactly the same problem. People became saints through saintly actions and the sources available for their lives, whether written, oral or material, were primarily geared to the substantiation of saintliness. Other attributes or personal characteristics were likely to be hard to find out, with the result that many a saint appears at first sight to be a pretty two-dimensional figure, a cardboard cut-out made to remind the reader of specific actions. 'Lives' are actually much more cleverly written than that, and actions are recounted in such a way as to cast light on the personal characteristics of the subject. The actions come first, and the deductions as to character are made afterwards by the reader. The author must, of course, make sure that the reader comes to the right conclusion.

That is exactly the technique adopted by Smiles. The expression 'humility in greatness' has been used several times in this book as summarising one of the key characteristics Smiles credits to George Stephenson. Smiles, however, nowhere uses that expression, nor any other directly comparable one.

Instead he provides a string of anecdotes about George in later professional life and in retirement from which it is intended that we cannot fail to arrive at the 'humility in greatness' conclusion.

It is true that some of the biographies have a section (as in the cases of Smeaton and Rennie) or even a whole chapter (in the case of Stephenson) which purports to be an assessment of the character of the subject. These sections are in fact constructed in the same way as the rest of the work, and concern themselves with accounts of events in the same way. The selection criteria are different, and the reader is prompted to make the intended deductions, but even so, these sections are still narratives of deeds: they are, as the Bollandists put it, *Acta*. George Stephenson was kind to animals, but instead of any extended explanation of why this was, and how it fitted in with the innumerable other facets of a complex character, we are given an account of his being nice to a poorly robin and are left to work out the rest for ourselves.

This could appear a crude literary technique in an age in which elaborate characterisation was considered an important ingredient in novels. Smiles, however, was rarely crude, and had recognised one of history's great techniques. A saint's 'Life' set out first to convince its reader that the subject was indeed a saint and, having achieved that, allowed the reader to form his own picture of the saint, according to his own perceptions of saintliness based on the information provided. The qualities of the subject were, therefore, in part the reader's own invention and likely to be afforded the special credibility we each conceitedly attach to our own views. There is not one 'character' of George Stephenson or Thomas Telford, but many, and each is tailored to the particular views and likings of its holder. As we go on to consider why it is that Smiles' work has lasted so well, we may recognise the guile with which he manipulated his readers through his adaptation of one of the all-time great literary forms to his own purpose. That he was able at the same time to cut the neo-medieval ground from under the feet of Carlyle indicates a man of unusual talent.

CHAPTER SIX

Variations on a Theme

The argument of the previous chapter suggests that, on the subject of engineering history as of the religious life, there was for Smiles only one overarching correct answer, but there were many ways of approaching it. If it is true that Smiles burgled the hagiographer's toolbox, we should not assume that he did not use any tools acquired from other sources. He was nothing if not versatile, and would use anyone's methods if they suited him. He wrote variations on other people's themes, but in the process inadvertently offered himself as the subject of further variations by others.

One of the key questions about Smiles, to which we return again and again, is how he managed to sell so many engineering biographies. He was not the first in the field, but Rickman's work on Telford, just as Muirhead's on Watt,[1] sold in small numbers to a specialist readership – or perhaps one should call it an ownership, since it seems that Rickman and Muirhead's works appealed as much to the professional piety of engineers as to any wider motive or public. The published version of Smeaton's reports – now a rare and highly esteemed work – sold like concrete lifebelts.[2] Smiles was the first to sell engineering biography in quantity, and while saintliness is part of their attraction, we may find other tricks of the literary trade employed to persuade the public that they wanted to read about people building things.

The idea that the history of engineering is boring is still alive and well, and is closely related to the idea that engineering itself is boring. This present work shared the fate of *Self-Help* in being turned down by a publisher who should have known better, and the author is aware of a new work on Froude which has amassed about fifteen rejections already. The neglect of Froude has been mentioned several times in passing. His work in hydrodynamics not only changed the relationship between science and technology but underpinned the continued success of the British shipping

and shipbuilding industries in the latter part of the nineteenth century –
when they were perhaps the only truly successful British industries apart
from armaments manufacture. Froude, one imagines, should be a man of
great interest to a fairly wide readership.[3] Could Smiles have sold a
biography of someone as 'boring' in popular perception as Froude, and if
so, how would he have gone about it? What were the secrets of a success
without precedent and which only L.T.C. Rolt has come close to emulating
since Smiles' death?

The first and most obvious factor is that the author must have some
involvement with the subject which extends beyond academic curiosity or
an intention to 'get it right' and engages with the subject and his or her life
and work at an emotional as well as a factual level. This present work was
born of a fascination with the variety of Smiles' interests, but soon acquired
an overlay of admiration for the energy and enthusiasm he put into those
interests and the way he was able to shape almost any subject to further
them. Of course it is possible to write about people without that kind of
involvement, but such works are perhaps better confined to the ranks of
PhD theses where, instead of paying to read them, the target readership (of
two or three) is paid to read them.

Smiles knew this very well: he was doubtful about embarking on
engineering biography in the first place, and his first subject, the one that
started him in the field, was (or was made) a complete exemplar of the
Smiles philosophy. But as we have seen, he turned down some very
lucrative commissions, notably to write the 'Life' of Brassey, and recorded
his dislike of writing the 'Life' of George Moore. These were people to
whom he did not warm, of whom he could not write 'full-hearted'. It is
widely believed that Smiles did not write about people of whom he did not
approve: this is generally true, but there are exceptions. In *Brief Biographies*
he wrote of a number of people of whom he disapproved, including
George Borrow and Theodore Hook.[4] But although his condemnation of
them is feeble stuff compared with his sanctification of, say, James Watt, he
was still able to write 'full-hearted' with a negative as with a positive
message.

It is nowadays considered pretty disreputable in academic historical
circles to adopt a judgemental approach to one's subject. Yet, if we see a
glimmer of truth in Marx's suggestion that most events appear twice on
history's stage, the first time as tragedy, the second as farce, we must

attempt to distinguish between the two. At one level it could be argued that history without judgement is a joke with no punch line: more seriously, history without judgement becomes a meaningless and unanalysed parade of useless data pertaining to the actions of dead people.[5] The gathering of such material is what research assistants are for (and Smiles used them thus), prior to the fruits of their labours being given shape and meaning by the historian. In their raw state, they are fit matter for the next reworking but one of the National Curriculum. Smiles was quite familiar with that sort of 'history' (and that sort of education) and had no time for it. His preface to *The Life of George Stephenson* has never been highly regarded as a contribution to the philosophy of history, but it does make clear his attitude to history as being essentially a human activity, valid only when endowed with human interest in human subjects.[6] The proper study of mankind was man.

Success in this quest for human interest was one of the factors which made Smiles' books so popular. The extent to which he borrowed the conventions of one age-old literary form, the saint's 'Life', has already been considered in some detail, and mention has been made of his employment of certain tropes in recounting the childhood of his subjects. These were by no means the only techniques he used.

One of the nineteenth century's more successful literary bandwagons was the revival of fairy tales, and more particularly the translation and adaptation of hitherto little-known foreign ones, mainly from France and Germany.[7] The appeal was ostensibly to children, but of course children did not make the decision to purchase, so the success or failure of a fairy tale depended on its appeal to adults. To take a modern analogy, cat food advertisements are designed to appeal to people, not to cats. While some fairy tales were of limited value as teaching aids, others conveyed messages of a suitably high moral tone to appeal to a notional *bonus paterfamilias*. One such tale was *Cinderella*, often misinterpreted by those who see the fairy godmother as a sort of supernatural Horatio Alger bringing tidings that Cinderella has won a fortune in a lottery. This is not at all what the story is about. From the outset Cinderella is noble by birth, by character and of right: no action of the fairy godmother seeks to change her. What is changed is the false perception of her which has arisen through the injustices of the world. What a comforting message it was: just keep on washing those pots with a pure heart and one day the irresistible power of the fairy godmother's wand will intervene. It will not directly elevate you to the status you deserve, but it will provide the situation in which you can elevate yourself.[8]

So it was with John Rennie and a stage coach. He was taking a trip to Scotland when the axle-tree failed. He and his fellow passengers would have been faced with sleeping a very uncomfortable night on the road, but Rennie was a skilled artisan by training and outlook. He removed the damaged part, and he and the coachman carried it to a smithy, where Rennie welded it and they then refitted it and drove on. Two of his fellow inside-passengers now viewed him askance, as he was obviously an artisan and no gentleman. The following morning one of them was greatly discomfited when he arrived to seek business with the Earl of Eglinton, only to find Rennie and the earl just finishing breakfast. Rennie, like Cinderella, was noble to start with but was wrongly perceived as menial through the spurious snobbery of lesser beings. Only when he was seen in his 'proper' surroundings, breakfasting with an earl, did the mistake come to light.[9] Smiles told this story in two different variants, and recorded his preference for the one more closely approximating to *Cinderella* in his *Autobiography*.

Jack the Giant-Killer is another uplifting tale. The essence of it is that the giant is not – cannot be – defeated by mortal prowess but only by the turning of his own gigantic strength against himself. The allegorical meaning of a puny little runt named George Stephenson defeating Ned Nelson, the works bully of Black Callerton Colliery, in a fight is very clear. George made no attempt to meet the giant on his own terms, but ducked and dodged until the giant had exhausted himself launching huge blows into fresh air, after which George's relatively puny, but accurate, blows proved effective and won the fight for him.[10] Smiles could write some good story lines, but why should he bother when he had age-old best-sellers, well out of copyright, to make his point for him?

It was not necessary to employ borrowed narrative. At one level, passing allusion to an already well-known narrative could be sufficient, as in the case of Smiles' mention of Excalibur.[11] He could have written pages about the development of traditional skills of metallurgy among the makers of medieval weapons: an oblique reference to King Arthur makes all that redundant while simultaneously reinforcing the favourite message, that his industrial and engineering heroes were heroes of *peace*. (Which is possibly the real reason why he never gave Sir William Armstrong the treatment for his achievements in hydraulics.) At another level, Smiles could borrow one of the fundamental precepts of legend, and simply adapt facts very freely to suit his purpose. It would nowadays be difficult to sell an account of Robin Hood which lacked the 'love interest' of the genteel Maid Marion who still knew how to handle weapons rather well, or the gluttonous and mildly comical Friar Tuck, yet both of these are sixteenth-century additions to the traditional stories.[12] It was precisely the strength of a story which would last, that it could assimilate such modernisation and become, through ongoing adaptation, a story for any time and for all time. The converse of that is that the essential message of the story, the bit without which all else becomes pointless, must be conceptually very simple indeed and must allow the reader to identify with its central character(s). Otherwise, when it is mangled by alteration it will succumb. Great author though she was, Jane Austen's work would not lie happily as a Hollywood musical, and the recent Austen mania and Brontë mania might be thought by some to bear this out. But the essential message of *The Life of George Stephenson* – overcoming poverty and a disadvantaged childhood by a combination of native talent and grinding perseverance could perfectly well be rendered by Fred Astaire as George, with Ginger Rogers as Miss Hindmarsh and (special guest appearance) Primo Carnera as Ned Nelson. That was the peculiar genius of Smiles: the best of his biographies, the ones he really cared most about, had assimilated the technique of immortal myth. It was like the *grand choeur* finale of a French toccata: the average listener would never remember all the twiddly bits played on the manuals, and would probably not notice if they were a tiny bit different next time – but he went away happy, whistling the big pedal tune.

Smiles wrote twiddly bits around other people's tunes – some of them pure invention in compliance with formulae upon which we have already touched – but he also wrote big pedal tunes all of his own. When you do that, other people will take them and improvise on them. Most did so not only privately, but unconsciously, so that each provided his own idealised picture of the subject based on Smiles' essentials. Like the saints' 'Lives' and immortal myths of King Arthur or Robin Hood, their longevity was guaranteed by the fact that each reader tailored his or her perception of them to his own liking.

But you, dear sceptical reader, are thinking that this cannot be: that what Smiles wrote is there in black and white to be believed or disbelieved, loved or loathed, as it stands. Not so. Let us consider another fairy tale plagiarism of Smiles. Once upon a time there was a young man called George Stephenson who was poor but very clever and hardworking. He fell in love with a rich girl called Elizabeth Hindmarsh, who loved him too, but her father would not let them fraternise because young George was not of the requisite social standing. Poor young George then trimmed his ambitions and successfully wooed, and married, Miss Hindmarsh's servant. As the reader, and indeed any fool except Mr Hindmarsh, could foresee, the frog he would not allow his daughter to kiss soon changed into a handsome, sickeningly rich and famous engineer, and the servant girl ended up far richer than her former mistress. But she died young, and George again made up to his former love, who graciously accepted him this time. Smiles must have been delighted when he picked up this story by oral tradition, and he published it long before the full biography. Later, he discovered that it was completely false and added a footnote to that effect.[13] Yet the error was perpetuated in Jeaffreson's well-documented biography of Robert Stephenson, and, over a century later, a serious historical work on George Stephenson by a respected authority on railway history went back to the original myth, as repudiated by its inventor.[14] Such is the power of the things we like to believe, the things which make a good story. At first hearing, the idea of a serious railway historian falling for the frog-kissing convention is ludicrous. The fact is that it happened, and it may perhaps suggest that at times Smiles unleashed stories more powerful in their ability to suspend disbelief than even he intended or realised.

The tailoring of Smilesian themes could lead to the most lamentable inaccuracies in later work by distinguished scholars. L.C.A. Knowles was a professor of economic history at Cambridge, no less, yet provides a fine example of the way in which Smiles' story-telling prowess can carry away even highly knowledgeable and sophisticated readers. According to Knowles, one of the objections to the Bill for the Liverpool & Manchester Railway came from 'a noble duke [who] thought it would damage his fox-covers'.[15] Reference to the source material would have revealed that there were no fox covers and there was no duke involved. There *were* the Earls of Sefton and Derby, who both objected to having a railway almost literally at the bottom of their gardens, as distinct from in some distant part of their estates, miles from their respective residences at Croxteth and Derby Halls. What went through Knowles' mind is a matter for speculation. The Select

Committee proceedings for the 1825 Liverpool & Manchester Railway Bill now survive in only four copies, all of them in Liverpool, but the author believes that at least one copy (in the House of Lords Record Office) was available in London before the Blitz. At first sight it seems possible that Knowles was simply being lazy by trusting Smiles. The remarkable fact is, however, that Smiles did *not* make this mistake: in his account the duke and the fox covers correctly belonged to the Stockton & Darlington, the earls and the 'pleasure grounds' to the Liverpool & Manchester Railway.[16]

Throughout this book it emerges clearly that much of Smiles' writing has a middling-to-high ideological content. The case of the aristocrats objecting to railways is one example. Smiles' old opposition to the Corn Laws and the Game Laws combined with his advocacy of the benefits of technological progress to produce an interpretation where aristocrats objecting to railways were cast as rich men denying material benefits to poor men in order to perpetuate their own frivolous, anomalous and anti-social pleasures. This was the 'big pedal tune' which Knowles went away whistling, and when he came to recount it in his book, some of the twiddly bits – those tedious things historians call facts – became a bit mixed up. Never mind: you could still recognise the tune. To bait de Maré a little more, this was no mean achievement for a man who was 'no thinker', comprehensively to mislead someone of Knowles' ability at the distance of half a century. Of course Knowles knew he should get his facts straight, which he could have done merely by rereading Smiles, but he remembered the story. He did, of course, remember the bit Smiles meant him to, because ensuring that was one of the things at which Smiles was outstandingly good. To put it another way, it's not the jokes, it's the way you tell them.

Much more recently, a scholar of high repute in the field of the history of science and technology wrote that 'It is strange but true, of course Smiles had never written about the Brunels'.[17] The reason for this is obvious: I.K. Brunel was about as unlike the Smiles engineering exemplar as he possibly could be. A mercurial genius who often promised more than he could or did deliver to the customers, an extravagant and extrovert man who became the undoubted Flash Harry of nineteenth-century engineering, he exhibited the very antithesis of the qualities which made the subjects of *Lives of the Engineers* the great men they were. Of course Smiles would not write about him, and his father, born with a silver spoon in his mouth and slightly foreign to boot, was just as improbable a subject.[17]

A persuasive line of argument: the only problem with it is that Smiles *did* write about the Brunels. They did not get anywhere near the canon of saints, indeed they were not even beatified at 'novelette-length' in *Industrial Biography* or *Brief Biographies*, but Smiles' substantial review of Beamish's work was published in the *Quarterly Review* and contains a good deal of observation of his own.[18] Buchanan, like Knowles, has been 'suckered' by Smiles: steeped in the Smiles message, he has believed without knowing, because he simply did not identify the need to check the facts. Clapham came part of the way to recognising this phenomenon when he wrote: 'Stories assumed to be familiar are apt to become good nesting places for legend.'[19] He could have gone further by suggesting that a top-class story-teller like Smiles could establish not just a nesting place but a large-scale commercial hatchery.

The credit for perpetuating the old anti-Corn Law view of the aristocracy obviously does not belong to Smiles alone: he was just one among many in a long tradition of radicalism, a tradition which in fact stretched back well before the Corn Laws. Because so many people read Smiles' books, and because he wrote them so cleverly, he nevertheless played a considerable part. It proved to be a remarkably durable view. Smiles would admit that some of the old aristocracy, notably the Duke of Bridgewater and the Earl of Stanhope, were worthy and practical men who applied their wealth and influence to beneficial purposes, but these were rather the exceptions. In the case of Rennie visiting the Earl of Eglinton, for example, we are not told why the engineer was going there. The earl was actually involved in a number of mining ventures and owned the harbour of Ardrossan, and we might think that he sought Rennie's advice in those contexts, but we are left to guess. More typical was the view he expressed in his biography of Samuel Bamford when writing of the Napoleonic Wars that they 'covered Britain with "glory", the aristocracy with stars and ribbons, and the people with taxes' and then added, 'The lords of England proceeded at once to celebrate their triumph by the enactment of a Corn Law'.[20] Furthermore, his oft-used expression a *truly* noble character must be taken as analogous to his use of *true* gentleman: that is to say that those normally thought noble or gentlemanly were in *truth* nothing of the sort. Another aspect of the argument emerges when Smiles writes about the Huguenots: persecuted by intolerant Catholic royalty and aristocracy, they proved to be an economic powerhouse whose migration was as much a blow to France as it was a benefit to the countries which received them. Here two favourite *bêtes noires* come together – aristocracy and religious intolerance. Small wonder that Smiles devoted two full-length books, several articles and dozens of passing references to Huguenot subjects. Their continuing popularity with editors of periodicals reflects the fact that this was one of the classic themes of middle-class radicalism, and remarkably durable it has proved to be.

As late as 1971, Ward and Wilson, in introducing a collection of papers under the title *Land and Industry,* found it necessary specifically to attack the traditional image of the effete, land-owning aristocrat.[21] That same image underlay the Weber thesis of what became known as the Protestant work ethic, though in fact Weber chiefly referred more specifically to Lutherans and Calvinists, excluding churches such as the Anglican which considered themselves catholic with a small 'c'.[22] Reduced to its simplest, this thesis argued that Protestantism made virtues of attributes which were particularly conducive to the gaining of wealth. These included a belief in the moral benefit of work for its own sake and an asceticism which led to willingness to sacrifice present consumption in favour of investment. That is why we find that so many prominent figures in the Industrial Revolution have emerged from obscurity to lead industrial empires. Use of images so contrasting as those of earnest Quakers such as the Darbys of Coalbrookdale and a caricature dandified aristrocrat seems to be justified by a simple difference in outlook on life.

This approach is open to two main forms of attack. The less damaging is that if Protestantism is almost a prerequisite of large-scale risk-taking in the application of novel plant and processes, then obviously we will not find many such things happening before the Reformation. At the time Weber was writing, this was broadly speaking believed to be the case, but that was a long time ago, and knowledge of medieval industry and technology was very slender. More recent research, particularly by Lynn White Jnr, has shown the premise to be false.[23] It appears that there was a perfectly effective monastic work ethic, which encouraged not just the erection of sacred buildings, but the application of water-powered machinery to the making and working of iron, leather and textiles. The Cistercian Order was particularly prominent as a diversified multinational conglomerate of great wealth and power, but the Benedictine contribution was substantial as well. White argues that there were long-term 'research programmes' to solve technological problems, particularly the need for a reliable clock. Monks not only developed and used new methods, they wrote about them as well, enabling the spread as well as the application of technology. White suggests that it was specifically the sanctification which Roman Catholicism gave to work which facilitated a proto-industrial revolution in twelfth- and thirteenth-century western Christendom.[24]

Not every one, of course, has agreed with White. Ovitt, for example, has questioned to what extent work was seen as a divine duty – *laborare est orare* – and to what an age-old punishment for the Fall. Ovitt's is a complex and detailed paper, but whatever the outcome of his deliberations they would serve only to reinforce the present argument, for it is not the reason for work being in some way or other virtuous, but the mere fact that it was, which need concern us here.[25]

Yet Weber's whole line of enquiry begins thus:

A glance at the occupational statistics of any country of mixed religious composition brings to light with remarkable frequency a situation which has several times provoked discussion in the Catholic press and literature, and in Catholic congresses in Germany, namely, the fact that business leaders and owners of capital as well as the higher grades of skilled labour, and even more the higher technically and commercially trained personnel of modern enterprises, are overwhelmingly Protestant.[26]

Weber's explanation of how Roman Catholicism did not encourage an entrepreneurial outlook dates originally from 1904–5. He specifically mentions the contribution of the Benedictines and the Cistercians to developing 'a systematic method of rational conduct'. The monk was 'a worker in the service of the Kingdom of God'.[27] The possibility of a monk working on systems of water supply or power transmission rather than systems of rational thought quite understandably did not occur to Weber, for remarkably little was then known about medieval industry. What is perhaps more surprising is that he does not seem puzzled by the erection of the huge Gothic abbeys. These were not merely great structures (on which he does remark), but undertakings of enormous expense and logistical complexity. Where did the money and the workers come from? Of course some of the money came from saying masses for the souls of recently departed rich villains (the medieval equivalent of corporate sponsorship of sport), but it is no coincidence that establishments of such exemplary splendour as Downside and Fountains were built in leading areas of wool production. Weber has argued that although monastic asceticism (i.e. adherence to a work ethic) existed, it was generically different from Protestant asceticism in that it did not extend into everyday life. Perusal of Kraus' substantial study of cathedral building must invite the question of whose everyday life we are talking about: the financing of great buildings had very far-reaching ramifications.[28]

Weber rightly distinguishes between the simple pursuit of profit and the continuous renewal of profit: only the latter is characteristic of capitalism, and that is to a measure governed by a necessary distinction between individual and corporate behaviour, and hence between individual and corporate property and profit. It was precisely that distinction which allowed ascetic orders such as the Cistercians to become egregiously rich. Nor did all such riches come from the hairy-chested blacksmiths and millwrights among the monks: some came from the pallid-faced forgers of deeds and charters in the *scriptorium.* These men, whom Weber clearly imagined as meditating on the goodness of God, were a classic example of one of the less desirable characteristics of modern corporate man: a willingness to do for the benefit of the body corporate that which they would regard as totally immoral if done for their own profit. One could go on: Weber suggests that the central role of the trained government official is a characteristic of a modern capitalist society; Cobban has shown that medieval universities held a key role in the training of just such people.[29]

More damaging is the attack launched by Rubinstein.[30] He points out that the evidence in favour of a Protestant work ethic is fundamentally unsound. To begin with it is anecdotal, depending on the detailed consideration of a small number of examples. Second, it concentrates chiefly on wealth generation by manufacturing, which is only one of a number of forms of work and of means of getting rich by it. Rubinstein analysed the grants of probate for those who died worth over £500,000 for the period 1830–1930, and what he found was that most very rich people had become so from old-style land ownership, from the investment of the fruits thereof in something else, or from commercial or mercantile, as distinct from manufacturing, activity. Furthermore, the great majority of very rich people subscribed to the Anglican Church. Now it may be argued that Rubinstein's evidence relates only to the situation in England, but since England's was both the prototype and still (just about) the archetype of the successful industrial capitalist economy it does not seem unfair to employ the available evidence. This two-pronged attack has left the Weberian thesis pretty well in ruins, and it would be surprising for any theory so broad-ranging as that to survive any longer than it did, so great has been the growth of historical knowledge since it was proposed.

The subplot of Weber was entirely consonant with the subplot of Smiles. Mixed in with its exemplary scholarship there are some pretty quaint suggestions, such as that Italians are lazy and that there may be an hereditary element in business success. Perhaps more than anything it is influenced by the old (pre-Smiles) school of the history of science and technology, which wallowed in the sufferings of Galileo *et al.* at the hands of a backward-looking Church. What Whewell and his followers failed to understand, as Smiles understood, was that persecution of scientists was only necessary or desirable when Protestantism existed to pose a threat. The idea that the same Church could, a couple of centuries earlier, have been the powerhouse of science and technology, escaped them because, lacking Smiles' breadth of vision, they identified specifically Catholic intolerance rather than intolerance *per se* as the enemy.

The end result (for present purposes) of the Weberian thesis was that until the 1980s a fair bit of the mud that Smiles and his ilk had thrown at the aristocracy continued to adhere, bound with the cement of such as Weber, whose own prejudices were constructed in a somewhat similar manner to those of Smiles and proved almost as durable.

The victories which canal and railway companies gained over the anti-social opposition of aristocrats and gentry form one of the sub-themes of the Whig interpretation referred to in the previous chapter. Smiles employed others, and they too were seized upon and embellished. Some, such as the benefits of 'progress' to ordinary people, have already been touched upon: here and in other cases Smiles employed techniques which were less truthful and not invariably wholesome. To show improvement, it is necessary to refer to the *status quo ante* and this was a manoeuvre particularly open to abuse. Thus Telford's achievements were enhanced by the almost complete omission of Jessop's.[31] The improvements wrought by the opening of the Liverpool & Manchester Railway were magnified by overemphasising the alleged inadequacies of the canals.[32] In this process it was possible to create major misunderstandings.

The most conspicuous and long-lasting example of this form of distortion is the question of roadbuilding. The lead-in to the 'Lives' of Metcalfe and Telford consists of a general history of British roads in five short chapters, totalling seventy-three pages. We are told that 'On the departure of the Romans from Britain, most of the roads constructed by them were allowed to fall into decay, on which the forest and the waste gradually resumed their dominion over them.' The impression is created, presumably deliberately, that this was through stupidity, since 'numerous attempts were made in early times to preserve the ancient ways and enable a communication to be kept up between the metropolis and the rest of the country'.[33]

Yet on the previous page, Smiles has shown us that he knew that Roman roads were primarily for military purposes. They were not there for driving animals to market or moving North Pennine lead down to navigable water. In medieval England they did not serve the main purposes for which roads were required. Can Smiles seriously expect us to believe that an age which could build excellent bridges and cathedrals, the best of which survive to this day, was incapable of mending roads if it wanted to? Writing in the capital city of the most centralised economy in the world it was perhaps difficult for him to conceive that things used to work so differently. As in other cases, his basic theme has been taken up by later writers, including those who ought to know much better. Savage, for example, disposes of a millennium of inland transport history in exactly nine lines. Pratt acknowledges some measure of Church involvement in road maintenance, but then goes on to suggest (literally) that the people responsible became fat and decadent and the condition of roads declined again.[34] This suggestion might be made because we all know what the story line is, namely that the country has only slowly emerged from the slough of ignorance into the glorious days of the railway age. If the story line is right, who cares about the detail? Once again, we find that Smiles' followers care even less than he did. In fact, the roads which common sense tells us *must* have been in an operable condition to serve the growing metal and textile industries of late medieval Britain did indeed exist, and many of their routes can still be traced quite readily – but it is only comparatively recently that such authors as Raistrick have made this known.[35] The monks at Fountains Abbey did indeed have a serviceable road to get their substantial output of wool and iron to navigable water. According to White, the cost of medieval land transport actually went down, as a result of the introduction of more effective harness.[36]

Like many of his contemporaries, Smiles was deeply convinced that the British were inherently superior to other people. Some of this was a matter of racial characteristics: he believed that in the racial mish-mash of ancient Britons, Anglo-Saxons and perhaps particularly Frisians, there was something very special. That is why he planned to write a book on race.[37] This is not to be equated with uncritical patriotism: we have seen enough examples already of situations in which Smiles thought British governments behaved deplorably both in peace and in war. Equally, the *Self-Help* series provides innumerable examples of British individuals or whole classes of them behaving badly or stupidly.[38] In matters of engineering history, however, British was best, and most of what was best about British was English. As a result, whole areas of the history of technology have become distorted. In the 1874 volume on roads, there is not a word of the French contribution to roadbuilding during the reign of Louis XIV. Nor do we find in the 'Lives' of Telford or Robert Stephenson that either of them was familiar with the work of French theoretical engineers – though each of them had access to such works and is extremely likely to have used them. We have two distortions in one: the importance of the French (as distinct from Huguenot) contribution to transport engineering and the growing role of theory in the scheme of things are both heavily undervalued.

The neglect of theory is another of the effects of the dictates of a good story. The development of engineering theory is almost entirely absent from several of the major engineering biographies: the account of Telford's Menai Bridge, for example, occupies eleven pages, yet it appears that the only 'theoretical' input was some experiments in the tensile strength of wrought iron and a calculation of the force needed to hoist the main chain cables after their chord had been empirically determined by hanging a piece of 'common chain' between the virtually completed towers.[39] Even in the case of Watt, whose theoretical contribution to the steam engine was of the greatest importance, Smiles largely confines himself to explaining Watt's early contacts with Robison and Black and his later involvement with the celebrated Lunar Society. What we do not get is any attempt to analyse or explain the importance of Watt's theoretical understanding, which some would argue was at least as important as his actual building and selling of engines.[40] In some cases a shortage of explanation was probably explained by the fact that Smiles' own understanding was limited, but his accounts of how Watt's improvements to the steam engine achieved their results suggest that in that case at least Smiles knew his stuff, and cut down on the explanation simply through a fear of boring or confusing his readers.

The end result was that as late as 1972, Musson was able to refer to 'the traditional view' of the Industrial Revolution *among professional historians* as being 'almost entirely the product of uneducated empiricism'.[41] The advocates of the scientific camp understandably overreacted, with the result that a balanced view is still hard to find. What is easy enough to find is who was responsible for the situation Musson set out to debunk, and why it was that enough others had followed him for his view to be described as 'traditional'. The word itself is redolent both of Smiles' didacticism and his persuasive power, for acceptance of a tradition is not the product of rigorous historical research nor even the slightest exercise of the critical faculties: a tradition is something handed down, and it is with the hander-down that the initiative rests. The recipient is passive – until, that is, he starts composing his variations. Let us end this chapter with an example in which the underlying message, that George Stephenson was 'very important', seems to have become entirely separated from any need for factual accuracy: 'In 1825 came the Stockton–Darlington line and George Stephenson's (1781–1848) *Rocket*.'[42] *Rocket* was constructed by Robert Stephenson in 1829 for the Liverpool & Manchester Railway. If it is not the most famous machine in all history it is certainly in the top ten, so the compression of three categorical errors into one brief (and inelegant) sentence is a compelling illustration of the continuing power of Smiles not merely to suspend disbelief, but to suspend even perception of the need to read, understand and remember what he wrote. Once again, the big pedal tune was enough – even with a few wrong notes.

CHAPTER SEVEN

Victorian Values

It may seem strange both to entitle and to end a serious book about a serious and important writer with reference to a catch-phrase from a political speech, but when Margaret Thatcher referred to 'good old Victorian Values' in that speech in 1983 she sparked off lines of thought which have not only been reflected in a number of books but which have brought Smiles and his kind to the forefront of popular (and unpopular) misconceptions of the past.[1] But while it may be tempting to dismiss the whole business as the perception of half-understood history peddled by a politician with a background in chemistry, it is also too easy.

It is *prima facie* absurd to characterise anything at all as 'Victorian', simply because the Good Queen reigned for sixty-three years, which is a long time for any archetype to endure. When she came to the throne, the population of Britain was about 23 million, and when she died it had risen to over 41 million. Despite that rise, fewer men and women worked in agriculture: all the extra people and more besides had added to the rapid and continuing process of urbanisation. Conditions in towns had so improved that where once England and Wales had consistently higher death rates than Scotland or Ireland, by 1900 the situation had reversed. Victoria's empire, from being a largely trading association (albeit backed by military force) had turned into a worldwide conglomerate sustained by a steam-powered merchant navy of unprecedented carrying power (over 2 million gross tons), guarded by a navy of armoured warships which was effectively invincible.[2] Increasingly improbable bits of the globe had been annexed, which bore less and less relationship to the original purposes of possessing an empire. One region of Britain after another in turn rose to become 'the workshop of the world' as its predecessors declined, and although by 1900 the competitive position of British industry had waned, Britain still held an impressive lead in many key industries.[3]

Social change was no less dramatic. The mercantile classes and the 'aristocracy of labour' perhaps changed least, though obviously their typical occupations changed with changing industrial patterns. But a good merchant could wheel and deal in a variety of goods, and a good craftsman or draftsman worked much the same way whatever the exact nature of whatever he was making or drawing. Perhaps the greatest change in their lives was the late nineteenth century's fascination with keeping servants in ever-increasing numbers and extending down the social scale to the point where a well-paid craftsman in a steady job could keep some pitiable little girl to light a fire for him before he got up to go to work.[4]

The changes came at the extremes. Those old land-based aristocratic families who had failed to move with the times by developing industries or moving into urban property speculation often found themselves in such financial difficulties that they were forced to marry off their heirs for money rather than see the family home fall down. In particularly distressing cases they were reduced to marrying Americans,[5] and in the case of the Dukes of Manchester they had to do it twice. At the same time their ranks were being infiltrated at an ever-increasing rate by wealthy men of no breeding, such as Lord Armstrong, who made his money from guns, and guns of a singularly unsporting kind at that. Although the real crunch would come only after the First World War, some old country houses were already crumbling and new ones were being built by parvenus such as Armstrong and the Rothschilds. More modest country houses built for the squirearchy commonly housed corn merchants or cotton brokers. Among the more striking changes which lay behind this visible phenomenon was the fact that it was now far more profitable to buy and sell imported corn (or meat) than to produce it. Britain had long been a net importer of food, but her net imports continued to increase.

At the other extreme, the condition of the unskilled and semi-skilled workers had improved almost beyond recognition. In 1837, many honest and hard-working men in regular employment could not be sure of continued subsistence. If they lived in the country they were grindingly poor beyond modern belief; if they lived in the towns they earned more, but did so only by enduring conditions which would almost certainly see them into an early grave.[6] By 1900, most towns had reasonably wholesome and plentiful water supplies and effective sewage disposal systems. Working hours had been radically reduced, so that in many industries men could go home in a less-than-totally exhausted state. The principle of employer's liability, while still a bit feeble, was enshrined in statute as of 1880, so that men disabled at work were no longer necessarily consigned to the workhouse. Possibly in hindsight the most radical change was that women could get reasonably well-paid jobs. They were no longer confined to sweat-shops in the rag trade or to light industries such as cigarette-making. There were openings in commerce, particularly for typists and telephonists, and the previously male world of Bob Cratchett was threatened as well.[7]

Working men were now voters, but they had also been metaphorically enfranchised for some time in other and perhaps more important ways. Such essentially gentlemanly facilities as libraries and art galleries – which had belonged in stately homes or the better kind of gentleman's club – had been provided by local authorities for the use of anyone who wanted them.[8] Music was held to have charms to soothe the savage (Chartist) breast and rich industrial municipalities installed huge concert organs to introduce the working classes to classical music through the medium of organ transcriptions.[9] Part-time adult education, which began with such organisations as mechanics' institutes, was widely available. It was even possible at some of the new red-brick universities for a bright working-class lad to get a job as a technician, be allowed to sit in on lectures and eventually take a degree. Furthermore, it was likely to be a degree in physics or engineering rather than dead languages.[10]

Which leads us into an area alien to 1980s politics, namely taste and the arts. Within the sixty or so years, every branch of literature, music, architecture, fine and applied arts changed beyond recognition. In 1837, Scott had only been dead five years and his books were still selling strongly; in 1900, Hardy was outgrowing his early unpopularity with the reading public. Any connection between Spohr's widely acclaimed *Calvary* (1835) and Elgar's *The Dream of Gerontius* (1899) is hard to find. Furniture design forms another interesting field of comparison, in that a piece of even reasonably good 1900 furniture was better made of better wood than its predecessor of 1840, but because it was made by machinery it lacked exactly those qualities of craftsmanship whose appreciation first made people interested in 'antiques' – and the Queen had not long been dead when people started using machinery to produce acceptable replicas of furniture with which she would have been familiar as a child. What is probably more important, though, is that by 1900 it was exceptional for even the really poor to possess no furniture whatever, whereas in 1840 it had been quite common.

These are just a few extremely perfunctory suggestions of the differences between early and late Victorian England. Any other author attempting the same task within the same compass might come up with completely different ideas of at least equal validity. If we now throw into the pot the reminder that, taking into account the people who were near the end of their lives in 1837 and those who were young in 1900, there were well over 100 million people we might call 'Victorians', then it becomes necessary to ask what, if any, values all these people, or even a working consensus of the opinion-formers among them, had in common. The immediate inclination is to answer 'none'.

That is too easy. The changes outlined above, and many others not even mentioned, did not happen by accident. They happened because people wanted them to happen. Can we find any distinctive Victorian values reflecting the want that those things should happen?[11]

There is a strong temptation to characterise the Victorian age as a harsh and uncaring one. It is fairly generally agreed that the new Poor Law, for example, was intended to make pauperism degrading and humiliating when all it needed to be was Spartan.[12] Those parents who could afford to do so sent young boys from their home and family at ages as early as seven to boarding schools, where they were at risk of their lives from a combination of inadequate diet and infectious diseases. Motivated chiefly by attempts to avoid corporal punishment which commonly crossed the dividing line between severity and brutality, they learned to read the banal accounts Julius Caesar wrote of his tedious military campaigns. Those parents who could not afford fancy schooling for their children often had no worthier aspirations for them than to pack them off into dead-end jobs, particularly, in the case of girls, into domestic service, at the earliest possible age.

Of course there is an element of truth in this. It is also true that there were employers who exploited their employees in the most ruthless manner. But before we become too smug about the virtues of the twentieth century, it is worth remembering one or two items which were current news at the time this chapter was being written. Two prominent businessmen were on trial for stealing from pensioners an amount of money it would have taken the entire Victorian footpad industry most of their lives to steal, assuming they lost no time by being caught and jailed. A well-known and previously respected football club was shown to have unilaterally revoked the contracts of at least two of its players and then placed absurd transfer prices on their heads, thereby rendering them both unemployed and unemployable in the only 'trade' they knew – and had acted entirely legally in doing it. Junior doctors in hospitals still worked longer hours than the most grossly down-trodden factory hands of the early 1840s, and the enquiry into an aeroplane crash revealed that the principal cause was fatigue on the part of the flight-deck crew.[13] Are these, perhaps, Victorian values to which we are returning?

SOME RATHER MORE CHEERFUL VICTORIAN VALUES

It may be that we owe it to the world of art and the aesthetes, or perhaps to the admirers of the Age of Reason, that we fail to recognise just how vile many aspects of life were in the late eighteenth century. While it may be true that eighteenth-century architecture has sometimes appealed to a more 'elevated' taste than the products of the following generations, yet among the issues floated above there is but one palpable example of deterioration according to modern values, namely the changes in the Poor Law. Under the old Poor Law, there was a good deal of luck involved, in the sense that some parishes were much wealthier than others, but there is no doubt that in a wealthy town such as Liverpool, paupers were relatively much better off than they are today. The workhouse was pretty grim, but not only was it less grim than the slums of downtown Liverpool at the time, it was also less grim than a cardboard box on the steps of a present-day department store. The food was not very varied, but nobody suffered from malnutrition, which was more than could be said for the worst-paid agricultural workers even when they were in full-time employment. (There were, of course, exceptions but it may be significant that the most notorious one occurred in rural Andover and under the new Poor Law.) The denizens of the workhouse did not even have to put up with allegations that they made a fortune begging and parked their Porsches round the corner before going sponging on honest citizens and taxpayers at the workhouse. The worst they had to endure was suggestions that the able-bodied among them should go and get a job and that receiving hand-outs was bad for the soul.

What has all this to do with Samuel Smiles? Quite simply, he believed in progress, and did so profoundly, consistently and completely. He believed that races, nations, states, industries and individuals progress. In the process, he adopted some philosophical approaches which are highly unfashionable now, but which were necessary parts of his overall philosophy, and some of them might even merit a slightly more sympathetic approach today.

As always, when we erect a fence of any kind, Smiles appears to straddle it, but in the case of the relativist/absolutist fence he seems to have rather more of his weight on the absolutist foot. Where we might look at the fraudulent activities of railway speculators and say, in our forgiving relativist way, that they were no worse than modern white-collar criminals or the cowboy investors of the canal mania, Smiles had no such doubts. What they were doing was wrong. Railways were potentially among the greatest sources of benefit available to mankind. They began by creating plentiful employment for navvies and continued by offering it to many thousands of railway officers and servants. While railway companies may not have been model employers in every possible respect (and in particular the accident rate of their employees was deplorable),[14] the way in which they modelled their organisations on military prototypes meant that they were the first large industry to offer the working-class lad a job for life as a norm. The large textile manufacturers probably could have done so, but as Smiles remarks, they chose not to. Railways also offered a career progression which could, at least in theory, reach absolutely to the top of the tree. It really was possible to start out as a junior clerk and end up as company treasurer or as a 'youth in the drawing office' and end up as chief engineer. Obviously many were called and few chosen, but it could and did happen.[15] Perhaps more to the point was the relative ease with which working-class lads could achieve the equivalent of warrant rank as a stationmaster or a workshop foreman.

Railways were much more than that. They were the largest single customer for the engineering profession, whether civil or mechanical, and Smiles knew well enough that the fortunes of that profession were of national importance. The issue of technological determinism will be briefly considered below, but at this stage we need only note that the railway companies were the largest corporate bodies in the country. They have been criticised for lack of research and development in such areas as the fundamental design of the steam locomotive (which pretty well ossified in general principle after about 1840) and for the reluctance with which they introduced continuous train brakes, high-speed freight trains and power-operated signalling systems.[16] All of these criticisms are at least partly justified, but they conceal much else. With a few obvious exceptions, such as Tower Bridge or the Barton swing aqueduct, almost every innovative bridge built in Britain between 1840 and 1900 was built to carry a railway, and the sheer volume of run-of-the-mill railway bridges was mind-boggling. Smiles could not quantify the contribution of railways to the British economy, and would probably have overestimated had he tried, but he knew their importance.[17]

That importance extended yet further. Later in Smiles' life, the railways brought fresh food to towns, even including fresh milk, and allowed people living inland to have fresh fish at affordable prices. Eventually they brought astonishingly cheap chilled meat from overseas, among the benefits of which was an end to the unhygienic practice of domestic pig-keeping. They stimulated competition between different areas of supply, offering better value to consumers of almost anything. They were, in short, the bringers of immense and varied benefits, both material and social. By Smiles' values, and remembering the example of Telford's Highland roads referred to above, it would probably be no exaggeration to add 'and spiritual'.[18]

This makes it easy to understand the uncharacteristic bitterness of Smiles, a man who was often angry but rarely bitter, when denouncing the railway speculators and the corrupt lawyers, accountants and engineers who supported them.[19] It was indeed a case for moral absolutism: these men were subverting what he perceived as the greatest single potential source of good for the population at large, for their own dishonest profit. In the process they did not just damage the careers of railway servants, they stole the savings of small-time investors who sought no reward other than the modest one normally attached to the exercise of thrift and the investment of the proceeds in something with a safe yield. They fully deserved the special execrations reserved not just for commonplace villains, but for traitors. Traitors to everything Smiles held good, traitors to the nation, traitors to progress, traitors to hard work, to thrift and to the manly independence which the fruits of thrift conferred. Traitors, in fact, to self-help, which as we have seen was nothing less than the solution to the 'Condition of England Question'. To fail to take an absolutist viewpoint would have seemed to Smiles to be a compromise with the untouchable: these men were bad, d'ye hear? BAD!

Sound Thatcherite stuff: no woolly-minded liberalism there. The problem is that the Smiles view was entirely in favour of the ordinary man or woman who worked or saved. The traitors were precisely the jobbers who profited most from the Thatcher regime as they adroitly moved money around without ever making or doing anything which was of visible benefit to the population at large. The City of London was littered with new office blocks whose expensive occupants seem mainly to have designed and built, mortgaged and insured, bought and sold – office blocks. Anything much further removed from Smiles' idea of honest, worthy, useful, true or manly work would be difficult to imagine. 'Speculative jobbery' was the term he used. Had he been allowed a vision of the future, his opinion of the rise of Saatchi & Saatchi would have been confined to a letter to Janet, for he would never have dared publish it. But he did suggest that the way to banish the traitors from the railway industry was to nationalise it.[20]

The converse was Smiles' admiration of physical work and craft skills. One after another of his great engineers is shown as being a skilled worker: Brindley and Rennie the millwrights, Watt the instrument-maker, Telford the stonemason, Stephenson the engine-wright, Newcomen the blacksmith. These men were the salt of the earth, and the yeast of civilisation. It was upon them that the wealth of the wealthiest nation on earth was founded:

> One of the most remarkable things about Engineering in England is, that its principal achievements have been accomplished, not by natural philosophers nor by mathematicians, but by men of humble station, for the most part self-educated. . . .
>
> Nor did any of the great mechanics, who have since invented tools, engines, and machines, at all belong to the educated classes. . . . These men gathered their practical knowledge in the workshop or acquired it in manual labour.[21]

This was truly a Victorian value: 'we' were richer and stronger than other people because of the skills of the workers and because society was sufficiently fluid to allow them to rise to the highest pinnacles of achievement – and wealth. These men, not the students of Latin and Greek, were the bone and muscle of the nation. Was it in honour of those values that Britain has closed most of its steelworks, its shipyards and its coal mines? Or was it because capital could be more profitably employed in providing unemployment insurance on hire purchase agreements for Japanese consumer goods? This brings us again to the distinctions drawn by Smiles and such others as Carlyle and Ruskin between 'true' and other work. It is amusing, albeit unproductive, to speculate on whether 1980s consumerism would have rendered Carlyle speechless.

Smiles was a firm advocate of technological determinism. He argued far more strongly than probably any living historian would that changes, normally for the better, arose from technological improvements. He did not claim that the improvements were completely mono-causal, in the sense that Boulton's part in not only financing Watt but also providing him with much-needed moral support was readily admitted. The benefits of the stationary steam engine were, however, attributed chiefly to the man who refined its design and construction to the point where it had the makings of a universal prime mover. Boulton's role was simply that of an important facilitator.[22] It was the same with railways: we might now quibble with many of the claims Smiles made for George Stephenson, but to Smiles, Stephenson was the father of the railways because he devised the complete ensemble, even if the component parts were made up of the ideas of others. What is perhaps significant is that Henry Booth, who has quite reasonably been styled the father of railway management, receives no plaudits from Smiles except for his (questionable) role in the design of *Rocket* and his invention of the screw coupling.

Smiles' love of the practical is a necessary logical stage in his overall philosophy. After the repeal of the Corn Laws, the Smiles agenda moved on towards artisan schooling and adult education, the provision of libraries and other cultural facilities and, eventually, working-class emancipation. Target number one was, therefore, the image of the working man. In the wake of the troubled times of the 1820s and '30s, working men were widely perceived as drunken, feckless, violent, lazy and dishonest. And those were just the nice ones: the nasty ones were dangerous Chartist revolutionaries. Such views were, of course, held by people who had little contact with members of the working classes and who only really noticed them when something unpleasant happened.

One of the main weapons Smiles deployed was the image of the working-man-turned-engineer and its singular effectiveness depended on the fact that it was two-edged. To the working man it said, 'Did you have a worse start in life than George Stephenson? No? Then stop wallowing in beer and self-pity, and get going, like he did', while to the middle classes it said, 'A lot of your creature comforts depend on the fact we have railways and other benefits of engineering, built for you by Intelligent Artisans: accord them the respect they deserve.' It worked, perhaps most effectively through such working-class institutions as the Co-op and the Oddfellows. These, like Smiles' original image, worked in both directions, showing workers and middle-class observers alike the benefits of self-help.

In the 1980s there was no recognition of any such thing as an intelligent artisan: the intelligent ones were assumed to have retrained as time-share salesmen and the ones who remained were those incapable of adapting to change. The possibility that they might have seen some dignity in making things – in 'true work' – was inexplicable. What they needed was to be made redundant and then to be retrained to make them fit for a proper job. What there was, however, was a burgeoning application of the expression 'self-help' which continues to this day.[23]

The famous passage in which Smiles castigated a personified 'Nobody' for a number of social ills brings out another aspect of his belief in progress, namely that there were some evils which had to be tackled by public agencies. The first such issue in which Smiles assumed a high profile was education, considered above, and the second was public libraries. The argument that the application of steam power in factories released men from brute toil and allowed them to go home with sufficient energy to do something creative is a familiar one advanced by such apostles of mechanism as Andrew Ure. Smiles has little to say of the moral improvements brought about by the factory system, but to him the public library was the most basic and essential tool of self-improvement: working men could afford to buy few, if any, books, and how else were they to learn? His own books were beyond the reach of all but the very best-paid workers.[24] Furthermore, it was essential that libraries were open in the evenings and at weekends, for those were the only times at which those who most needed them could use them. He had seen the mechanics' institutes infiltrated by the middle classes, and could probably have foreseen the day when public libraries would have their opening hours so curtailed as to be chiefly useful for suburban housewives to drive there in their Volvos, to borrow the Princess of Wales' work-out book. Where now are the resources for working men to emulate the scholarship of Edwards or Dick? The Open University and access courses at other universities seem to offer far better opportunities than they had, but even university libraries' opening hours have had to be cut to a point which can make life difficult for part-time students with full-time jobs.

One of the most puzzling features of Smiles' work is how little he wrote about public health. He was a doctor, his father had died of cholera and he was a shrewd enough observer of current affairs to be well aware that London's water supply, managed by private companies, continued to be of execrable quality well after the 'filth theory of disease' had been proven empirically and the transmission of cholera had been shown beyond doubt to be effected by infected water supplies.[25] The logical missing link was identifying exactly which organism was transmitted – which mattered not a jot. On that excuse, the London water companies continued to sell dilute sewage as drinking water for decades after go-ahead municipalities such as Liverpool, Birmingham and Glasgow had invested heavily in large-scale improvements, bringing in pure water from as far away as they needed to. The 'Nobody' passage is a clear allusion to that, but where are the biographies of such engineers as Newlands (Liverpool and Britain's first borough engineer), Bateman (saviour of Manchester's poor) or Rawlinson, who was chief engineer to the local government board and national doyen of municipal engineering, or a dozen others? We search in vain, and as one might expect, those whom Smiles neglected, other biographers have neglected too, so that most of them remained obscure until the publication of Binnie's work in 1981.[26]

There are three exceptions to be made to the above. The first is the usual one: *Brief Biographies* often provides exceptions to supposed rules about Smiles, and there he partly sets the balance straight with an account of Edwin Chadwick, but it is not really comparable in terms either of length or of saintliness with any of the major subjects, or indeed of some of the minor ones such as Murdock. The second is in *Thrift*, where a chapter on 'Healthy Homes' reproduces much of the material on Chadwick. There is heavy emphasis on individual effort, but on the other hand it is acknowledged that individual effort alone is not sufficient, of which more below. The third is that in *Lives of the Engineers* there is quite a lengthy account of Sir Hugh Myddleton, engineer of the New River. Yet neither in his description of the *status quo ante,* nor in a statement of the benefits of the construction of the New River, is there any mention of disease. Water became cleaner, but perhaps more important was the fact that it became cheaper and more plentiful. Myddleton is admired, but is not given the 'full treatment' and is certainly not made an exemplar of self-help. He seems, in fact, to be included mainly to provide historical background to canal engineering in the much longer 'Life' of James Brindley which follows.

By the time Smiles made his last revision of *Lives of the Engineers* it was pretty clear that 'big municipal government', run by rich city councils, was the answer to the urban problem. It is also true, however, that the Metropolitan Board of Works was a by-word for corruption and inefficiency, and a number of other local authorities in the metropolis had been engaged in practices which were either illegal to start with or which were made so shortly after their profitability was demonstrated! But when railway companies betrayed the trust he placed in them, he set out to show the benefits which were possible and which people were entitled to expect, then castigated the traitors. Why his faith in progress failed him in the case of water and sewage remains a mystery.

There may be a partial explanation, but it is certainly no more than that, in his faith in ordinary people and common sense. Smiles was perfectly capable, if he so chose, of providing footnotes giving the authorities for statements and the precedents for arguments, but he only rarely did so. That is because his technique, of making a relatively simple statement and then providing strings of anecdotes and examples, amounted to writing the notes into the text – except for the fact that without the 'notes' the text would have been very brief indeed. It was a clever technique, for it made things seem obvious to the intelligent lay reader, even when he or she had little or no previous knowledge of the subject. It turned his argument into an appeal not to formal logic, but to a blend of logic, intuition and emotion. That is exactly the mixture we call common sense when we agree with its outcome, though we think of different names for it when we disagree.

The appeal to common sense is not a peculiar or distinctive Victorian characteristic, but it is a noticeable one. The common law, for example, came to depend heavily on 'the reasonable man', later personified as 'the man on the Clapham omnibus', and the offence of affray was defined in terms of causing alarm to three or more 'persons of reasonable stolidity'.

All these expressions equate to common sense. In another field, that of 'liberal education', a refined and sharpened common sense was held to fit its possessor for practically anything. You wanted to be a forest manager in Burma, or a railway manager in Bombay? The last thing you went to learn about was forestry or railways: what you learned about was one stage on from J. Caesar Esq. and his tedious wars, such as the sex life of Catullus. This was the great British tradition of amateurism, memorably satirised in the strictures of Flanders and Swann on foreigners' attitude to sport:

> They argue with umpires, they cheer when they've won,
> And they practise beforehand, which ruins the fun.

If the commonsensical amateur can be regarded as some kind of Victorian stereotype, then his values have struck home recently in two entirely different ways. The first is a belief in management as a specific skill, which sounds initially like the exact antithesis of amateurism. Yet at bottom, it is no more reasonable to expect the holder of a master's degree in business administration to know anything about Burmese forests than it is to expect it of someone with a degree in Classics. We have actually reverted to amateurism from a position where the top man was a forester who knew his job, with minions to deal with the finance, administration and marketing of the product. It may also be significant that it has now become normal to refer to services as 'products'. A bank loan is a 'product' with the singular advantage that it entirely eliminates the need to have people like foresters at all. What used to be the product can be bought in, using the bank loan, from someone else, repackaged and sold on. It is remarkably similar to the way in which the natives did the forestry under British 'supervision'.

The other revival in common sense is in the fields of architecture and town planning. During the 1980s, a situation came about where professional experts in these fields had to submit themselves to often quite abrasive questioning by amateurs from the 'conservation lobby' in what became known as 'consultative processes'. The reason for this apparently foolish and expensive attack of common sense was the excesses of those professions in the 1960s and '70s when, talking only to each other at conferences, they made dramatic changes to the urban environment in manners which offended large numbers of ordinary but articulate people.

They would have got away with it, on the basis of their expert status, subject to two conditions. The first was that their schemes had to work and they frequently did not. Tower blocks became a social disaster, inner ring roads isolated whole districts, indoor shopping precincts were frequently unsuccessful and pedestrian subways became the home of petty criminals. Construction standards were often low, leading to early onset of 'concrete sickness'. Dogma did what dogma often does and produced such absurdities as Liverpool Moorfields station, where one climbs a staircase to first-floor level in order to get the escalator down to the underground railway.

All that was lacking was something to create an issue in the national press, and the willingness of the Prince of Wales to put his head above the parapet provided it. He spoke as an educated and intelligent layman, and struck a chord with millions like him. Sadly, his well-timed, well-intended and entirely beneficial intervention could be linked to other fields where similar ideas might have different consequences.

As we have seen, Smiles was ambivalent about experts. In his view, the real experts, the engineers and their ilk, were largely self-taught and certainly owed nothing either to a liberal education in the Matthew Arnold mode or to the professional qualifications of academies or institutions. If we go back to Chapter 1, we find that he held the professional skills of schoolteachers in little esteem. It may be true that one should not pay too much attention to experts, and especially not to economists when they offend under the Vagrancy Acts by purporting to tell the future by mystic devices, because they always get it wrong. Unfortunately, it is a short logical step from there to disbelieving anyone who can be categorised as having a professional vested interest. The result is that we now have a Parliament inhabited by people who know more about teaching than the teachers, more about social work than the social workers, more about crime than the criminologists and probably the criminals as well. This has led to such anomalies as the head of the prison service being recruited from the world of private business. (Stop Press: by the time this page was re-edited he had been sacked.) That is truly an early Victorian value, for it is directly comparable with the view that anyone who was 'the right kind of chap' and would pay for a commission would make a good army officer. Such attributes as training, experience and proven commitment could, and can be, dismissed as irrelevant. Virtually any professional or academic skill which is remotely comprehensible to politicians has come under attack, and those which are incomprehensible have either been denounced as arcane and irrelevant or have simply had their funding cut. But we must not mock, for this is a reflection of a genuine Victorian value.

Paradoxically, it cuts directly across another one, which is the concept of duty in public service, a subject on which Smiles is remarkably quiet, despite having written a book entitled *Duty*. His duties are, of course, individual ones – or are they? As it happens, they are not, for Smiles expects society to provide an army and a navy to protect the nation as a whole, and a police force to protect some parts of it from others. But he also expects people who sell short measure or adulterated goods to be prosecuted.[27] We know by whom they would be prosecuted, namely by the town clerk's department of the local authority, using evidence provided by the local authority's weights and measures or public analyst's department. But we search in vain for any recognition even that such people exist, much less that in discharging a function he considered necessary, they might exhibit a genuine sense of duty to society. So it was with housing: after a passage mocking the idea of Arcadian bliss, Smiles tells us that 'The first method of raising a man above the life of an animal is to provide him with a healthy home.'[28] Do we read you right, Dr Smiles? What has happened to self-help, manly self-reliance and that triumph over difficulties without which no achievement is truly worthy? In fact, Smiles is not being inconsistent, for the idea that some people need to be provided with houses is entirely in accordance with his idea that some problems are beyond individual solution and require state intervention. When he wrote *Thrift* he knew perfectly well that Liverpool had long since built the first municipal housing in the country and that while it was pretty cramped and Spartan, it offered standards of hygiene which were formerly the preserve of those earning at least £100 per annum to those earning half that. It is also worthy of remark that in this section Smiles' normal denunciations of working-class drinking are tempered with a measure of sympathy: 'Mr Chadwick once remonstrated with an apparently insensible workman on the expenditure of half his income on whisky. His reply was, "Do you, Sir, come and live here, and you will drink whisky too."'[29]

Smiles does not specifically endorse the workman's point of view, but his use of the word 'apparently' clearly implies that the reply was reasonable.

Here is another authentic Victorian value which is alive and well today. No politician has ever been elected on a platform of 'What we need is more bureaucrats', but plenty have been so on the promise of the fruits of the labour of bureaucrats. When some new benefit is offered to us, be it the last Labour government's Price Check scheme or the Major government's Citizen's Charter, we all know, if we stop to think about it, that what we are being offered is more bureaucrats. Nobody has ever loved bureaucrats, so when things go wrong it is bureaucrats who are to blame, whereas when things go right it is to their employers that the credit accrues. The Victorian age, despite its alleged *laissez-faire* inclinations, saw a steady growth of bureaucracy in both central and local government, and it happened for two reasons: society wanted the product, and newspaper proprietors found that stories about inept or corrupt bureaucracy sold newspapers. The latter Victorian value is also with us today, and is responsible for elaborate procedures designed to prevent bad publicity, which, of course, employ many bureaucrats. Accountability costs, and the more people to whom an organisation is accountable, the more it costs. When we read about a local government scandal in the newspaper, we would be wise to wring the maximum enjoyment from it, for we have paid handsomely for it – and the scandal is, in a very real sense, our own property being sold back to us by a newspaper.

One very tempting characteristic of the Victorian age is what Girouard terms 'earnestness', which is virtually the converse of Houghton's suggestion that just about the only unforgivable Victorian sin was levity. As the reader will have long since gathered, earnestness is not this author's strong suit, and if levity be a deadly sin then stick your harp and pass me a shovel. Smiles may seem very earnest, though his report to Janet that 'Your Mither [*sic*: Smiles often slipped in bits of phoneticised Scottish accent in his correspondence] was blessed by the Pope today, but seems none the worse for it' supports Aileen Smiles' view of him as a man who often had a twinkle in his eye. Sadly, earnestness seems to be making a comeback. When Erasmus Darwin jokingly coined this ultimate circumlocution for a spade, 'Metallic blade wedded to ligneous rod, wherewith the rural swain upturns the sod', he could hardly have foreseen expressions like 'person of colour', or he would have given up on parody as a bad job. We joke about Victorian prudery, but in fact we are quite as prudish in different directions, and no less given to euphemisms or circumlocutions. There is even a direct parallel in our reasons for adopting them. The Victorians saw themselves as having overcome animal instincts and were therefore prudish about sex: on the other hand they had yet to invent orthopaedic surgery,[30] so someone who had lost a couple of limbs in an industrial accident was called a cripple. Our society recognises it has not overcome animal instincts and therefore has few inhibitions about sex, but has endless faith in its surgeons, so that words like 'cripple' are embargoed in favour of euphemisms like 'differently abled' which are quite as absurd as anything applied to sex in Victorian times. We are are not expressionally crippled like they were: we are just differently hibited.

None of this relates to what Margaret Thatcher really meant when she spoke of her 'good old Victorian values'. She meant that Victorian people exhibited a sturdy self-reliance in the face of difficulties, and one may give her credit for a sincere belief in the idea that the receipt of hand-outs was debilitating. This was, of course, myth. There are some things that change from age to age, and others which do not. Among the latter category we find the instincts of a Benthamite majority, who balance the enjoyment of pleasure against the disagreeable necessities of life which make the maximisation of that enjoyment possible. What she failed to realise is that ideas of pleasure vary: to some, self-denial is itself a pleasure, and one which can impinge just as unpleasantly upon others as other forms of self-indulgence – for that is what it paradoxically becomes. Smiles knew this, and the power of the story-telling appeal of *Lives of the Engineers* is matched in the *Self-Help* series by an understanding of the aspirations of his readers. What went wrong in this aspect of the 'Victorian Values' theme was that Smiles knew his audience and his history. Mrs Thatcher certainly knew her audience at least as well, possibly better, but she lacked Smiles' historical perspective. He would never have perpetrated such an anachronism as having a female prime minister advocate a return to the values of an age in which women were not allowed to vote, much less to be elected to Parliament. There we find an essential collision: if earnestness and hard work were features of Victorian England, then those qualities needed to be extracted from it and applied to the study of it before making pronouncements about it. Thatcherite Victorian values were constructed without applying them to the process of their own construction.

Obviously there are certain areas in which we can find a genuine revival, or at least a genuine attempt at revival, of something which might be considered a framework of Victorian values. The remarkable thing about this process is that one political speech should have caused a large amount of serious historical thought. The end result of that thought tends to a consensus that while it is not possible to substantiate a complete corpus of ideas which can be packaged as the essence of the Victorian age, there are certain values which may properly be termed Victorian and some of them can be reconstructed in today's society.

It might be objected that what are suggested as Victorian values are not necessarily the values of real people at all, but only those of authors, journalists and politicians – those people current politicians deride as 'the chattering classes', apparently forgetful of the fact that one of the better-paid jobs as a professional chatterer is that designated by the letters MP. Therein lies the invalidation of the objection: we can never know the real values of an age; we can only make an intelligent guess based on the sources available, and those sources will always and inevitably be tilted in favour of those who are paid, or otherwise motivated, to talk and to write. At the time I am writing this, a man is welding pieces back into the underside of my car. But if I were doing it myself (which, as a truly manly character in the Rennie mould, I could), you would not get his views instead of mine, because he would be welding pieces into somebody else's car. All that would happen is that I would upset my publisher by over-running my deadline. We cannot deal in real Victorian values, only in received ones. But the greater the attention one pays to the simple task of tuning a radio, the better the reception.

I have attempted to meander around a fairly wide variety of ideas which might be termed Victorian values. In the first chapter of this book, I suggested that Hughes' description of Smiles as a typical Victorian deserved some slightly sceptical scrutiny. If Smiles can in any sense be held to exhibit typically Victorian values, then they must be reduced to the simplest of highest common factors. He believed in self-reliance based on thrift, which broke the wage-slave economy by removing the threat of imminent poverty. We may make a well-informed guess at what his view would have been of the present tendency in the British economy away from permanent employment and towards increasing casualisation of labour. Privatisation of the railways, following on the failure of the private railway companies and their fusion into a relatively coherent national system, would surely have mystified him. The modern doctrine that you motivate rich men by paying them more and poor men by paying them less would be not merely mystifying, but alien. So far as may be told, nothing in Smiles' lifetime ever made him despair until he realised, in his senility, that he had outlived all but one of his children, but the suggestion that the doctrine of self-help could be perverted to such ends would surely have done so. As perversion goes, it ranks close to Hitler's use of quotations from the New Testament.

But this is too complex: we must simplify further. If there is a single, simple idea which runs through the writings of Smiles, it is that of the perfectibility of mankind through progress. Progress involves looking forward, not back. Of course Smiles looked back, but he looked back for personal qualities, not for global values. The distinction is important: the admiration of, say, Telford as an individual does not imply any espousal of the values current in Telford's lifetime: as we saw in Chapter 2, Smiles despised many of them. Smeaton was long buried before the public whipping of women was abolished by statute, and we know what Smiles thought of corporal punishment. His view of Smeaton was not coloured by the legal environment in which Smeaton lived and worked, and neither was his view of that environment softened by the existence within it of such as Smeaton. They were separate issues.

We cannot re-create the Victorian age, and if we could we would be remarkably foolish to do so. To begin with, your beloved author would probably have been dead before he got round to writing this book, and so too would quite a high proportion of you out there who would have been reading it had I lived long enough to write it. Of course there were benefits attached to this uncertainty of life, in that a lot of the people who now flood us with too much administration would, in the good old days, have gone to bore the nether garments off long-suffering Indians, died quite soon of fever, drink, VD or being eaten by tigers, and been replaced by more of their ilk who would have done likewise. The loss of the empire has meant that people like that stay in Britain to plague *us* rather than the inhabitants of the Indian subcontinent. The White Man's Burden is heavy indeed, but on balance we would not want 1890 back.

That is the true connection. Smiles was just like the architects of his day: he was an historical eclectic, and that was a genuine Victorian value. But neo-Gothic architects did not insist on their designs being executed by monks, any more than neo-classical architects insisted on theirs being constructed by slaves. (Which in some cases would have been the only way they might have kept to budget.) Like Smiles, they looked forward and borrowed ideas from the past which they felt could aid the cause of progress, without the slightest intention or pretence of adopting the totality of the past.

At first hearing, the expression 'Victorian values' implies an attempt at reconstructing and adopting a complete value system which is difficult to define and undesirable to adopt. Precisely because we have to simplify the value system, we end up with just a few of its underlying assumptions, one of which was that it was entirely legitimate to borrow ideas from the past without having to assimilate the value system that went with them. It is easy to show that Smiles has been invoked for purposes completely alien to his own carefully developed philosophy, but it must regrettably be admitted that he who lived by the sword has perished by it. If he has suffered from the current outbreak of Victorian values, that suffering has occurred under rules to which he himself subscribed.

But that is a downbeat note on which to end. If we were to indulge in a little very amateurish counter-factual speculation we should ask how society in 1900 would have been different had Smiles never written. Clearly, some of the great causes he fought for, such as the abolition of the Corn Laws, would have been won anyway: they had become socio-economic anomalies which could not survive much longer than they did. Legal changes to protect the consumer, such as the Sale of Goods Act and the application of the common law principle of fundamental breach, were part of a wider movement to spread the protection of the law to the man in the street. Much has been made over the last few years of the effects of the supposedly anti-entrepreneurial values of 'Muscular Christianity' and the 'liberal education'. Smiles' books, both directly and through a host of imitators, reached a very wide readership. Who is to say that the simple values of what we might term 'secular decency' – honesty, forbearance, consideration for others, a dislike of ostentation, which were still being taught in public schools a century after Arnold wrote his supposedly seminal *Culture and Anarchy* – were derived from the lesser-read author rather than the more-read? Those were probably the values which Margaret Thatcher was really advocating, but she was wrong in calling them Victorian. They are timeless values, which have been more observed in some ages than in others.

It has been suggested above that Smiles attempted a philosophical synthesis resolving several of the nineteenth century's great debates, in which the secret of success was cooperation. It is also suggested that the key to the success of Smiles' biographies was that he prompted people to think that they were forming their own ideas about his subjects. If we put these two ideas together and apply them to the self-help philosophy, we can see that what appear to us to be Smilesian values are in fact values formed for themselves by his readers. He did not construct Victorian values, but he erected the scaffolding.

Notes

Where no author is stated, except in obvious cases like the Bible, the author is Smiles. Shortening of titles is mostly self-explanatory, as in *Autobiography* = *The Autobiography of Samuel Smiles*, LLD. Slightly less obvious are:
LofE plus a date means *Lives of the Engineers*, edition of the date given.
'Harper' means *Lives of the Engineers* in the edition published by Harper, New York, 1868.
'A. Smiles' means Aileen Smiles, *Samuel Smiles and his Surroundings*.
'Travers' means T. Travers, *Samuel Smiles and the Victorian Work Ethic*.

CHAPTER ONE

1. Haddington Library has a good collection of cuttings, including a newspaper article by J.H. Jamieson, ref. AK25.8, 'Haddington School of Arts a hundred years ago', which set the local scene.

2. A. Smiles gives a simplified family tree in an unpaginated preface and an account of Haddington which is partly based on the *Autobiography* and partly on 'fieldwork'.

3. *Autobiography*, p. 13. But note that Travers suggests, on the evidence of the Preface to *George Moore* (London & New York, 1878), that this was incorrect.

4. Quoted in *ibid.*, p. 6. The quotations from Smiles from this point to the superscript for n. 5 are from *ibid.*, pp. 8–12. For young James Brindley, see *LofE* (1966) I, pp. 312–18.

5. Travers, p. 137.

6. *Autobiography*, p. 24.

7. *ibid.*, p. 27 ff.

8. T.P. Hughes, Introduction to *LofE*, abridged edn, Massachusetts, 1966, p. 1.

9. A. Briggs, *Victorian People*, Harmondsworth, 1965; title to his essay on Smiles, *Autobiography*, p. 398.

10. A. Burton, *The Rainhill Story*, London, 1979, p. 21.

11. K. Joseph, Introduction to *Self-Help*, abridged edn, Harmondsworth, 1986, p. 16.

12. H. Ritvo, 'Pride and Pedigree: The Evolution of the Victorian Dog Fancy', *Victorian Studies* 29 (1986), p. 257. Cross reference to Chapter 3, n. 16 below, for Smiles' categorical condemnation of reliance on luck.

13. Travers, p. 66.

14. *LofE*, 1966, II, pp. 281–2 and III, pp. 468–9.

15. *ibid.*, I, p. 475.

16. *ibid.*, II, p. 68.

17. *Autobiography*, p. 396.

18. The Preface to his *History of Ireland and the Irish People under the Government of England* (London, 1844) minces no words: the English treated the 'natives as Helots and slaves and with a cruelty that has

never been exceeded in any age or country'. Worse, 'All the evils springing out of the Conquest of Ireland have been greatly aggravated by *religious* causes [Smiles' italics].' For Huguenots, see the bibliography, and for St Ignatius Loyola and John Knox see, for example, *Self-Help*, 1859, pp. 322 and 273, and *Character*, pp. 24 and 156.

19. *Character*, pp. 10, 73, 176. The *Dictionary of National Biography* implies that she was not nearly so agreeable in her private life as her Quaker background (she was the daughter of Samuel Galton, of Lunar Society fame) might suggest, but coyly refrains from explanation. C.C. Hankin (ed.), *Life of Mary Anne Schimmelpenninck* (London, 1858), contains some truly vile passages, and I beg forgiveness for quoting this example: 'When that which is noble, devout, tender or great is the subject then I think the writer should put forth his historical powers and add colour and the effects of light and shadow on the naked outline and seek to reproduce in indelible lineaments on the heart of the reader the images before him, to bring them, as it were, in the full light of the Sun of Righteousness whose beams may photographise them on the mind and heart.'

It is possible that this 'interesting and bewitching' woman had some influence on Smiles: the above passage bears on the themes of Chapters 4 and 6, below.

20. A. Smiles, 1956, p. 128. One wonders why the name of the deist Robert Owen sprang to Aileen Smiles' mind.

21. R.J. Morris, 'Samuel Smiles and the Genesis of Self-Help', *Historical Journal* 24 (1981), pp. 89–109, at p. 96.

22. The obvious example is Aileen Smiles, who entitled the first section of her first chapter 'Religious Martyrdom' (and see especially pp. 19–20).

23. This somewhat perfunctory account is loosely based on J.H.S. Burleigh, *A Church History of Scotland*, London, 1960.

24. *Autobiography*, p. 18.

25. Though Aileen Smiles thought Sam Jnr was the favourite. His gradual recovery is indicated by a very clumsily written letter to 'Gingers' dated 31 May 1872; West Yorkshire Record Office, hereafter WYRO, SS/A1/38.

26. Notably, though by no means exclusively, the engineers. One of the themes which I hope emerges in this book is that the true benefit of the implementation of self-help was the achievement of the purpose of the Creator.

27. This account is derived from Jamieson (see n. 1 above).

28. *Autobiography*, pp. 31 and 52–8.

29. Burleigh, *Church History of Scotland*, pp. 318–29.

30. J.M. Robertson, *A History of Freethought in the Nineteenth Century*, 2 vols, London, 1929; Vol. 1, p. 17.

31. A.L. Drummond and J. Bullock, *The Scottish Church 1688–1843*, Edinburgh, 1973, pp. 174–5, 164–5.

32. Burleigh, *Church History of Scotland*, p. 329.

33. *Autobiography*, p. 29.

34. *ibid.*, pp. 30 and 52.

35. Robertson, *History of Freethought*, pp. 9–10 and 92–5.

36. Travers, *Work Ethic*, p. 287; Smiles, *Duty*, pp. 48–50.

37. *Autobiography*, p. 106.

38. *Duty*, London, 1880, p. 366; hereafter *Duty*.

39. There are exceptions, of which a couple are discussed in Chapter 6.
40. *Robert Dick*, London (1878), 1905, p. vii; hereafter *Robert Dick*.
41. *ibid.*, p. 234. Hugh Miller was editor of the evangelical newspaper *The Witness*. He appears in *Self-Help*, *Thrift*, London, 1875 (hereafter *Thrift*), *Duty*, and *Life and Labour*, London, 1887 (hereafter *Life & Labour*).
42. *Life & Labour*, London, 1887, p. 279.
43. *Robert Dick*, p. 235. If any reader can tell me what 'an ignorant W.W.' is, I would love to know.
44. *ibid.*, p. 237.
45. *ibid.*, p. 307.
46. *ibid.*, p. 310.
47. *ibid.*, p. 410.
48. Verses 2, 6 and 18, quoted from the Authorised Version.
49. *Robert Dick*, p. 412.
50. *The Huguenots: Their Settlements, Churches and Industries in England and Ireland*, London, 1867, p. 162.
51. *Duty*, p. 110.
52. *ibid.*, pp. 99 and 112.
53. A. Smiles, pp. 139–40. At p. 142 she claims that he was required to refer to George Moore's shop as his 'place of business' because that sounded more genteel.
54. *Autobiography*, pp. 323–35, and WYRO, SS/A/I/85.
55. Chapter 18 of *George Moore* lays great stress on his tolerance in matters of denominational religion. See also p. 435.

CHAPTER TWO

1. L.T.C. Rolt, 'The History of the History of Engineering', *Transactions of the Newcomen Society* XLII (1969–70), pp. 1–10.
2. *LofE*, 1966, II, p. 326.

3. *ibid.*, p. 329.
4. R.A. Buchanan, 'Gentleman Engineers: The Making of a Profession', *Victorian Studies* 26 (1983), pp. 407–29, at p. 409.
5. E.J. Hobsbawm, *The Age of Revolution*, New York, 1962, p. 222, quoted in A. Tyrrell, 'Class Consciousness in Early Victorian Britain: Samuel Smiles, Leeds Politics, and the Self-Help Creed', *Journal of British Studies* IX (1970), pp. 102–25. P.D. Anthony, *The Ideology of Work*, London, 1977; Chapter 4 is entitled 'The Official Ideology: *Laissez-Faire* and Self-Help'. Smiles detested *laissez-faire* (see p. 26), which rather damages Anthony's chapter.
6. K. Fielden, 'Samuel Smiles and Self-Help', *Victorian Studies* XII (1968), pp. 155–78. Much the fullest study of Smiles' early work is in Travers, *Work Ethic*.
7. In all of his papers mentioned in the bibliography. Travers is sceptical for reasons which will appear in Chapter 3.
8. *Autobiography*, p. 43.
9. Joseph, *Self-Help*, p. 9.
10. *Thrift*, p. 376. The idea of personalising 'Nobody' was not new: Dickens had done it (*Little Dorritt* was originally to have been entitled *Nobody's Fault*), and he in turn may have seen *The Odd-Fellows Magazine* VII (new series, Jan. 1844–Nov. 1845, pp. 17–19), and borrowed it from the article by John Dent Jnr, 'Reflections on Nobody'. Smiles himself had done it before in *Eliza Cook's Journal* V (1851), pp. 223–4.
11. *ibid.*, p. 378.
12. Joseph, *Self-Help*, p. 12.
13. For George Stephenson's entrepreneurial activities, see V. Haworth, 'A Case Study:

George Stephenson, 1781–1848, Enginewright and Railway Promoter', in *Nineteenth Century Business Ethics, papers presented at a research day school at Merseyside Maritime Museum, 31 October 1992.*

14. *LofE*, 1966, III, pp. 374–5. G. Alderman, *The Railway Interest* (Leicester, 1973) makes it clear that, while Smiles may have been defending his engineers, he was if anything understating the conflict of interest within Parliament.

15. *ibid.*, p. 376.

16. *Autobiography*, p. 49.

17. Those of a trusting disposition sometimes think parliamentary papers should be taken at face value. As in the case of the enquiry into local government which led to the Local Government Reform Act of 1835, the answers they produced could be, and were, preconditioned by the terms of the warrant. Furthermore, evidence could be choreographed in advance. Parliamentary sleaze is an enduring value.

18. 'The Industrious Poor', *Quarterly Magazine of the Grand United Order of Odd-Fellows* (hereafter *OFM*) No. 1 (February 1850), p. 1.

19. While this particular example comes from *OFM* for February 1852, p. 16, it is a form of comparison which Smiles used repeatedly: as late as 1875, an extended version appears in *Thrift*, occupying pp. 47–53.

20. For influences of Rousseau, see Travers, *Work Ethic*, pp. 98–9, and T.H.E. Travers, 'Samuel Smiles and the *Origins of "Self-Help"*', *Albion* 9 (1977), at pp. 168–9. Smiles' later 'mentions' of Rousseau: *Character*, p. 377; *Life and Labour*, p. 388.

21. W. Cobbett, *Cottage Economy* (1822), Oxford, 1970, p. 20.

22. For a sympathetic overview of Cobbett, see D. Green, *Great Cobbett: The Noblest Agitator*, Oxford, 1985.

23. T. Carlyle, 'On Chartism' in *Critical and Miscellaneous Essays*, repr. London, 7 vols, 1872; Vol. 6, pp. 109–86, at p. 110.

24. S. Smiles, *Address to the Members of the Bradford United Reform Club, 14 February 1841*, Leeds, 1842, p. 15 (hereafter *Bradford Address*); Carlyle, 'On Chartism', Vol. 4, pp. 184–211, at p. 203. The 'Corn Law Rhymer', Ebenezer Elliott, receives many favourable mentions in Smiles' work. He is one of the subjects of S. Smiles, *Brief Biographies*, Boston, 1860 (hereafter *Brief Biographies*).

25. *Bradford Address*, p. 11.

26. *ibid.*, p. 14.

27. Rare because only one edition was published in his lifetime, and most of that went to Australia (*Autobiography*, p. 63). *NUC* shows a new edition, edited by Sir J. Beevor, published in 1905, but the only copy I have seen is in the Bodleian.

28. Samuel Smiles, *Physical Education*, Edinburgh, 1838, p. 1.

29. *Bradford Address*, pp. 6–7. Similar themes appear in other places, e.g. his description of the powers and responsibilities of the press in 'What are the People Doing to Educate Themselves?', *People's Journal* 1 (1846), pp. 229–30.

30. Smiles wrote at least two articles on Robert Nicoll: *Howitt's Journal* 3 (1848), p. 135, one of series entitled 'Poets of the People'; *Good Words* XVI (1875), pp. 313–14.

31. S. Smiles, *The Education of the Working Classes*, Leeds, 1845, p. 11.

32. 'What are the People Doing to Educate Themselves?', p. 223.

33. 'Hints to working men about providence and the duty of economy', *OFM* (February 1852), p. 16.

34. On 10 March 1884 he wrote to 'Gingers' complaining that Dr Parr had forbidden him his port and his whisky and jokingly enquired, 'Is life tolerable on these terms?' WYRO, SS/A/I/174. A decade later, a similar fate befell his cigars: letter to Jack, 17 December 1894, WYRO, SS/A/J/250.

35. *People's Journal* 1 (1846), p. 136.

36. *Thrift*, p. 113 ff.

37. R.J. Morris, 'Samuel Smiles and the Genesis of Self-Help: The Retreat to a Petit Bourgeois Utopia', *Historical Journal* 24 (1981), pp. 89–110.

38. *Bradford Address*, p. 9.

39. For dock expansion and the export of dock engineering technique, see A. Jarvis, *The Liverpool Dock Engineers*, Stroud, 1996.

40. But see E.H. Kinmouth, 'Nakamura Kein and Samuel Smiles', *American Historical Review* 85 (1980), pp. 535–56, which deals with the highly successful Japanese translation of *Self-Help*. The original form of the book addressed social problems (and customs) which did not exist in Japan, and the 'translation' therefore involved a fair amount of adaptation. The argument of the paper is that it appealed almost solely to the less wealthy members of the Samurai class – who might equate, in nineteenth-century England, with declining rural gentry.

41. These editions are still common: they have a red buckram binding with gold blocking and are printed on thick, pulpy paper of high acid content. Lord Leverhulme *inter alia* gave away hundreds of them, and a fair proportion of surviving copies have gift or prize bookplates in them. I own six of Smiles' works in these editions, only one of which does not bear such a plate.

42. Travers, *Work Ethic*, Appendix F.

43. See references to railway speculation both above and below, and also his approbation of Bulwer Lytton, in *Brief Biographies* (Boston, 1860, pp. 107–36), as well as various quotations. Lytton's *Paul Clifford* caused outrage at the time of its publication by its comparison of the ethical values of the financial speculator with those of the highwayman. In the novel, the highwayman won the heroine, and in the process the concept of white-collar crime was invented.

44. *National Education*, Manchester, 1851, p. 1.

45. *People's Journal* 1 (1846), p. 222.

46. *Eliza Cook's Journal* 5 (1851), p. 145.

47. *Bradford Address*, p. 6.

48. *Thrift*, p. 321.

49. This, of course, has an interesting bearing on the suggestion by Travers that Smiles was influenced by an underlying long-term Calvinism. I differ from him: 'salvation' in Smilesian terms is achieved by a combination of (mostly) character and good works and (to a much lesser extent) the help of others. The abiding message is that *nothing* is predetermined.

50. The only copy I have seen is in WYRO, printed by Harper of Huddersfield, and entitled 'Industrial Education'.

51. *ibid.*, p. 10.

52. Astonishingly, there is no full-length biography of Rankine, but D.F. Channell, 'The Harmony of Theory and Practice: The Engineering Science of W.J.M. Rankine', *Technology & Culture* 23 (1982, pp. 39–52), provides some consolation.

53. Possible reasons for the omission of these two uninspiring persons are suggested above.

54. See his life of Hartley Coleridge

(one of his least favourite biographees) in *Brief Biographies*.

55. *Self-Help*, p. 321; Sir Joshua Reynolds, *Discourses*, ed. P. Rogers, Harmondsworth, 1992, Discourse 3.

56. Telford's books are, of course, still at the Institution of Civil Engineers; the library of the Newcastle 'Lit & Phil' is rich in such works, as is the Manchester Central Library. The Liverpool Lyceum Club Library's contents were unfortunately dispersed, but its catalogue survives and establishes that similar facilities were available there.

57. D.S.L. Cardwell, *From Watt to Clausius*, New York, 1971.

58. *LofE*, 1874, V, p. 407.

59. *ibid.*, p. 409.

60. For a more recent appraisal of the importance of these contacts, see R.E. Schofield, *The Lunar Society of Birmingham*, Oxford, 1963.

61. *LofE*, 1874, V, p. 71.

Chapter Three

1. R. Blatchford, 'Of Samuel Smiles and Self-Help', *The Clarion*, 13 July 1923, p. 3.

2. If, of course, one wishes to trace Social Darwinism back to Herbert Spencer's invention of the phrase 'survival of the fittest', Smiles still predates it: *Self-Help* was published in the same year as *The Origin of Species*, but had been offered (complete) to Routledge, who turned it down, in 1855. But most people would accept that Sir Francis Galton's *Hereditary Genius* (1869) was the real starting point.

3. Mentions of racial characteristics appear in many places, e.g. *Character*, pp. 280–5; 'Hugh Miller' in *Brief Biographies*, p. 85; *Self-Help*, pp. 223–4. At one point Smiles considered writing a book specifically on race: it seems to have been laid aside at the time of his stroke and never taken up again.

4. Lecture, delivered 22 May 1840, published as the final chapter of *On Heroes, Hero-Worship and the Heroic in History*, London, 1841.

5. This is the central thesis of Travers' *Work Ethic*; perhaps the most forceful statement of it by Smiles is in the earlier part of Chapter 1 of *Thrift*.

6. A. Briggs, *Centenary Introduction*, p. 28: 'They [Smiles and Carlyle] did not distinguish between work and drudgery.' T. Carlyle, *Past and Present* (1843), London, 1912, p. 147; for activity or employment which did not count as work, see the account of 'Plugson of Undershot', *ibid.*, p. 181 ff.

7. Just one of Hudson's many sins was that he was the 'King of Scrip': Carlyle used the analogy of organic growth – 'flowery umbrageous scrip' – but clearly he knew that many people worked in the financial services sector he so deplored. However, that was not work at all, just as to Smiles it was not 'true work'. T. Carlyle, 'Hudson's Statue', *Latter Day Pamphlets* No. 7, London, 1850.

8. Carlyle, *Past and Present*, p. 204.

9. Cobbett, *Cottage Economy*, p. 3. The reason is that 'such content is proof of a base disposition, a disposition which is the enemy of all industry, all exertion, all love of independence'. It was the independence which was the key, to Smiles as to Cobbett.

10. Carlyle, *Past and Present*, p. 64.

11. 'Thomas Carlyle', in *Brief Biographies*, at p. 271.

12. Blatchford, 'Of Smiles and Self-Help'.

13. *Self-Help*, p. 4.
14. *ibid.*, p. 66; the patent was no. 11,103 of 1846.
15. *ibid.*, pp. 101–2. One cannot help but feel that Carlyle's reaction to such a misfortune striking someone with whom he disagreed might have been less gracious.
16. *ibid.*, pp. 207–11. See also *Thrift*, p. 180: 'It is not luck, but labour, that makes men. . . . Luck lies in bed and wishes the postman would bring him news of a legacy; Labour turns out at six and with busy pen or ringing hammer lays the foundations of a competence.' After several similar examples: 'Luck slips downwards to self-indulgence; Labour strides upward, and aspires to independence.'
17. *Self-Help*, p. 311.
18. *ibid.*, p. 301.
19. *ibid.*, p. 295.
20. E. de Maré, Introduction to *The Lives of George & Robert Stephenson*, London, 1975, pp. 15–16.
21. *Self-Help*, p. 294.
22. *ibid.*, p. 301.
23. For example, his account book (WYRO, SS/B/71) shows his investment portfolio as worth some £19,000 in 1874 and over £25,000 by 1882. This was at a time when he was incurring heavy expenditure on the education of his grandchildren.
24. *Self-Help*, p. 295.
25. For young Brindley's indiscretion, see H. Malet, *Bridgewater, The Canal Duke 1736–1803*, Manchester, 1977, p. 57; Robert Stephenson was the godfather of Robert Stephenson Smyth, 1st Baron Baden-Powell of Gilwell (1857–1941). Henrietta Powell came from Naples, where it was, at the time, customary to use the term 'godfather' in a euphemistic manner. Victoria Haworth, to whom I am indebted for the information, has amassed a good deal more circumstantial evidence for this and other philanderings of Robert. She also suggests that the one-third share of his large estate left to his solicitor was possibly for ex gratia maintenance payments.
26. This was widely known at the time, because in 1850/1 Hartley went through the long and complex procedure to obtain a divorce, which until 1857 required a private Act of Parliament.
27. This theme occurs in many places: its fullest explanation forms the subject of Chapter 2 of *Character*.
28. For Florence Nightingale, see *Duty*, pp. 265–9; for Grace Darling, *ibid.*, pp. 281–3.
29. *Character*, pp. 168–72.
30. 'What passes by the name of "etiquette" is often of the essence of unpoliteness and untruthfulness. It consists in a great measure of posture-making, and is easily seen through', *ibid.*, p. 259.
31. In, for example, F. Engels, *The Condition of the Working Class in England*, London, 1892, p. 276, and compare G. Smith, *op cit*: 'the boat women used to strip and fight like men' (p. 81); 'I have frequently seen women in a half-nude state washing over the sides of the boat as it was moving along . . .' (p. 95); such behaviour was naturally followed, as in the mines, by a very high rate of illegitimacy, *passim*, e.g. p. 111. Extracts relating to agricultural gangs and chainwrightettes are in P. Hollis, *Women in Public: The Women's Movement 1850–1900*, London, 1979, at pp. 57 and 80. For prurient journalism, see T. Doyle, *Black Swine in the Sewers of Hampstead*, New York, 1989. (And particularly the case of

the bare-breasted servant girl, *ibid.*, pp. 35–8.) I should record that Simon Dentith disagreed with me on this point, but I think he's just too nice a man to believe what was going on.

32. *Character*, p. 65.

33. J. Arch, *From Ploughtail to Parliament*, repr. London, 1986, Chapters 8 and 9; *Duty*, p. 377.

34. This is another recurrent theme: *Physical Education*, pp. 3–7; *Eliza Cook's Journal* No. 157 (1 May 1852), pp. 1–3; *Thrift*, the latter part of Chapter XV. Note that these references span thirty-seven years.

35. Comments on the evil effects of incompetent cookery achieved almost the status of a journalistic genre. My wife found literally dozens of examples – without specially looking for them – in preparing A.M. Jarvis, 'The Technology of Cooking', unpublished MSc dissertation, University of Liverpool, 1996. (History of Science & Technology.) Note that in the *Eliza Cook's* article cited above, Smiles quotes W. Lee, superintending inspector to the Board of Health, in support of his own statement that 'Another enormous moral and physical evil to the inhabitants of unwholesome localities, is the extent to which the passion for intoxicating drinks, opium &c. is developed. . . .'

36. *Character*, p. 330, and see below, on the subject of Harriet Martineau. On the other hand, in *Life and Labour* he argues that the education of girls, more particularly than that of boys, must avoid 'cramming' and 'over brain-work', *ibid.*, p. 303.

37. In *Character* 'help-mate' is used, but Chapter IX of *Life and Labour* is entitled 'Single and Married – Helps-Meet'.

38. *The Music Makers* might be held to be an exception, but worthy work though it is, much of it is a musical reprise of ideas which had received Alice's seal of approval before she died – including the great tune of the 1st symphony, which was now set to words.

39. *Brief Biographies*, p. 499.

CHAPTER FOUR

1. *LofE*, 1862, p. vii; J. Scott Russell, 'Memoir of George Stephenson', *Proceedings of the Institution of Mechanical Engineers*, October 1848, p. 2.

2. This appeared in parts in the *Civil Engineer and Architect's Journal* 11 (1848), pp. 297–300, 329–33, 361–4, and 12 (1849), pp. 68–72, 103–7, 170–3, 205–9.

3. These comings and goings are recounted in introductions to various editions and in greater detail in *Autobiography*, Chapters XIII and XIV.

4. *LofE*, 1862, Introduction.

5. I. McNeil, *Hydraulic Power*, London, 1972, p. 121.

6. Though it must be admitted that much of *Brief Biographies* was reworked from earlier anonymous articles, particularly from *Eliza Cook's Journal.*

7. See his unkind remarks about Trevithick and Blenkinsop, among others.

8. This is reflected in W.J.M. Rankine's celebrated textbook *The Steam Engine and Other Prime Movers*, which appeared in numerous editions from 1859 onwards, and continued to remind students of the fact, and to provide means of comparing the relative efficiencies of muscle as against mechanical power.

9. *LofE*, 1862, II, pp. 388–9.
10. For the origins of tartan, see J.T. Dunbar, *History of Highland Dress*, London, 1962. In Chapters 8–10, Dunbar examines at length the document known as *Vestiarum Scoticum*, which was published in 1842 and allegedly dated back to the sixteenth century. His conclusion is that it was an early nineteenth-century fraud. See also H. Trevor-Roper, 'The Invention of Tradition: The Highland Tradition of Scotland' in E.J. Hobsbawm and T. Ranger (eds), *The Invention of Tradition*, Cambridge, 1983. The poems of Ossian were an assemblage of ancient fragments published in 1762–3 by James Macpherson. They were undoubtedly genuine in parts, but Macpherson has been widely suspected of doing more 'editing' than he admitted, indeed it was at one stage believed that he had written them *in toto*.
11. This line of argument is derived from P.J. Bowler, *The Invention of Progress* (Oxford, 1989), which provides many useful further references.
12. S. Smiles (ed.), *James Nasmyth, Engineer, An Autobiography*, London, 1885, Preface, p. vi.
13. Travers, *Work Ethic*, p. 88.
14. *LofE*, 1874, I, p. viii.
15. *ibid.*, Chapter 2: quotation, p. 47.
16. Malaria was still common in the Lincolnshire fens and the Somerset Levels into the nineteenth century. M.J. Dobson, 'Marsh Fever: the geography of malaria', *Journal of Historical Geography* 6:4 (1980), pp. 357–89.
17. This is a source of pollution which has come into prominence again quite recently as mines closed and pumping stopped, changing the flows again. The pollution of rivers by mining was hotly denied with a suspicious degree of unanimity by witnesses called before the Royal Commission on River Pollution.
18. Smith, *op. cit.*, pp. 101–2.
19. *LofE*, 1862, I, p. 415.
20. *Railway Property*, Leeds, 1850, p. 24.
21. *Robert Dick*, p. 2.
22. J.A. Cantrell, 'James Nasmyth and the Steam Hammer', *Transactions of the Newcomen Society* 56 (1984–5), pp. 133–8.
23. C. Hadfield, *Thomas Telford's Temptation*, Kidderminster, 1993; J. Griffiths, *The Third Man*, London, 1992; H. Torrens, 'Jonathan Hornblower and the Steam Engine: a Historiographic Analysis' in Smith, *op. cit.*
24. For example, the claim that it was the first locomotive with smooth wheels (1857, p. 54) does not appear on the corresponding page (p. 82) of the 1864 edition.
25. 'EMSP', *The Two James's and the Two Stephensons*, London, 1861; O.D. Hedley, *Who Invented the Locomotive Engine?*, London, 1859.
26. *Life of George Stephenson*, 1857, p. 410.
27. This issue is explored in some detail in A. Jarvis, 'Engineering the Image: The Censoring of Samuel Smiles', *Journal of the Railway and Canal Historical Society* 31 (1993), pp. 176–85
28. *LofE*, 1862, III, p. 374.
29. A similar incident occurred late in his life when he was threatened with action for defamation over a passage in *Thrift*. Some angry letters, urging no retraction, survive in the archives of John Murray. In this case, no retraction was made.
30. *LofE*, 1862, III, pp. 443 and 448.
31. S. Smiles, *The Life of George Stephenson*, New York, 1868 (hereafter Harper edn).
32. *ibid.*, pp. 86–7; Harper edn, p. 74.

33. Smiles did not try to explain how it came about that the two Georges went to Durham together and jointly purchased the Durham Junction Railway – apparently for cash! D.M. Evans, *Facts, Failures and Frauds*, London, 1859, p. 26.

34. It has been said of my friend Victoria Haworth that her enormous knowledge of early railways is vitiated by her hero-worship of Robert Stephenson. Be that as it may, she has confessed to me that in her opinion Robert was perfectly capable of being thoroughly devious.

35. Hartree Papers, Devon Record Office, 1119 ME/11 and E11.

38. O.J. Vignoles, *Life of Charles Blacker Vignoles*, London, 1889; F. Trevithick, *Life of Richard Trevithick*, London, 1872; Miss Gurney did not attain hard covers, but wrote to *The Times* (11 April 1879) and a string of letters to the *Royal Cornwall Gazette* between January and May 1879.

39. This occasion is recounted in J.C. Jeaffreson, *The Life of Robert Stephenson*, 2 vols, London, 1866; Vol. I, p. 258. There were 350 people present: the claim for George was made by Sir Thomas Liddell. George spoke as well, and the chairman was George Hudson.

40. *LofE*, 1862, III, p. 346; Lambert, *op. cit.*, p. 110.

41. J.R. Leifchild, *Our Coal and Our Coal Pits*, 1856, repr. New York 1968, pp. 228–40. 'Some of them [i.e. anecdotes passed on to him by John Bourne] were traditional and had gathered, in the course of re-telling, accretions which were more or less fictitious', *Autobiography*, p. 162.

CHAPTER FIVE

1. A.O.J. Cockshutt, *Truth to Life*, London, 1974, p. 105. This may also be the appropriate place to remark that Cockshutt is not the only one to have trouble finding the time to read Smiles: I found a substantial number of the pages of the Bodleian's copy of the first printing of the first edition of *The Life of George Stephenson* still uncut on 10 April 1990.

2. 'The most glorious exploits do not always furnish us with the clearest discoveries of virtue or vice in men': quoted in *Character*, pp. 301–2.

3. Bede, *A History of the English Church and People*, trans. L. Sherley-Price, London, 1964, p. 33.

4. L.T.C. Rolt, Introduction to *LofE*, 1966, III.

5. *Character*, p. 301.

6. J.R. Stanfield, *An Essay on the Study and Composition of Biography* (1813), repr. New York & London, 1986, p. 133.

7. G. Bentley, 'Sincerity in Biography', *The Temple Bar*, 1881, repr. in Ira B. Nadel (ed.), *Victorian Biography*, New York & London, 1986, pp. 329–36; for Poe see *Brief Biographies*.

8. There is a good deal of recent literature on neo-medievalism. As a general guide, M. Girouard, *The Return to Camelot* (Yale & London, 1981), is both scholarly and readable.

9. K.L. Morris, *The Image of the Middle Ages in Romantic and Victorian Literature*, London, 1984; R. Faber, *Young England*, London, 1987.

10. K.H. Digby, *The Broadstone of Honour, or Rules for the Gentlemen of England*, London, 1823, p. 549.

11. *ibid.*, p. 542.

12. *ibid.*, p. 178.

13. G. Willans and R. Searle, *The*

Compleet Molesworth, London, 1984, p. 58.

14. Digby, *The Broadstone of Honour*, p. 535.

15. S. Dentith, 'Samuel Smiles and the Nineteenth Century Novel' in Smith, *Perceptions of Great Engineers*.

16. *ibid.*, p. 47; the quotation is from *Bleak House*.

17. *LofE*, 1862, I, pp. 311–18.

18. *ibid.*, p. 470.

19. For Jacquard's escape, *Self-Help*, p. 60. For 'martyr-inventors', *LofE*, 1874, V, p. 381.

20. *LofE*, 1862, III, p. 449.

21. Harper edn, 1868, p. 297 n.

22. *LofE*, 1862, I, pp. 23–4. Guthlac is omitted from the 1874 edition, presumably because by then Smiles had read H.T. Riley (ed.), *Chronicle of the Abbey of Croyland*, London, 1854.

23. *LofE*, 1862, II, pp. 45–6.

24. *LofE*, 1874, V, pp. 198–9; *Men of Invention and Industry*, p. 127.

25. Swithun appears as a bridgebuilder in *LofE*, 1874, III, p. 45. The sources are cited in a footnote. The reference to St Benezet on p. 51 is unlikely to have come from anywhere other than *Acta Sanctorum*.

26. *Proceedings of the Institution of Mechanical Engineers*, October 1848, pp. 1–13.

27. Eadmer, quoted in R.W. Southern, *St Anselm and his Biographer*, Cambridge, 1963, p. 278.

28. Note my 'generally'. There are a few exceptions, most of them in *Brief Biographies*.

29. The fact that Murdock, as Watt's agent in Cornwall, fought a duel with Trevithick's father probably did little to endear the Trevithick clan to Smiles either.

30. Though, at the the risk of being frivolous, the account Smiles gives of Guthlac's encounter with demons sounds more like the product of a session on fermented elderflower stalks or whatever other halucinogenic substances were available at the time.

31. *LofE*, 1862, III, pp. 209–10.

32. This was made clear by W.H. Bailey, 'A new chapter in the history of the Manchester & Liverpool [*sic*] Railway', *Transactions of the Manchester Association of Engineers*, 1889, pp. 23–9.

33. Though he might be thought to let the cat out of the bag in Harper, 1868: 'A minute was concocted, purporting to be a resolution of the Old Quay Canal Co to oppose the projected railroad by every possible means and calling upon landowners and others to afford every facility for making such survey of the intended line as should enable the opponents to detect errors in the scheme of the promoters. . . .' But Smiles would no more have thought that the use of forged documents to enable trespass was wrong than Eadmer thought it was wrong to forge title deeds to monastic lands – which was a standard medieval practice. It's the circular argument about saintliness again.

34. Brindley in *LofE*, 1862, I, pp. 352–3; Middleton in *ibid.*, pp. 110–13; Albion Mills in *ibid.*, II, pp. 140–1.

CHAPTER SIX

1. J.P. Muirhead, *The Origin and Progress of the Mechanical Inventions of James Watt*, London, 1854.

2. C. Hutton (ed.), *Reports of the late John Smeaton*, 4 vols, London, 1798 onwards. For details of publication and sales, see G. Watson, *The Smeatonians*, London, 1989.

3. In fact, the only book on him is

A.D. Duckworth (ed.), *The Papers of William Froude, MA, LLD, FRS, 1810–1879*, London, 1955. Its target readership is naval architects and marine engineers.

4. The account of Borrow is at first fairly sympathetic, but then gets round to Borrow's love of 'the glories of pugilism', which Smiles considers as barbaric as bull-baiting (p. 168). Theodore Hook, a novelist whose work Smiles would elsewhere have described as 'intellectual dram-drinking', and who moved in exactly the social circles Smiles despised, is presented not as a villain but as an object of pity (p. 349).

5. M.C. Duffy has been particularly strong in his condemnation of history devoid of philosophy or analysis; see for example, his excoriation of popular railway histories in his 'Technomorphology and the Stephenson Traction System', *Transactions of the Newcomen Society* 54 (1982–3), pp. 55–78.

6. See above, pp. 69–72, for a summary of Smiles' attitude to taking on George Stephenson.

7. J. Zipes (ed.), *Victorian Fairy Tales: The Revolt of the Fairies and Elves* (New York & London, 1987), has a useful introduction and commentary, and a formidable bibliography.

8. I. Opie and P. Opie, *The Classic English Fairy Tales*, London, 1974, pp. 117–21, for an analysis of *Cinderella.*

9. *LofE*, 1862, II, pp. 281–2. See also *Autobiography*, pp. 254–5.

10. Opie and Opie, *The Classic English Fairy Tales*, pp. 47–50: *LofE*, 1862, III, pp. 35–6.

11. 'This famous sword was afterwards sent by Richard I as a present to Tancred', *Industrial Biography*, Newton Abbot, 1967, p. 18n.

12. R.B. Dobson and J. Taylor, *Rymes of Robyn Hood*, Gloucester, 1989, pp. 41–2.

13. For the original version, *Eliza Cook's Journal* I, No. 5 (1849), pp. 55–7; for the correction, *LofE*, 1862, III, p. 159.

14. W.O. Skeat, *George Stephenson: The Engineer and his Letters*, London, 1973, p. 38. The myth also recurs in L.T.C. Rolt's generally sound *George and Robert Stephenson*, Harmondsworth, 1978, pp. 8–9.

15. L.C.A. Knowles, *Industrial and Commercial Revolutions*, London, 1926, p. 255.

16. Of the Stockton & Darlington: 'The measure was however, strongly opposed by the Duke of Cleveland because the proposed line passed near one of his fox covers', *LofE*, 1862, III, p. 151; of the Liverpool & Manchester, *ibid.*, p. 193.

17. R.A. Buchanan, 'The Lives of the Engineers', *Industrial Archaeology Review* IX (1988), pp. 5–15, at p. 8.

18. 'The Brunels', *Quarterly Review* 112 (1862), pp. 1–39; R. Beamish, *Memoir of the Life of Sir Marc Isambard Brunel*, London, 1862.

19. Quoted in S. Fairlie, 'The Corn Laws and British Wheat Production 1829–76', *Economic History Review*, 2nd series, XXII (1969), pp. 88–116, at p. 88.

20. *Brief Biographies*, p. 419.

21. J.T. Ward and R.D. Wilson (eds), *Land and Industry*, Newton Abbot, 1971. This is a main theme of the Introduction.

22. M. Weber, *The Protestant Ethic and the Spirit of Capitalism*, trans. T. Parsons, 2nd edn, London, 1976.

23. L. White, 'Introduction: The Study of Medieval Technology 1924–1974: Personal Reflections', in his *Medieval Religion and Technology: Collected Essays* (Berkeley & Los

Angeles, 1978), gives a clear outline of the development of, and major contributions to, the study of medieval technology.

24. Argued in detail in the essay 'Cultural Climates and Technological Advance in the Middle Ages', in *ibid.*

25. G. Ovitt Jr, 'The Cultural Context of Western Technology: Early Christian Attitudes toward Manual Labor', *Technology and Culture* 27 (1986), pp. 477–500.

26. Weber, *Protestant Ethic*, p. 35.

27. *ibid.*, pp. 118–19.

28. *ibid.*, pp. 119–21; H. Kraus, *Gold was the Mortar: The Economics of Cathedral Building*, New York, 1994.

29. A.B. Cobban, *Universities in the Middle Ages*, Liverpool, 1990, pp. 29–32. The notes of this pamphlet provide numerous further references.

30. W.D. Rubinstein, *Men of Property: the very wealthy in Britain since the Industrial Revolution*, London, 1981.

31. Jessop's name is mentioned seven times in *LofE*, 1862, II, and once in III. There is a brief memoir of him at II, p. 197. Although he is more than once described as 'eminent', no one would imagine that they were reading about Britain's most successful and prolific canal engineer. The balance was not redressed until the appearance of C. Hadfield and A.W. Skempton, *William Jessop, Engineer*, Newton Abbot, 1979.

32. See C. Hadfield and G. Biddle, *Canals of the North West*, Newton Abbot, 1970. Vol. I, Chapter 5.

33. *LofE*, 1874, III, pp. 1–73, at p. 4.

34. C.I. Savage, *An Economic History of Transport*, London, 2nd edn, 1966, p. 11; E.A. Pratt, *A History of Inland Transport and Communication* (1912),

repr. Newton Abbot, 1970, pp. 11–13. While some might think Pratt well named, Savage held a chair in economics in a very reputable department.

35. A. Raistrick, *Industrial Archaeology*, London, 1972, pp. 127–32, and see also Chapter 12. G.H. Martin, 'Road Travel in the Middle Ages: Some Journeys by the Warden and Fellows of Merton College, Oxford, 1315–1470', *Journal of Transport History*, 2nd series, III (1975–6, pp. 158–78), puts some flesh on the bones of medieval road travel.

36. L. White, *Medieval Technology and Social Change*, Oxford, 1962, p. 66.

37. For British superiority, see *Self-Help*, p. 27; for Teutonic energy, *ibid.*, pp. 223–4; for assorted other racial characteristics, *Character*, pp. 278–85; for the proposed book, see A. Smiles, pp. 111–12.

38. Even *Character*, which is perhaps the most positive of the series, has sections on Idleness, Pandering to Popularity, Evils of Strong Temper etc. (see table of contents.). It also draws an important distinction between 'noble and ignoble patriotism' (p. 30).

39. *LofE*, 1874, III, pp. 266–77.

40. For the importance of Watt as one of the founding fathers of thermodynamics, see D.S.L. Cardwell, *From Watt to Clausius*, Ames, Iowa, 1989, Chapter 3.

41. A.E. Musson (ed.), *Science, Technology and Economic Growth in the Eighteenth Century*, London, 1972, p. 3.

42. M.S. Gregory, *History and Development of Engineering*, London, 1971, p. 48. (The reader may feel I am unkind to Gregory. Not so; had I wished to be I would have mentioned that the *Ladybird Book of Early Railways* has it right.)

CHAPTER SEVEN

1. In addition to those I have cited, we find, for example: G. Himmelfarb, *Victorian Values and Twentieth-Century Condescension*, London, 1987; E.M. Sigsworth, *In Search of Victorian Values: Aspects of Nineteenth-Century Thought and Society*, Manchester, 1988; J. Paradis and T. Postlewait (eds), *Victorian Science and Victorian Values*, New Brunswick, NJ, 1985; G. Marsden (ed.), *Victorian Values: Personalities and Perspectives in Nineteenth-Century Society*, London, 1990. See also my letter to the editor, *Independent on Sunday*, 9 January 1994.

2. Figures of British steam tonnage are most conveniently found in B.R. Mitchell, *British Historical Statistics*, Cambridge, 1988. The invincibility of the Royal Navy may be judged from early (pre-Dreadnought) editions of *Jane's Fighting Ships*. A spectacular illustration was provided in the aftermath of the so-called Hull outrage. The Channel Fleet was despatched to see off the Russians: against their force of 5 modern battleships, Beresford was able to deploy 8 at once and a further 20 shortly afterwards. See also *The Memoirs of Admiral Lord Charles Beresford*, 2 vols, London, 1914; Vol. 2, pp. 494–5: 'a fight would have been murder'.

3. The decline was *relative*, which, as Gordon Jackson once remarked to me, means that if a chicken in Poland lays an egg, the British egg industry suffers relative decline.

4. A state of affairs which enraged the Liverpool journalist Hugh Shimmin: see J.K. Walton and A. Wilcox (eds), *Low Life and Moral Improvement in Mid-Victorian England*, Leicester, 1991, pp. 146–9.

5. This process forms the main theme of M.E. Montgomery, *Gilded Prostitution: Status, money and transatlantic marriages 1870–1914*, London, 1989.

6. P. Horn, *Labouring Life in the Victorian Countryside*, Gloucester, 1987: F. Engels, *The Condition of the Working Class in England*, London, 1892 (innumerable reprints).

7. It has to be admitted that for some time these were mainly middle-class occupations: L. Holcombe, *Victorian Ladies at Work*, Newton Abbot, 1973.

8. The Public Libraries Act and its successor, the Public Museums Act, authorised local authorities to spend public money for these purposes.

9. The instruments in Birmingham Town Hall and St George's Hall, Liverpool, were successively the largest in the world. W.T. Best, organist at St George's Hall, published literally hundreds of transcriptions of orchestral music. Edwin le Mare, widely and wrongly expected to succeed Best at St George's Hall, published even more.

10. I apologise for another 'home-town' example, but see T. Kelly, *For Advancement of Learning: the University of Liverpool, 1881–1981*, Liverpool, 1981.

11. Many authors have attempted to identify common themes and values. An early and relatively convincing one is W. Houghton, *The Victorian Frame of Mind*, London, 1957, while more recently a collection of papers, T.C. Smout (ed.), *Victorian Values (Proceedings of the British Academy* No. 78) Oxford, 1990, approaches the problem from a variety of viewpoints.

12. But there has been substantial debate on the extent to which this

intention was carried into practice. For a round-up of views on a subject with a large historiography, see P. Wood, *Poverty and the Workhouse*, Stroud, 1991.

13. This was written in the week beginning 8 January 1996.

14. A number of governmental enquiries considered this issue; see, for example, BPP 1898 (366) LXXXII.251 *Return of Accidents to Railway Shunters*.

15. For contrasting examples, see Alfred Williams, *Life in a Railway Factory* (1915), repr. Stroud, 1984, and E.J. Larkin, *Memoirs of a Railway Engineer*, London, 1979.

16. D.H. Aldcroft, 'The Efficiency and Enterprise of British Railways', repr. in D.H. Aldcroft, *Studies in British Transport History 1870–1970* (Newton Abbot, 1974), gives an overview of, and further references for, the problems of the railways.

17. G.R. Hawke's pioneering attempt to quantify the railway contribution, in his *Railways and Economic Growth* (Oxford, 1970), puts the figure at not more than 10 per cent.

18. The 1874 edition of the *Lives of George and Robert Stephenson* has a 32-page introduction almost entirely devoted to the benefits of railways.

19. Even in the introduction mentioned in n. 18, he remembers earlier outbursts: 'whatever may be said of the financial management of railways . . . railways which have exhibited the most "frightful financial jobbing". . .' (p. xxxii). For the original outbursts, see pp. 27–8 above.

20. S. Smiles, 'The Great Railway Monopoly', *Quarterly Review* Vol. 125 (1868), pp. 287–329.

21. Introduction to 1874 edition, *Brindley and the Early Engineers*, pp. xvi–xvii.

22. *ibid.*, p. xx.

23. For example, entering 'Self-help' in the University of Liverpool Library catalogue produced twenty-one 'hits', not including the prototype, which is 'Self-Help'. These included works purporting to cure anything from poverty to obesity. Issue 157 (20–26 November 1995) of *The Big Issue* (sold by, and in aid of, the homeless) bears the words 'Self help' in large letters on its cover.

24. Obviously references for such a favourite theme are legion: perhaps the best single one is his chapter 'Astronomers in Humble Life' in *Men of Invention and Industry*, London, 1884.

25. C. Hamlin, *A Science of Impurity*, Bristol, 1990. The central chapters are a fearful indictment of the companies and of the chemists who scripted their excuses – whence the *double entendre* of the title.

26. G.M. Binnie, *Early Victorian Engineers*, London, 1981.

27. *Thrift*, pp. 377–8.

28. *ibid.*, p. 359.

29. *ibid.*, p. 363.

30. (Sir) Robert Jones is generally regarded as the first orthopaedic surgeon and could perhaps be said to have become so when he was appointed to take charge of accident cases during the construction of the Manchester Ship Canal, 1885–94; see F. Watson, *The Life of Sir Robert Jones*, London, 1934.

Bibliography

There have been two previous serious attempts at producing a bibliography of Smiles' writings: my own in *Industrial Archaeology Review* and T.H.E. Travers' in his *Samuel Smiles and the Victorian Work Ethic*. Travers put a great deal of effort into identifying Smiles' work in *Eliza Cook's Journal*, which places his bibliography ahead of mine. I claim the merit of having spent more time investigating the different editions of Smiles' major printed works, and also any credit due for recognising the importance (which I think considerable) of his *Brief Biographies*.

Computers are wonderful things, and I shudder to think how long it would have taken me to finish this book without using one. They can be, and frequently are, misused. There are databases freely available which allow me to carry out literature searches for particular combinations of words. I can enter 'Self-Help' as a search term and one of the 'hits' I get will be P.H.J.H. Gosden's excellent but largely irrelevant book on benefit societies. I may wish to show the pervasive influence of Mrs Thatcher's speech on 'Victorian values' and enter that as a search term. One work I will turn up is that by J.A. Banks on the history of family planning, published two years before *that speech.*

So here, dear reader, is a Quality Assurance statement: this bibliography is not as long as it might be, but I have read almost every item in it. The few exceptions are marked *, as having been taken on hearsay from a source I regard as reliable. I should also emphasise that I have no intention of supplanting Travers' bibliography: those that require a full picture, especially of Smiles's minor writings, must refer to that as well.

Travers has remarked on the dangers of dating particular opinions of Smiles from their occurrence in his better-known works. He did this in the light of his discovery in the pages of *Eliza Cook's Journal* of material often thought to have originated in, say, *Character*. He did not do as I have done and attempt to find every article which Smiles wrote in periodicals, but what emerges from the extra references I have turned up is only a reinforcement of the suggestion that Smiles was completely ruthless about re-using material several times, sometimes over a period of decades. His article on John Harrison, chronometer maker, appears four times to my knowledge, and there may yet be other occurrences which I have not found.

For it must be understood that there *is* more to be found. The 1872 *Memoir of the Author* (see below) describes *Brief Biographies* as a reworking of articles published anonymously in London journals 'many years ago'. But where? Not one of the subjects appears in Travers' diligently compiled list of Smiles' work in *Eliza Cook's Journal*. Some correlate loosely with articles in *The People's Journal* or in *Howitt's Journal*, but the essays in *Brief Biographies* are several times the length of any we might claim as antecedents. A few of the subjects, such as Robert Stephenson or James Watt, appear in Smiles' articles in more substantial periodicals but these are almost contemporary with *Brief Biographies*.

The issue may be even more complicated in that while Smiles is not known to have written under any pseudonym(s), and I cannot claim to have proved that he did, there is one instance in which I suspect he may possibly have done so. In his *Autobiography* he mentions writing articles on benefit societies at an unspecified date in the late 1840s or early '50s. I have not traced these and neither has Travers, but what I have found are four articles in the *People's Journal* (see below) attributed to a Dr Beard. These laud the objectives and good intentions of such societies but also criticise them heavily for a number of organisational failings as well as for poor actuarial practice. At the time these articles appeared, Smiles was writing a good deal for the Howitts (see below), but he was also editor of the *Odd-Fellows Magazine* (Grand United Order) and thus closely associated with people to whom such views would be highly unpalatable. I therefore make the tentative suggestion that 'Dr Beard' is in fact a pseudonym for a bearded doctor – named Smiles. When we look at the level of output he could sustain over a couple of years (and he was said by Sir Arthur Helps to be able to dictate text so fast as to need two shorthand writers), the use of a pseudonym or two during times when he seemed to be writing less is an identifiable and distressing possibility.

The works in Sections 1, 2 and 3 are listed in chronological order of publication; those in Section 4 are given alphabetically.

SECTION 1: BOOKS ABOUT SMILES

Green, T.B., *The Life and Work of Samuel Smiles*, London, 1904.
Smiles, A., *Samuel Smiles and his Surroundings*, London, 1956.
Travers, T.H.E., *Samuel Smiles and the Victorian Work Ethic*, New York & London, 1987.

SECTION 2: PAPERS ABOUT SMILES

2.1 Introductions to reprints of Smiles' works
Briggs, A., *Self-Help*, centenary edn, London, 1959.
Rolt, L.T.C., *Lives of the Engineers*, reprint of 1862 edn, New York and Newton Abbot, 1966.
Rolt, L.T.C., *Industrial Biography*, Newton Abbot, 1967.
Harrison, J.F.C., *Self-Help*, London, 1968.
de Maré, E., *The Lives of George and Robert Stephenson*, London, 1975.
Joseph, Sir K., *Self-Help*, abridged, Harmondsworth, 1986.
Hughes, T.P., *Lives of the Engineers*, abridged edn, Massachusetts, 1996.

2.2 Papers in journals or collections
Briggs, A., 'Samuel Smiles and the Gospel of Work', in *Victorian People*, London, 1954.
Harrison, J.F.C., 'The Victorian Gospel of Success', *Victorian Studies* 1 (1957), pp. 153–64.
Fielden, K., 'Samuel Smiles and Self-Help', *Victorian Studies* 12 (1968), pp. 155–76.

Tyrrell, A., 'Class Consciousness in Early Victorian Britain', *Journal of British Studies* 9 (1970), pp. 102–25.

Travers, T.H.E., 'Samuel Smiles and the Pursuit of Success in Victorian Britain', *Canadian Historical Association, Historical Papers*, 1971 (Ottawa), pp. 154–68.*

Travers, T.H.E., 'Samuel Smiles and the Origins of "Self-Help": Reform and the New Enlightenment', *Albion* 9 (1977), pp. 161–87.

Kinmouth, E.H., 'Nakamura Kein and Samuel Smiles', *American Historical Review* 85 (1980), pp. 535–56.

Morris, R.J., 'Samuel Smiles and the Genesis of Self-Help', *Historical Journal* 24 (1981), pp. 89–109.

Stephens, M.D. and Roderick, G.W., 'Samuel Smiles and Nineteenth Century Self-Help in Education' in M.D. Stephens and G.W. Roderick (eds), *Nottingham Studies in the History of Adult Education*, Nottingham, 1983.

Thornton, A.H., 'The Smilesian Philosophy', in Stephens and Roderick, *op. cit.*

Jarvis, A., 'An Attempt at a Bibliography of Samuel Smiles', *Industrial Archaeology Review* XIII (1991), pp. 162–71.

Jarvis, A., 'Engineering the Image: the Censoring of Samuel Smiles', *Journal of the Railway and Canal Historical Society* 31 (1993), pp. 176–85.

Jarvis, A., 'The Story of the Story of the Life of George Stephenson' in D. Smith (ed.), *Perceptions of Great Engineers*, London, 1994.

2.3 Short papers, articles and contributions

Obituary, *The Times*, 18 April 1904.

Blatchford, R., 'Of Samuel Smiles and Self-Help', *The Clarion*, 13 July 1923.

Scott, E.K., 'Samuel Smiles of "Self-Help" fame', *North Wales Weekly News*, 21 October 1937.

Morris, R.J., 'The History of Self-Help', *New Society*, 3 December 1970, pp. 992–5.

Page, M., 'The Samuel Smiles Set', *Observer Magazine*, 13 December 1970, pp. 52–7.

Tyrrell, A., 'The Origins of a Victorian Bestseller: An Unacknowledged Debt', *Notes and Queries* 17 (1970), pp. 347–9.

Travers, T.H.E., 'The Problem of Identification of Articles: Samuel Smiles and *Eliza Cook's Journal*, 1849–54', *Victorian Periodicals Newsletter* VI (1973), pp. 41–5.

Milstadt, D., 'Eliot and Smiles', *English Language Notes* 14 (1977), pp. 189–92.

Briggs, A., 'Samuel Smiles: the Gospel of Self-Help', *History Today* 37 (May 1987), pp. 37–44.

Note: I have not included contemporary reviews of Smiles' works, but many examples may be readily located by referring to the *Combined Index to Book Reviews in Humanities Journals, 1802–1974*. Shorter reviews of his works may be found from the CD-ROM edition of *The Times*.

SECTION 3: SMILES' PUBLISHED WORKS

3.1 The hardbacks

For numbers of printings, see my 'Attempt at a Bibliography'. Citations of the editions of *Self-Help* alone occupy two and a half pages of the *National Union*

Catalogue. Quantities sold are sometimes difficult to establish, but Smiles' *Account Book*, West Yorkshire Record Office, SS/B/71, gives some idea. Travers has worked out what seem convincing sales figures for *Self-Help.*

Physical Education; or the Nurture and Management of Children, Edinburgh, 1838.
History of Ireland and the Irish People under the Government of England, London, 1844.
Railway Property: its Conditions and Prospects, London, 1849.
The Life of George Stephenson, London, 1857.
The Story of The Life of George Stephenson, London, 1859 (abridgement of above).
Self-Help, London, 1859.
Brief Biographies, Boston, 1860.
Workmen's Earnings, Strikes and Savings, London, 1861.
Lives of the Engineers, 3 vols, London, 1862.
Industrial Biography, London, 1863.
Boulton and Watt, London, 1865.
The Huguenots: Their Settlements, Churches and Industries in England and Ireland, London, 1867.
A Boy's Voyage Around the World, ed. Samuel Smiles Jnr, London, 1871.
Character, London, 1871.
The Huguenots in France after the Edict of Nantes, London, 1873.
Lives of the Engineers, new edn in 5 vols, London, 1874.
Thrift, London, 1875.
Life of a Scotch Naturalist: Thomas Edward, London, 1876.
George Moore, Merchant and Philanthropist, London & New York, 1878.
Robert Dick, Baker of Thurso, Geologist and Botanist, London, 1878.
Duty, London, 1880.
Men of Invention and Industry, London, 1884.
James Nasmyth, Engineer, an Autobiography, ed. Samuel Smiles, London, 1885.
Life and Labour, London, 1887.
A Publisher and his Friends. Memoir and Correspondence of the Late John Murray, London, 1891.
Jasmin. Barber, Poet, Philanthropist, London, 1891.
Josiah Wedgwood, his Personal History, London, 1894.
The Autobiography of Samuel Smiles, LLD, ed. T. Mackay, London, 1905.

There are some 'pseudo-Smiles' works whose exact authorship and copyright status I have not determined, including *Higher and Higher*, published by the Christian Knowledge Society (London, 1876), and described as a book for children containing 'stories, with two exceptions . . . adapted . . . from *Self-Help*'. There is also a quite amazingly bad play by one C. Bolton entitled *The Engineer*, which is an adaptation of *The Life of George Stephenson*. WYRO, SS/A/IX/72, mentions this work as being performed in the Victoria Theatre which, we are told, is 'a place now thoroughly cleaned out and started under new management'. Judging from the script (BL, Additional MS 53020), it is hard to imagine standards from which the Victoria could have risen. But if there are any theatre directors reading this, I am open to offers to play the part of George Stephenson. My talents match those of Mr Bolton.

3.2 Pamphlets and longer articles

These become problematical. Pamphlets, especially political ones, can be pretty ephemeral, and the ones listed are simply those of which I have found copies, mostly in WYRO or in Manchester City Library. The ones I have found contain important material. The articles in this section are those which are either published under Smiles' name or are attributed to him in *Poole's Index*, and which are more than three pages long. I confess that I have read very few of the articles in *Good Words* and the *Eclectic Magazine*, since a sampling suggested that of all them are rehashes of other articles listed here. This is why I give only the starting page in such references.

Address to the Bradford United Reform Club, Leeds, 1842.
The Diffusion of Political Knowledge among the Working Classes, Leeds, 1842.
The Education of the Working Classes, Leeds, 1845.
Railway Property, Leeds, 1850.
National Education: Is the Voluntary Principle adequate to our exigencies?, Manchester, 1851.
'Difficulties of Railway Engineering', *Quarterly Review* 103 (1857), pp. 1–28.
'Iron Bridges', *Quarterly Review* 104 (1858), pp. 75–106.
'James Watt', in *ibid.*, pp. 410–51.
'Robert Stephenson: In Memoriam', *Fraser's Magazine* 60 (1859), pp. 661–7.
'Strikes', *Quarterly Review* 106 (1859), pp. 485–522.
'Cotton-Spinning Machines and their Inventors', *Quarterly Review* 107 (1860), pp. 45–85.
'Workmen's Earnings and Savings', *Quarterly Review* 108 (1860), pp. 80–120.
'The Brunels', *Quarterly Review* 112 (1862), pp. 1–39.
'Workmen's Benefit Societies', *Quarterly Review* 116 (1864), pp. 318–50.
'Iron and Steel', *Quarterly Review* 120 (1866), pp. 64–105.
'A French Church in Canterbury Cathedral', *Good Words* 7 (1866), p. 253.*
'Cugnot and his Vehicle', *The Engineer*, 21 December 1866.
Industrial Education of Foreign and English Workmen, Huddersfield, 1867.
'The Great Railway Monopoly', *Quarterly Review* 125 (1868), pp. 287–329.
'Frederick Koenig, Inventor of the Steam Printing Press', *Macmillan's Magazine* 21 (1870), p. 135 (repr. in the *Eclectic Magazine*).*
'Life Assurance Companies', *Quarterly Review* 128 (1870), pp. 18–49.
'The Police of London', *Quarterly Review* 129 (1870), pp. 87–149.
'A Visit to the Country of the Vaudois' (2 parts), *Good Words* 11 (1870), pp. 40, 451.*
'The Country of the Camisards', *Good Words* 11 (1870), pp. 641, 645.*
Memoir of the Author, London, 1872. (This was prepared for the Italian edition of *Character* on the assumption that by the time the translation was completed Smiles would be dead: it was published only in the technical sense of being printed and distributed to a plurality of third parties; copy in WYRO.)
'Charles Bianconi and what he did for Ireland', *Good Words* 15 (1874), pp. 15, 23, 114.*
'Robert Nicoll', *Good Words* 16 (1875), pp. 313, 414.*
'The Persecutions of Samuel de Pechel', *Good Words* 18 (1877), pp. 99, 265.

'Reform at Woodhouse Moor', *Good Words* 18, p. 386.
'Paul de Rapin-Thoyras', *Good Words* 20 (1879), pp. 407, 762, 845.*
'John Harrison, Chronometer Maker', *Longman's Magazine* 1 (1882), p. 256 (repr. in the *Eclectic Magazine*).
'John Stephens Henslow', *Longman's Magazine* 2 (1883), p. 147.
'Authors and Publishers', *Murray's Magazine* 7 (1890), pp. 48, 207.

3.3 Shorter articles

I do not intend to enumerate all of these since they are already easy to find, if not always to identify positively. There are the following main categories:

The *Leeds Times*. Smiles was appointed editor in 1839, and continued until the end of 1842. It is unclear whether he actually wrote everything himself, but it cannot be doubted that at the very least he wrote the leaders and controlled the rest. He was successful in raising the paper's flagging circulation, but found the job something of a treadmill existence.

The *Odd-Fellows Magazine*. Smiles edited this magazine from its establishment in 1847 until about 1852 (the date he gives, 1845, in his *Autobiography* is clearly wrong since the magazine he edited was that of the Leeds-based Grand United Order: in 1845 only the Manchester Unity had a magazine, and its editor was John Rogerson, not Smiles). As with the *Leeds Times* it is difficult to tell what, if any, part anyone else played. Many of the articles were republished from elsewhere, and both their selection and the style and inclination of the new articles suggest that we should not go far wrong in attributing all or virtually all of the latter to Smiles. One article cited in the main text seems to me particularly important: 'The Industrious Poor', *Quarterly Magazine of the Grand United Order of Odd-Fellows*, No. 1 (February 1850), p. 1.

Howitt's Journal and *The People's Journal*. It seems to have been a characteristic of Smiles' article-writing that he had phases of writing almost exclusively for one journal or another for a few years and then changing his allegiance. From 1846 to 1848 he enjoyed such a relationship with William and Mary Howitt. Each volume of both publications for those three years had multiple contributions by Smiles, and they form a fertile browsing ground for the student of his work at that period. As mentioned in the main text, Smiles made few concessions to respectability in his choice of subject, especially in the two series of potted biographies, 'Men of the People' and 'Poets of the People'. But it was also in *Howitt's Journal* that he published an important short article on 'A Scheme of Free Libraries' and in *The People's Journal* he published some quite substantial multi-part articles including: 'What is Doing for the People of Leeds?' and 'What the People are Doing for Themselves' (Vol. 1, pp. 136, 222, 229; 'Factory Women', Vol. 2, p. 238 and Vol. 3, pp. 52, 143.

Eliza Cook's Journal. Smiles started to write for Eliza Cook in 1849, initially one article per week. This increased rapidly, and Travers estimates that Smiles wrote a total of about 580 articles in the next five years. Of these, I have found just two which are actually attributed; a few are identified by Smiles in other works and

Travers has identified a further twenty-five which he feels he can attribute with confidence. These attributions are important, because they reveal origins of Smiles' ideas and a good deal about his methods of work as well. See Appendix D of Travers, *Work Ethic.* In addition (one he has not mentioned) in Vol. 2, pp. 225–7 is an anonymous account of 'A Last Visit to Ebenezer Elliott' which is re-used in *Brief Biographies* and the *Autobiography.*

Other untraceables. Smiles' first paid writing work was for the *Edinburgh Weekly Chronicle,* but no-one has yet managed to ascertain what he wrote for it. Even more puzzling is his reference in his *Autobiography* to editing, in or about 1841, what he called 'a little penny paper' entitled *The Movement.* Only two journals of that name seem to have existed, one being the Secular Society publication which was definitely edited by G.J. Holyoake and the other an electoral reform paper which ran for nine issues in 1833 and cost 7*d!*

SECTION 4: OTHER WORKS CITED IN THE NOTES

Aldcroft, D.H., *Studies in British Transport History 1870–1970,* Newton Abbot, 1974.

Alderman, G., *The Railway Interest,* Leicester, 1973.

Anthony, P.D., *The Ideology of Work,* London, 1977.

Arch, J., *From Ploughtail to Parliament,* repr. London, 1986.

Bailey, W.H., 'A new chapter in the history of the Manchester & Liverpool [*sic*] Railway', *Transactions of the Manchester Association of Engineers* (1889), pp. 23–9.

Beamish, R., *Memoir of the Life of Sir Marc Isambard Brunel,* London, 1862.

Bede, *A History of the English Church and People,* trans. L. Sherley-Price, London, 1964.

Bentley, G., 'Sincerity in Biography', *The Temple Bar,* 1881, repr. in Ira B. Nadel (ed.), *Victorian Biography,* New York & London, 1986.

Binnie, G.M., *Early Victorian Engineers,* London, 1981.

Bowler, P.J., *The Invention of Progress,* Oxford, 1989.

Buchanan, R.A., 'Gentleman Engineers: The Making of a Profession', *Victorian Studies* 26 (1983), pp. 407–29.

Buchanan, R.A., 'The Lives of the Engineers', *Industrial Archaeology Review* IX (1988), pp. 5–15.

Burleigh, J.H.S., *A Church History of Scotland,* London, 1960.

Burton, A., *The Rainhill Story,* London, 1979, p. 21.

Cantrell, J.A., 'James Nasmyth and the Steam Hammer', *Transactions of the Newcomen Society* 56 (1984–5), pp. 133–8.

Cardwell, D.S.L., *From Watt to Clausius,* New York, 1971.

Carlyle, T., *Past and Present* (1843), London, 1912.

Carlyle, T., 'Hudson's Statue', No. 7 in *Latter Day Pamphlets,* London, 1850.

Carlyle, T., 'On Chartism' in *Critical and Miscellaneous Essays,* repr. London, 7 vols, 1872, Vol. 6, pp. 109–86.

Channell, D.F., 'The Harmony of Theory & Practice: The Engineering Science of W.J.M. Rankine', *Technology & Culture* 23 (1982), pp. 39–52.

Clark, Hyde, Articles on George Stephenson, *Civil Engineer and Architect's Journal* 11 (1848), pp. 297–300, 329–33, 361–4, and 12 (1849), pp. 68–72, 103–7, 170–3, 205–9.

Cobban, A.B., *Universities in the Middle Ages,* Liverpool, 1990.

Cobbett, W., *Cottage Economy* (1822), Oxford, 1970.

Cockshutt, A.O.J., *Truth to Life*, London, 1974.

Dentith, S., 'Samuel Smiles and the Nineteenth Century Novel' in D. Smith, *op cit.*

Dickens, C., *Little Dorritt*, London, 1857.

Digby, K.H., *The Broadstone of Honour, or Rules for the Gentlemen of England*, London, 1823.

Dobson, M.J., 'Marsh Fever: the geography of malaria', *Journal of Historical Geography* 6:4 (1980), pp. 357–89.

Dobson, R.B. and Taylor, J., *Rymes of Robyn Hood*, Gloucester, 1989.

Doyle, T., *Black Swine in the Sewers of Hampstead*, New York, 1989.

Drummond, A.L. and Bullock, J., *The Scottish Church 1688–1843*, Edinburgh, 1973.

Duckworth, A.D. (ed.), *The Papers of William Froude, MA, LLD, FRS, 1810–1879*, London, 1955.

Duffy, M.C., 'Technomorphology and the Stephenson Traction System', *Transactions of the Newcomen Society* 54 (1982–3), pp. 55–78.

Dunbar, J.T., *History of Highland Dress*, London, 1962.

Engels, F., *The Condition of the Working Class in England*, London, 1892.

Evans, D.M., *Facts, Failures and Frauds*, London, 1859.

Faber, R., *Young England*, London, 1987.

Fairlie, S., 'The Corn Laws and British Wheat Production 1829–76', *Economic History Review*, 2nd series, XXII (1969), pp. 88–116.

Girouard, M., *The Return to Camelot*, Yale & London, 1981.

Green, D., *Great Cobbett: The Noblest Agitator*, Oxford, 1985.

Gregory, M.S., *History and Development of Engineering*, London, 1971.

Griffiths, J., *The Third Man*, London, 1992.

Hadfield, C., *Thomas Telford's Temptation*, Kidderminster, 1993.

Hadfield, C. and Biddle, G., *Canals of the North West*, Newton Abbot, 1970.

Hadfield, C. and Skempton, A.W., *William Jessop, Engineer*, Newton Abbot, 1979.

Hamlin, C., *A Science of Impurity*, Bristol, 1990.

Hankin, C.C. (ed.), *Life of Mary Anne Schimmelpenninck*, London, 1858.

Hawke, G.R., *Railways and Economic Growth*, Oxford, 1970.

Haworth, V., 'A Case Study: George Stephenson, 1781–1848, Enginewright and Railway Promoter' in *Nineteenth Century Business Ethics: papers presented at a research day school at Merseyside Maritime Museum, 31 October 1992.*

Hedley, O.D., *Who Invented the Locomotive Engine?*, London, 1859.

Hobsbawm, E.J., *The Age of Revolution*, New York, 1962.

Holcombe, L., *Victorian Ladies at Work*, Newton Abbot, 1973.

Hollis, P., *Women in Public: The Women's Movement 1850–1900*, London, 1979.

Horn, P., *Labouring Life in the Victorian Countryside*, Gloucester, 1987.

Houghton, W., *The Victorian Frame of Mind*, London, 1957.

Hutton, C. (ed.), *Reports of the Late John Smeaton*, 4 vols, London, 1798 onwards.

Jarvis, A., *The Liverpool Dock Engineers*, Stroud, 1996.

Jarvis, A.M., 'The Development of Cooking Technology and how Women Used and Perceived it', unpublished MSc dissertation, University of Liverpool, 1996. (History of Science & Technology.)

Jeaffreson, J.C., *The Life of Robert Stephenson*, 2 vols, London, 1866.

Kelly, T., *For Advancement of Learning: the University of Liverpool, 1881–1981*, Liverpool, 1981.

Knowles, L.C.A., *Industrial and Commercial Revolutions*, London, 1926.

Kraus, H., *Gold was the Mortar: The Economics of Cathedral Building*, New York, 1994.

Larkin, E.J., *Memoirs of a Railway Engineer*, London, 1979.

Lytton, Bulwer, *Paul Clifford*, London, 1829.

McNeil, I., *Hydraulic Power*, London, 1972.

Malet, H., *Bridgewater, The Canal Duke 1736–1803*, Manchester, 1977.

Martin, G.H., 'Road Travel in the Middle Ages: Some Journeys by the Warden and Fellows of Merton College, Oxford, 1315–1470', *Journal of Transport History*, 2nd series, III (1975–6), pp. 158–78.

Mitchell, B.R., *British Historical Statistics*, Cambridge, 1988.

Montgomery, M.E., *Gilded Prostitution: Status, money and transatlantic marriages 1870–1914*, London, 1989.

Morris, K.L., *The Image of the Middle Ages in Romantic and Victorian Literature*, London, 1984.

Muirhead, J.P., *The Origin and Progress of the Mechanical Inventions of James Watt*, London, 1854.

Musson, A.E. (ed.), *Science, Technology and Economic Growth in the Eighteenth Century*, London, 1972.

Opie, I. and Opie, P., *The Classic English Fairy Tales*, London, 1974.

Ovitt, G. Jnr, 'The Cultural Context of Western Technology: Early Christian Attitudes toward Manual Labor', *Technology & Culture* 27 (1986), pp. 477–500.

Paine, E.M.S. (published under the pseudonym 'EMSP'), *The Two James's and the Two Stephensons*, London, 1861.

Pratt, E.A., *A History of Inland Transport & Communication* (1912) repr. Newton Abbot, 1970.

Raistrick, A., *Industrial Archaeology*, London, 1972.

Rankine, W.J.M., *The Steam Engine and Other Prime Movers*, London, 1859.

Reynolds, Sir Joshua, *Discourses* (ed. P. Rogers), Harmondsworth, 1992.

Riley, H.T. (ed.), *Chronicle of the Abbey of Croyland*, London, 1854.

Ritvo, H., 'Pride and Pedigree: the evolution of the Victorian dog fancy', *Victorian Studies* 29 (1986).

Robertson, J.M., *A History of Freethought in the Nineteenth Century*, 2 vols, London, 1929.

Rolt, L.T.C., 'The History of the History of Engineering', *Transactions of the Newcomen Society* XLII (1969–70), pp. 1–10.

Rolt, L.T.C., *George and Robert Stephenson*, Harmondsworth, 1978.

Rubinstein, W.D., *Men of Property: the very wealthy in Britain since the Industrial Revolution*, London, 1981.

Russell, J. Scott, 'Memoir of George Stephenson', *Proceedings of the Institution of Mechanical Engineers*, October 1848, pp. 1–13.

Savage, C.I., *An Economic History of Transport*, London, 2nd edn, 1966.

Schofield, R.E., *The Lunar Society of Birmingham*, Oxford, 1963.

Skeat, W.O., *George Stephenson: The Engineer and his Letters*, London, 1973.

Smith, D. (ed.), *Perceptions of Great Engineers*, London, 1994.

Smout, T.C. (ed), *Victorian Values, Proceedings of the British Academy* No. 78, Oxford, 1990.

Southern, R.W., *St Anselm and his Biographer*, Cambridge, 1963.

Stanfield, J.R., *An Essay on the Study and Composition of Biography* (1813), repr. New York & London, 1986.

Torrens, H., 'Jonathan Hornblower and the Steam Engine: a Historiographic Analysis' in D. Smith, *op. cit.*

Trevithick, F., *Life of Richard Trevithick*, London, 1872.

Trevor-Roper, H., 'The Invention of Tradition: The Highland Tradition of Scotland' in E. J. Hobsbawm and T. Ranger (eds), *The Invention of Tradition*, Cambridge, 1983.

Vignoles, O.J., *Life of Charles Blacker Vignoles*, London, 1889.

Walton, J.K. and Wilcox, A. (eds), *Low Life and Moral Improvement in Mid-Victorian England*, Leicester, 1991, pp. 146–9.

Ward, J.T. and Wilson, R.D. (eds), *Land and Industry*, Newton Abbot, 1971.

Watson, F., *The Life of Sir Robert Jones*, London, 1934.

Watson, G. *The Smeatonians*, London, 1989.

Weber, M., trans. T. Parsons, *The Protestant Ethic and the Spirit of Capitalism*, 2nd edn, London, 1976.

White, L., *Medieval Religion and Technology: Collected Essays*, Berkeley & Los Angeles, 1978.

Willans, G. and Searle, R., *The Compleet Molesworth*, London, 1984.

Williams, A., *Life in a Railway Factory* (1915), repr. Stroud, 1984.

Wood, P., *Poverty and the Workhouse*, Stroud, 1991.

Zipes, J. (ed.), *Victorian Fairy Tales: The Revolt of the Fairies and Elves*, New York & London, 1987.

Index